Only One Chance

ENVIRONMENTAL ETHICS AND SCIENCE POLICY SERIES
General Editor: Kristin Shrader-Frechette

Environmental Justice
Creating Equality, Reclaiming Democracy
Kristin Shrader-Frechette

In Nature's Interests?
Interests, Animal Rights, and Environmental Ethics
Gary E. Varner

Across the Boundaries
Extrapolation in Biology and Social Science
Daniel Steel

Taking Action, Saving Lives
Our Duties to Protect Environmental and Public Health
Kristin Shrader-Frechette

Is a Little Pollution Good For You?
Incorporating Societal Values in Environmental Research
Kevin C. Elliott

A Perfect Moral Storm
The Ethical Tragedy of Climate Change
Stephen M. Gardiner

What Will Work
Fighting Climate Change with Renewable Energy, not Nuclear Power
Kristin Shrader-Frechette

Only One Chance
How Environmental Pollution Impairs Brain Development—
and How to Protect the Brains of the Next Generation
Philippe Grandjean

Only One Chance

How Environmental Pollution Impairs
Brain Development—
and How to Protect the Brains of the Next
Generation

PHILIPPE GRANDJEAN

OXFORD
UNIVERSITY PRESS

UNIVERSITY PRESS

Oxford University Press is a department of the University of Oxford.
It furthers the University's objective of excellence in research, scholarship,
and education by publishing worldwide.

Oxford   New York
Auckland   Cape Town   Dar es Salaam   Hong Kong   Karachi
Kuala Lumpur   Madrid   Melbourne   Mexico City   Nairobi
New Delhi   Shanghai   Taipei   Toronto

With offices in
Argentina   Austria   Brazil   Chile   Czech Republic   France   Greece
Guatemala   Hungary   Italy   Japan   Poland   Portugal   Singapore
South Korea   Switzerland   Thailand   Turkey   Ukraine   Vietnam

Oxford is a registered trademark of Oxford University Press in the UK
and certain other countries.

Published in the United States of America by
Oxford University Press
198 Madison Avenue, New York, NY 10016

Library of Congress Cataloging-in-Publication Data
Grandjean, Philippe, 1950–
Only one chance : how environmental pollution impairs brain development—
and how to protect the brains of the next generation / Philippe Grandjean.
pages cm.—(Environmental ethics and science policy series)
Includes bibliographical references.
ISBN 978–0–19–998538–8 (hardback : alk. paper)—ISBN 978–0–19–998539–5 (updf)—
ISBN 978–0–19–998540–1 (epub)   1. Prenatal influences.
2. Fetus—Abnormalities—Etiology.   I. Title.
RG627.5.G73 2013
618.3'2686—dc23
2012036713

9 8 7 6 5 4 3 2 1
Printed in the United States of America
on acid-free paper

CONTENTS

Introduction

Brain Matters

ONLY ONE CHANCE TO DEVELOP A BRAIN

The brain makes us who we are. "I think, therefore I am," French philosopher René Descartes wrote. We think, we read, we write, all due to this exceptional and complex organ called the brain. Still, our sophisticated brains evolved over thousands of generations to serve needs prevalent during prehistoric life conditions. Modern society provides highly different challenges and potentials for our paleolithic nervous system. And now our brains are being put to an extreme test. It is double-edged.

Problems that we create often demand an even greater ingenuity to control the consequences. This is particularly true of chemical pollution. We have been enormously successful in generating useful industrial chemicals, but some of them accumulate in the environment, contaminate our food, or leak into our drinking water, thereby creating exposures that may be dangerous—a problem we often discover with much delay.

In addition, some of that pollution can attack brain development—a form of toxicity that I call chemical brain drain. Such effects may damage the thinking that we will badly need to counter the very risks to brain development. Will managing chemical brain drain require a level of thinking that is no longer possible? This is the question that worries me, a worry that made me write this book.

Having studied brain toxicity for 30 years, and having become more and more concerned about the consequences of chemical brain damage, I realized that I must speak up. As I shall argue in this book, brain drain can be easily overlooked, and it may appear to be silent, as it is frequently not accompanied by a formal medical diagnosis.

My own perspective as a physician changed, because I met victims of different types of brain drain. Although many of them had one or more traditional medical diagnoses, none was identified by the diagnosis that they truly had in common—chemical brain drain.

When I was a medical student at the University of Copenhagen, Denmark, in the early 1970s, the word "environment" had just entered the common vocabulary.

The TV news began to feature pollution problems and showed crippled victims, whose nervous system had been damaged by chemicals. I became fascinated by the likely impact of pollution on human health. Physicians needed to play an active role beyond diagnosis and treatment, I thought. However, our discoveries on disease etiologies are only slowly being translated into prevention, if at all. Why is that? Should we not try to protect brains and not limit ourselves to diagnosis and treatment after the damage has already happened?

After graduation from medical school, I started a career in environmental medicine and epidemiology research. I wanted to understand better why the medical community failed to prevent chemical damage to children's brains. I soon encountered some surprises that medical school had not prepared me for, surprises that were fundamental to our understanding of human development and the frailty of the human brain. The human physiology that I was taught at the university specified that the fetus is well protected inside the pregnant mother's womb. Contrary to this comforting notion, however, the placenta does allow toxic chemicals to seep through. Once within the fetal circulation, some of these compounds can cause damage to the sensitive processes going on in the developing brain. The mother may escape completely unscathed, but for her child, the damage can be catastrophic. Early brain development molds the brain functions that will be available for the rest of one's lifetime. You get only a single chance to accomplish that.

Our understanding has improved only slowly through scattered studies on single chemicals, such as lead, mercury, and alcohol, now known to be toxic to the developing brain. From these bits and pieces of information, a more general pattern is now becoming apparent and is changing our perspective on the health risks brought on by environmental chemicals. This new knowledge developed only gradually, often hampered when narrow economic interests countered the emerging evidence that could hurt an industrial company's bottom line. Only recently has it become clear that the brain is both crucial for our being who we are and at the same time also extremely vulnerable, especially during its development. Brains need vigorous protection.

Understanding the implications is not just a matter of biochemistry and statistics. Real people, children, victims are affected. Their lives are changed forever. Early in my medical career, I had the benefit of being a Fulbright Fellow for two years at Mount Sinai Hospital in New York, where Professor Irving J. Selikoff was my mentor. He taught me this: "Never forget that the numbers in your tables are human destinies, although the tears have been wiped away." So this book is also meant as a tribute to the sufferers of chemical brain drain. Many were not recognized as pollution victims but instead endured stigmatism and lack of rehabilitation and compensation.

I am embarrassed that the medical profession—and society—have not risen to the challenge. The effects on brain development may often be silent, but they are serious and demand a loud response. This book is meant to be very loud!

The Human Brain Is Unique

Compared to body size, the adult human brain is the largest in the biosphere, taking up about 2% of our body weight. It is about four times the size of that of a gorilla or chimpanzee. Much of this size difference is due to an expansion of the cerebral cortex—the cell-rich outer layers of the brain. The human brain is not the largest in the animal world, though. Whales and elephants have brains up to five times greater in size. Much of that weight is occupied by the complex wiring that is needed by the formidable size of these animals. In contrast, primate brains are built in a space-saving manner that allows highly efficient packing of cells within the skull. Among primates, humans by far have the largest number of brain cells.[1] Hence, it is not the weight or the actual size that makes a difference (Einstein's brain weighed only 1,230 grams and was no bigger than an average brain).

So brain size alone does not determine our cognitive abilities. Nevertheless, the sheer number of cells in the human brain is unusually large. The exact number of nerve cells, or neurons, is unknown, but a fair estimate is that each of us probably has close to 100 billion nerve cells packed between the ears. That is a hundred times one thousand times one thousand times one thousand. If this number is not impressive, then consider that the brain also houses supporting glia cells that provide nutrients, general housekeeping, and the insulation of nerve fibers. The glia cells outnumber the nerve cells almost everywhere in the brain.

For comparison, many insects make do with less than 1 million neurons, and even that small number in a mosquito or a honeybee is sufficient for some quite sophisticated functions.[2] So despite our substantial superiority in terms of brain cells, our understanding even of the brain functions of insects is quite limited (and they do manage to bite).

As with other animals, your highly sophisticated brain started out as a tiny strip of cells. By a couple of weeks after conception, these cells were ready to multiply. At the peak, about 12,000 cells were generated every minute—200 per second. Most cells did not remain in the same place, but aimed to specific locations within the developing brain. Moving by themselves to their final positions, some cells had to find their way across a distance up to 1,000 times their own size. When settled at their destination in the brain cortex or elsewhere, they began to develop extensions of the cell membrane to establish contact with other cells, probably hundreds of such extensions, to set up joint functions.[3]

So the brain develops by multiplication, migration, maturation, and messaging— complex steps, each of which has to happen in a specific fashion, in the correct order, and at the right time. These biological processes are extremely complex and are only superficially understood so far. The morphological changes and biochemical mechanisms are portrayed in current textbooks in the field. But there is no authoritative review so far that highlights how environmental hazards can damage brain development and what we need to do to protect the vulnerable developmental processes. Still, we are beginning to appreciate that the intricate timetable of closely connected and complex processes is very sensitive to interference and that obstacles can have serious consequences. If some disruption happens, brain development will be incomplete or abnormal, and there will be little, if any, time and opportunity for repair. Thus, brain functions will be curtailed, whether attention, spatial orientation, muscular coordination, memory, or some other crucial aspect. Thus, the final product, the mature brain, will not express the full potentials that we inherited from our parents.

Brains Are Vulnerable

We get only one chance to develop a brain. The damage that occurs to a brain of a fetus or child will likely remain for the rest of his or her life. The consequences can therefore be dire. Neurodevelopmental delay or neurological disease are thought to occur in about one of six children in the United States.[4] The adverse conditions range from serious diagnosed disease, such as mental retardation, cerebral palsy, and autism to less clearly defined disorders like attention deficit hyperactivity disorder (ADHD) and more subtle deviations like learning disabilities and sensory deficits. An estimated 2 million children in the United States suffer from ADHD, and about 1.7 million from autism spectrum disorder. Some of these conditions seem to be increasing in prevalence, thus probably not being of genetic origin. Although the causation in most cases is unknown, environmental factors are likely culprits. This book will discuss what we know and what we can reasonably infer about industrial chemicals as likely and suspected causes of brain damage. I refer to such damage as chemical brain drain, as it may be subtle and insidious, yet the overall effects can be devastating. I will summarize different types of research and their interpretations, and I shall also discuss how we may responsibly act to protect the developing brains of the next generation.

The brain is different from other organs. Our overall health and well-being will not be negatively affected by donating a kidney for transplantation. Also, we generally don't depend on the maximal capacity of the liver or most other organs. However, the complete and optimal function of the brain is essential to each and every individual. To keep the nerve cells functioning, we reserve 15% to 20% of our blood supply for the brain and 25% of the energy used at rest—a 10-fold higher need for calories and oxygen compared to the rest of the body. So the heart and blood vessels inherently favor the brain to deliver the nutrients and energy required by the nerve cells. However, something is clearly going wrong when neurodevelopmental disease in children is among the most common types of childhood disorders, apparently even increasing in prevalence. However, the less obvious decreases in brain function are not recorded by the medical statistics, although even small degrees of brain damage can negatively impact human welfare and income.

We care for a child's well-being and prospective success in life, and any parent would worry about a slight delay in the child's brain development. As adults and parents, we want our children to get a head start, to develop and utilize their talents and to enjoy the benefits of life to the fullest possible extent. Yet, we are changing the environment and unwittingly exposing the next generation to chemicals that may change early brain development into a toxic head start.

Through evolution, our brains have developed to deal with acute dangers, whether saber cats or thunderstorms. Our nerve connections will ensure that we become aware of the dangers and react to them to protect ourselves, being alerted by their pungent smell, their threatening looks, or their scary noise. But nothing in our past has prepared us to deal with the insidious chemical threats that endanger the development of the next generation's brains. On the contrary, we are thoroughly enjoying the immediate benefits of attractive consumer goods, efficient technologies, and handsome profits that we generate from producing and disseminating hazardous chemicals. Our senses are not geared toward detecting the underlying dangers. The irony is that the resulting brain drain may wipe out some of those senses that we badly need to manage this very problem.

While we are polluting our food, drinking water, and air with chemicals that may harm brain development, we have been acting as if the risk of chemical brain drain is nonexistent. True, convincing proof is available for only a few well-researched chemicals. The best documentation available is in regard to lead pollution, which has ruined the lives of countless children. While we were slowly gathering detailed scientific documentation, a whole generation of Americans, and children around the world, suffered loss of brain function due to the pollution from our careless use of lead as an octane-booster in gasoline, as paint pigment, and as applications in myriads of consumer products. Only when the scientific evidence became truly overwhelming was a consensus finally reached that the public should be protected against this brain drainer.

We are now discovering similar evidence about other chemicals, such as mercury, polychlorinated biphenyls (PCBs), arsenic, some solvents, certain pesticides, and other industrial compounds. Again, we hesitate to act, because we prefer to have convincing proof before making restrictions against activities and products that are useful to society. In an attempt to translate the science into terms that may help priority-setting, economists have begun to calculate the costs to society due to chemical brain drain. In terms of lost income alone, the losses add up to billions of dollars per year. Despite the enormous costs, we have been reluctant to control the hazards that endanger brains.

Brain Drainers Are Not Easily Identified and Eliminated

We are up against substantial challenges when seeking information on chemical brain drain. One complication is that each toxic chemical may not appear by itself to cause any obvious or serious risk to our brains. The damage may only be detectable from the effects of a combination of chemicals. Even so, only the most severe deviations from optimal development are likely to trigger a medical diagnosis, but they may nonetheless lead to fundamental deficits like learning or memory problems.

To make the situation even more difficult, our traditional research methods are inefficient tools to obtain the documentation we desire. Proper proof may take decades to gather for each individual chemical, one by one. Thus, useful knowledge has been accumulated only for a small number among the thousands of environmental pollutants. A few years ago, I scrutinized the scientific and medical literature to identify the industrial chemicals that had caused brain toxicity one way or another. I found that more than 200 industrial chemicals can be toxic to the human brain, although the majority of cases relate to poisonings of adults (see the updated Appendix list of known brain drainers).[5] These chemicals are obviously able to gain access to the nervous system and to exert damage to brain cells. It seems evident that these substances can also be hazardous to the brain during development. Due to the vulnerability of developing brains, chemicals that are toxic to adult brains are probably even more of a threat to young brains and at much lower doses.

Unfortunately, such evidence on damage to children's brains is available only for a handful of chemicals. This lack of information cannot be due to developing brains being resistant to toxic chemicals—in fact, they are more vulnerable. The reason is more likely the obstacles and time constraints in conducting research in this area. Our ignorance is further upheld because testing industrial chemicals for developmental brain toxicity is not mandatory. Further, scientists generally express their conclusions in a subtle language that tends to underestimate the risks. As a result of these three flaws (which I call the "triple whammy"), we do not know the potential of most environmental pollutants for causing brain drain. Without systematic evidence, we are left in the dark and at great risk.

Worse, we often require an unrealistic high level of understanding of each chemical and its adverse effects before we make decisions on restricting its use and initiating preventive efforts. A convincing proof is typically demanded by the affected industry that stands to lose revenue if a chemical is considered toxic with consequent loss of market. For 50 years, powerful economic interests resisted restrictions to the use of lead additives in gasoline, insisting that documentation did not exist that lead pollution was dangerous. True, regulatory agencies also have a desire for detailed documentation, and so do ambitious scientists, who aspire to disentangle the innermost secrets of biochemical mechanisms.

With time, regulatory efforts result in a gradual tightening of rule-making for an increasing number of toxic chemicals. Thus, the vast majority of official exposure limits have decreased as better information became available. Initial regulations are often found to be too lax and optimistic, so that adverse effects at lower levels of exposure are recognized only after the fact. Even worse, evidence on neurotoxicity is usually not available and is therefore not considered in regulatory decisions. And tightened regulations barely keep pace with the increasing complexity of environmental pollution. Although the 200 known neurotoxicants are recognized as toxic hazards, only a few are regulated to protect developing brains.

It may take decades and substantial resources to generate the documentation that regulators desire before deciding to control a brain-draining chemical. Although lead poisoning and other brain toxicity have been extensively described, they are usually looked upon as a specific aspect of toxicology only related to individual substances, and not as a reflection of a hazard of general relevance. Again and again, doubt and skepticism, especially from the side of vested interests, pose obstacles to prudent protection of developing brains. Our insights are therefore only slowly being translated into prevention due to what journalism professor William Kovarik calls "historical amnesia."[6] While waiting for prevention policies to happen, exposures disseminate and increase, and persistent chemicals accumulate in food chains. As a result, our knee-jerk demand for detailed documentation leaves the brain power of the next generation in harm's way.

We are faced with a paradox. When we test new drugs, we conduct research studies on volunteers. But with environmental chemicals, we cannot conduct controlled clinical trials where children or pregnant women would be given a test chemical every day. Even if the high dose did not exceed the maximum exposure occurring in society, the study would certainly be considered unethical, especially in vulnerable populations, and would and could not be approved by ethical review boards. So while a controlled study of suspected brain drainers to support our documentation is not allowed, the insidious and undesirable exposures to children and pregnant women remain. In most cases, we do not even attempt to keep track of possible adverse health effects. And while we are pondering the research on a small number of chemicals that have been studied in some detail, action is being postponed for thousands of other substances that have not yet been evaluated.

The consequences, in regard to disease and organ dysfunction, may be subtle and hard to detect in the individual child. Most negative effects on brain development barely affect standardized, routine health statistics, and any changes are slow and can take many years to recognize. On the other hand, we are facing a massive prevalence of brain dysfunction, autism, and many other signs of ill health due to developmental insults. Because the exposures to toxic chemicals happen worldwide, the adverse effects are appearing now as a silent pandemic.[7]

Chemicals serve useful purposes in society, and we routinely have faith in modern technology as being inherently safe, a belief that is also supported by comforting statements from industry. This view is now being challenged, as we realize that many technologies have been introduced without proper attention to their risks. When new legislation on chemicals control was introduced in the late 1970s, existing chemicals in current use were not required to be tested for toxicity. Even the current European Union (EU) legislation does not require any specific tests for brain toxicity. This flawed rationale awarded all existing chemicals and production processes the right to be considered innocent or innocuous unless the opposite was proven. This logic makes less and less sense, and it is especially dangerous in regard to adverse effects on the developing brain.

Confronting the Challenge

We need to raise the question "What should be done about it?" Because most chemicals have been poorly studied so far, we have a very incomplete understanding of the role of each of them in causing adverse effects. New chemicals introduced during the last 30 or so years must by law, at least within the European Union, be examined for toxic effects. However, we do not require such information for the majority of the currently used industrial chemicals because they were initially marketed before stricter laws were enacted. They were "grandfathered" in, according to regulatory slang, although this wording gives the false sense of comfort as if grandpa cares more about industrial chemicals than his grandkids' well-being.

Parents do not need to rely on official health statistics to decide that abnormal brain development should be curbed. But they are not well positioned to decide how to avoid poisoning by toxic chemicals in everyday life. We have certain options as consumers, such as choosing organic foods and healthy lifestyles thought to be beneficial, and we can try to avoid specific chemicals known to be toxic. However, most toxicants are not listed on the labels of consumer products, and you cannot see, taste, or smell them. One batch of toys may contain a large amount of toxic substances like phthalates, but the release of these substances when a child chews on the toy may be negligible compared to the release from another product with a lesser concentration. Some stores now require that the products they sell must be without toxic chemicals, such as phthalates or perfluorinated compounds, and this seems like a good approach from the viewpoint of the consumer. But what if the toy then contains an alternative or substitute of unknown potential toxicity?

These issues are complex and leave the parent or consumer with little chance of avoiding chemical risks by her own actions or choices. Therefore, industrial companies also need to make healthy choices as they produce and use chemicals, and they must make responsible decisions regarding toxicity testing and pollution abatement. Mechanisms are available to put such a strategy into place, should we choose to do so. But they may require a new way of thinking and of decision making, where health risks are taken into account even though they may as yet be considered unconfirmed. That would be in accordance with the so-called precautionary principle. Although often criticized in the United States, this decision rule is part of the EU treaty and allows policy choices to counter serious health risks in the absence of a complete proof of the hazard. Chemical brain drain should be considered a public health threat serious enough to evoke precautionary intervention with the aim of protecting the brains of future generations.

Prevention of chemical brain drain may seem costly in the short term, but I shall argue that it is cheaper in the long run and may be one of the best investments we can make. Moreover, if we don't act, our children and grandchildren may not forgive us. My hope is that this book will help to inspire more responsible decision making to protect the brains of the future. As a first step, we should allow no more grandfathering of chemicals that threaten brain development.

The Strategy

Having now given an overview of the book let me explain what the individual chapters will cover. Each chapter in the book can be read independently of the others, although together, they build toward the conclusions of the final chapter. Chapter 1 lays out the foundation for the book by explaining why the early stages of brain development are so vulnerable to the effects of toxic chemicals. Even medical textbooks do not discuss brain development from the point of view of vulnerability to toxic damage, so this summary will also contain something new for specialists.

Chapter 2 reveals how we optimistically counted on the placenta to protect the fetus, and how sad experience rectified that error. I focus on discoveries made in Australia and France and how they paved the way, very slowly, for a wider recognition of the vulnerability of the fetus, especially in regard to brain development. We now know that hundreds of industrial chemicals circulate in the fetal blood as a sign of chemical invasion. Thus, in hindsight, we were naïve and wrong to assume that the fetus was protected in the womb.

In the following chapters, I will highlight more mistakes, each chapter focusing on a specific brain drainer. Lead poisoning (chapter 3) was first thought of as a potentially life-threatening disease, which, in survivors, left no trace at all. Accordingly, lead exposure was not considered a hazard, unless clinical signs of poisoning developed. With time, research in the United States and elsewhere disclosed that brain drain is a continuous response, where the extent of the damage is proportional to the exposure, and that even small doses are hazardous.

Chapter 4 describes how early reports from Japan on brain toxicity due to mercury in seafood were ignored at first. The belief was that seafood was healthy and could therefore not be hazardous to anyone's health. Again, more refined research documented adverse effects at lower and lower exposure levels. However, public health action was delayed for several decades because healthy food items were considered resistant to pollution risks. Again, a naïve assumption hampered the interpretation of brain toxicity research and therefore delayed prevention.

It is not only during prenatal development that the brain is vulnerable to toxic chemicals. It took the poisoning of thousands of infants to make us recognize brain toxicity due to arsenic-contaminated milk powder (chapter 5). Although this discovery of life-threatening, acute effects must have been shocking, one untoward effect of the embarrassing tragedy was that the long-term fate of the victims was never examined. Even recent, authoritative assessments of arsenic toxicity have ignored the effects of arsenic on brain development. But I have met victims, whose suffering clearly shows that the toxicity does not disappear simply because it is ignored by the perpetrators. This certainly also applies to persistent organic chemicals that resist breakdown (chapter 6). Once absorbed, they remain in our body, and they can be passed on to the next generation. This is particularly true for a highly successful industrial chemical called PCB, first produced in the 1920s in Anniston, Alabama. Now this community is one of the world's most polluted towns, and the residents carry some very high PCB burdens. The PCB will go away only very slowly, and the pollution will likely continue to affect developing brains in many years to come.

We should have learned from the blunders, misfortunes, and new insights on brain drain caused by lead, mercury, arsenic, and persistent chemicals. But brain drain is not just a matter of a few annoying substances, as I will describe in chapter 7. Pesticides are often designed to interfere with the neural functions of pests, especially insects. Unfortunately, the brain biochemistry differs little between species, and the pesticides can therefore cause neurotoxicity also in humans. There are many other brain toxicants. I have included as an Appendix the updated list of chemicals that are known to be toxic to the brain. This list is incomplete, to a great extent because brain toxicity is almost never tested. This lack of information is dangerous, as the vulnerability of the developing brain is a physiological characteristic that creates exceptional susceptibility toward toxic chemicals in general, not just toward lead, mercury, and a few other poisons.

Disrupted brain development can have severe consequences. Even subtle brain damage has a tremendous personal and societal dimension, which is often overlooked or ignored. Chapter 8 puts these costs into perspective. Such damage may not be recorded as a medical diagnosis, but affected children may need special education in school; they may become less successful in life, contribute less to society in terms of income and tax revenues, and become involved in delinquency, substance abuse, and other problems because of their deranged behavior. In terms of dollars, decreased IQ and loss of lifetime income due to brain drain costs us billions of dollars per year in the United States alone. These expenses are usually hidden and ignored, as the victims and the causation are generally unknown.

Chapter 9 discusses how inertia in science is a hurdle, but not the only one. Thousands, perhaps millions, of children may suffer adverse effects that could have been prevented while expert committees contemplated the evidence. This inertia is augmented by the chemical manufacturers and other companies that question the validity of the evidence and demand more documentation. These vested interests have repeatedly manipulated brain-drain research, and they have manufactured uncertainties to raise doubt about the conclusions and the credibility of scientists. There are of course uncertainties, but the costs of brain drain are simply too enormous for us to accept that our incomplete understanding should allow continuing damage to the next generation's brains.

The final chapter outlines how chemical brain drain can be prevented. Test methods are available, although some need further validation, some are expensive, and they all have limitations, but they are helpful in identifying substances that are suspect. The consumers' own choice of a healthy lifestyle is only a partial solution. More to the point, there are healthy potentials in the use and production of chemicals. Cleaner production and safe products should take into account benefits to today's children and their children. We need to act as true parents and grandparents. Precautionary thinking and prudent intervention are needed. While we can't rely on technofixes, special diets, or neuroenhancers, we can choose green technologies and responsible innovation that do not put brains at risk.

I realize that any book on a hot neuroscience or public health topic may be outdated fairly soon. But to cover the research frontline is only one part of my purpose in writing this book. We already have plenty of evidence to support actions to protect against brain drainers. What we need most is therefore, as said by Gustave Speth, dean at Yale University, a new consciousness and a transformation in politics.[8] Such mechanisms may at first seem impossible, but they must nonetheless be implemented on behalf of our children and grandchildren. While chemical brain drain appears as a silent pandemic without impressive statistics on mortality or disease, the impacts are serious enough to demand a loud response. To promote discussion and exchange of information, a website has been generated at www.chemicalbraindrain.info, where news and reader comments will be gathered. I look forward to hearing from you. But I first want to share with you what I have found out.

CHAPTER 1

Sensitive Development

COMPLEXITY CREATES VULNERABILITY

Highly complex brain functions make it possible for me to write these lines, and for you to read them. Both you and I rely on sensory perception, cognitive processing, motor coordination, and many other brain functions. Optimal functioning depends on the interplay of many brain cells and brain regions. This extreme complexity also means that the entire brain development is enormously complicated. Thus, much can go wrong, and the intricate biological processes involved are therefore vulnerable, too. This logic might seem straightforward, but the concern that industrial chemicals can be devastating to brain development is very recent.

How do brains develop and why are environmental chemicals often so damaging to them? We get only a partial answer from the embryology and neuroanatomy textbooks, as they have a different focus.[1] Answering these questions explains why vulnerability during development is solidly based on biology and that chemical brain drain is not an unusual condition that happens only after exposure to a few substances like lead and mercury.

The human brain starts out from a bunch of cells quite similar to what other animals have at early stages. First, a thickened layer of these precursor cells (the so-called ectoderm) forms a groove that then closes up to form a tube. The distal part eventually becomes the spinal cord, at the same time as the rest expands to form the beginnings of a brain. This starts to happen during the third and fourth weeks of gestation, before the woman is certain that she is pregnant. Soon, the embryonic human brain begins to differ from the less complex organs that fish, frogs, and felines have to be content with. The cells multiply and start to differentiate to develop into the cell types that eventually build the brain—the neurons and the supporting cells called glia cells.

Most brain cells do not remain in the same spot where they started out, and cortex cells generally have to navigate a substantial distance to find their final positions. Some of the cells—the progenitor cells—have to travel more than one centimeter, in some cases close to an inch. Such distances are huge when compared to the size of the brain cells. The body of each nerve cell is about 10 micrometers, so a cell would have to travel its own width 1,000 times to have moved one centimeter. The migration requires a network of supporting glia cells to develop a structure within the space that is eventually taken up by the brain. The nerve cells then move along the lianas strung out by the glia cells. The process is complex and incompletely understood. In addition to a series of hormones, several transmitter substances, such as acetylcholine (to which I shall return shortly), are thought to play a role as "guidance" molecules that help nerve cells find their way.[2] Such functions would also explain why acetylcholine occurs widely in the brain before the nerve cells have begun to use it as a transmitter substance.

The mature neuronal circuitry depends on each cell having reached the right place at the right time. This intricate process is sensitive to a variety of external forces. Animal studies show that alcohol, cocaine, mercury, radiation, and other hazards may result in misplacement of brain cells. Upsetting the architecture of the brain has serious functional consequences, as it affects the construction of the cell network.

During brain growth, different portions of the expanding tissue generate the two hemispheres with cerebral cortex or gray matter, white matter, basal ganglia, pituitary gland, and all the other structures of the brain. By the seventh month of gestation, the outermost cell-rich layers of the brain that have already formed the cortex start folding into convolutions called gyri and sulci. But at this time the brain also weeds off some of the neurons it has formed—there are too many, and the unneeded cells must wither away. Perhaps as many as half of the brain cells are eventually eliminated.

Specialization of Brain Cells

Each neuron has to develop into a brain cell appropriate for its location and function, with the proper transmitter system for signaling. This is just like the transistors in a computer that need to be in the right position and able to connect. But development does not stop once the neurons are formed and located in their precise positions. Now the neurons need to interconnect—the cells are said to arborize. They generate dendrite extensions that form whole tree crowns of branches that reach out. The shape of the dendritic trees varies between brain regions, and thus the number and relative location of synapses that allow transfer of information between cells. The transmission of signals at the synapses and the integration of inputs from all the synapses that each neuron receives constitute the basis of the astounding information-processing capacity of the brain.

In newborn kittens, neuroanatomists have shown a burst of buddings on the dendrite trees, with an increase from an initial few hundred synapses to over

10,000 per cell. Much less is known about human brains, but on average, we probably generate about 1,000 new synapses every second during the first few years of life. Although many initial synapses do not last, the total number of synapses in the mature human brain is thought to be about 100 trillion. That is 100 followed by 12 zeros. A thousand or more for each brain cell, at least in the cortex—the large number of neurons in the cerebellum have comparatively few connections. While you are reading this, billions of synapses in your brain are signaling, not because this sentence is particularly demanding, but because the linkage between visual perception, information processing, memory, and other functions requires interaction between numerous brain regions.

Each neuron has no more than one axon, a slender projection for conduction of electrical impulses away from the cell body, sometimes stretching out thousands of times the width of the cell body from which it arises. Axons must recognize the target cells, whether other neurons, muscle cells, or other specialized cells, to form stable contacts. They produce transmitter substances at the terminal end in response to the arrival of electrical impulses that are conducted along the axon surface from the cell body and the dendrites. In the newborn child, the longest nerve cell extensions are about one foot (30 cm). In adults, the length of an axon may be up to a meter. Billions of axons are needed to transmit messages to and from all parts of the body. If all axons from a single person were lined up, they would reach four times around the globe.

The cortex consists of discrete subdivisions, each of which processes specific aspects of sensation, movement, and cognition. The parcelation of the cortex into these processing areas happens as a result of both intrinsic programming and extrinsic stimuli.[3] Thus, both pre- and postsynaptic electric activity governs the maintenance of each synapse, and over time, also the shape of the dendritic tree. In other words, usage promotes function and structure, as the connectivity of the brain cells is shaped by responses to environmental stimuli. This refinement of the circuitry is guided by activity and experience during early postnatal life and thereby forms the basis for learning and memory.[4] As a result, some cells and connections are withdrawn due to little or no activity, and eventually the number of synapses decreases to a much lower level than originally generated. The overall process seems to create the optimal connections between nerve cells based upon their use, and this refinement of the dendritic tree is guided by chemical signals.[5] Yet, we do not know precisely how this process works in regard to our developing special talents, be it singing, running, or dreaming.

Once the developmental period of neurogenesis is complete, most parts of the brain stop generating new nerve cells, even if some of the cells later on are damaged or die. Thus, we are essentially born with all the nerve cells we need. Still, stem cells have been found to remain, and a few brain regions are therefore able to add new neurons throughout life. So some cushioning is available, with possible repair, but it is certainly not a luxury that we can rely on to compensate for chemical brain drain in general.

The final outcome of this complex development still requires an extraordinary amount of energy for its functioning and maintenance. Forming neurotransmitters, distributing them, firing electrical signals, and rewiring the connections all require energy, and these processes never rest, even when we sleep. The amount of energy that you use while reading this book averages a mere 20 watts, which may not seem like a lot. That amount will provide a good reading light only if you use an energy-saving bulb. But this represents 25% of the basal metabolic rate of the whole body. This means, on a weight basis, that the brain requires 10 times more calories for maintenance than the rest of the body does. This energy is consumed by the chemical processes that produce our brain functions, whether we write, read, or think.

Chemical Brain Functions

To transmit a signal, the neurons use chemical messengers, or transmitter substances. Once contact has been made between sending and receiving cells, these special molecules are exchanged to ensure proper contact and harmonize matching specialization. There are more than 100 different neurotransmitters in operation in the brain, one of the most common ones being acetylcholine. The neurotransmitters activate, inhibit, and modulate the functions of the other cells that receive the signal. After its release, the transmitter is broken down by an enzyme before being reassembled and reused all over again. Acetylcholine is broken down by cholinesterase, a critical enzyme that has achieved toxicological importance: Inhibition of this enzyme is utilized in many pesticides to kill insects, which like humans, depend on the very same biochemical mechanism for crucial brain functions.

These transmitters also contribute toward the biochemical basis for the development of brain function. Thus, during nervous system development, neurons often express and release the very same neurotransmitters before contacts are established with target cells. It seems that the substances serve as trophic factors, or stimulants, that influence important processes, such as cell proliferation, differentiation, and development of neuronal circuits.[6] All major transmitter substances seem to play a role. Thus, if a foreign chemical causes interference with one of the transmitters, it can likely also cause interference with brain development. The chemical can thereby affect the imprinting by parental inheritance that switches genes on and off, in part mediated via the transmitter substances.[7]

A variety of hormones play a role in the control of brain development. Thus, brain hormones like the brain-derived neurotrophic factor (BDNF) trigger cell differentiation. BDNF is one of the targets affected by methylmercury exposure (see chapter 4). Sex hormones also exert powerful functions on brain development, leading to sexual dimorphism in certain brain areas. Receptors activated by specific hormones can bind to the DNA and trigger expression of certain genes that control specific stages of brain maturation. Androgen receptors that respond to the male hormone testosterone are already present in several parts of the brain during early development. Some industrial chemicals can disrupt hormonal functions, and developmental processes triggered by these hormones may therefore be sensitive to chemical exposures, sometimes with different effects in boys and girls. For example, Dutch boys exposed to estrogen-mimicking chemicals showed less masculinized play, while the exposed girls engaged in more.[8] The long-term implications of these findings are unknown.

While the total number of synapses in an adult can be counted in trillions, the numbers change substantially during brain development. The small infant sends out clouds of dendrites to form contacts with other neurons, a process that peaks at 2–3 years of age. Many of these connections are useless and get pruned away later on. At the peak of pruning, as many as 100,000 synapses may get cut every second. Those that have been frequently used get strengthened. The second wave of synapse growth occurs at 7–11 years of age. Again, much pruning occurs once the child becomes a teenager. As a result, an adult retains about half as many synapses as a 2-year-old, although many of them, perhaps most, are not the same.[9]

Once these connections are in place, the infant becomes able to control movements and manage to crawl, stand, and walk. Within the first year of life, the brain doubles in weight and size, mainly from generating insulation around the nerve cell extensions. This insulation is made of a substance called myelin and allows electrical signals to travel faster. By age 5 years, the brain is about 95% its adult size, and the remaining increase is a result of the myelination that continues until early adulthood. The frontal lobes—site of such functions as judgment, insight, and impulse control—are the last to be connected via high-speed axons as the final step in brain maturation.

Hence the neurons and the positions of the cell bodies do not change much after birth, but their connections do. The synapses are constantly being rewired during childhood. This is crucial for learning processes and memory. Synapses may be weakened or lost if they are not activated correctly. This way, synaptic activity can exert a direct influence on the connections between the brain cells. This flexibility (sometimes called plasticity) will continue to some extent for our entire lifetime, especially in regard to learning and memory. However, accomplishment of basic nervous system structure and function is possible only during early development. Later on, this potential—which we call plasticity—is no longer present. This has been demonstrated in famous laboratory experiments.

Development Depends on Stimulation

Sensory signals can determine the development of nerve cell connections. The first studies to show this effect were carried out in the early 1960s by Torsten Wiesel and David Hubel, who both received the Nobel Prize for their work.[10] In young kittens, visual stimulation was shown to cause electric responses by nerve cells in the occipital cortex in the back of the head. The nerve cells in this part of the brain are known to register and process signals from the eyes and thereby result in what we call vision. However, if a kitten had one eye blindfolded, these responses did not occur, and the animal later on became physiologically blind in that eye. Thus, within a fairly narrow time frame, the kitten uses light stimuli to help program the nerve cells, allowing the animal to "see." If the cues are not presented in due course, that is, within the first 3 months of life, development is halted, and the cat will never be able to use that eye. Once again, cholinergic signaling is responsible for determination of the ocular dominance, but only within this short time span. So the juvenile brain possesses a high capacity for plasticity and repair, while this potential is severely restricted or absent in adulthood.[11]

Similar and more specific results were obtained from other experiments with cats. Their motor cortex develops representation of all the body parts between 8 and 13 weeks after birth. The experimenters prevented forelimb movements by restraint or by intramuscular injection of botulin toxin (popularly known as Botox used for wrinkle treatment). This interference resulted in deficient development of the specific brain areas that would normally control the movement of the forelimbs.[12] Without the cortex cells to regulate movement, the cat will limp the rest of its life. Thus, it seems that repetitive exercising of motor skills is necessary to allow normal development of the brain's control of motor function. Further, intensive training of forelimb movements during this period stimulates development in the brain's motor function area, but the brain reverts back to ignoring these extra functions if the motor tasks are not maintained.[13]

Rodent studies showed similar results. Nerve fibers carry signals from each of an animal's whiskers to a particular region of the brain, where the nerve cells then organize into so-called barrel structures within the first few days after birth. However, if the whiskers are clipped, so that the sensory input is prevented, the barrels fail to form, and the perception is lost. Recent studies have shown that receptors using glutamate as transmitter are crucial for barrel formation.[14] Further, young rats that are reared in an enriched social environment have more branching of the nerve cell connections than rats reared alone or in an impoverished environment. Sound and visual stimulation during this period are also associated with specific changes in neuron morphology.

The synaptic dynamics illustrate that the brain develops as a tissue designed for continuous modification to allow for learning and memory development. The addition and loss of synapses probably serve to optimize performance in particular settings and environments. Both addition and elimination of synapses improve the specificity of the neural connections. Although these processes are particularly intense during specific phases of development, some of them continue throughout life, albeit at a reduced level, thus allowing for some degree of plasticity of the mature organ.[15] For all of this to become possible, the brain must have completed multiple and complex developmental stages in the right sequence and at the right time.

Brain Plasticity

Most studies in laboratory animals focus on sensory or motor function as accessible functions in experiments. Although these functions are quite similar to those of the human nervous system, we cannot be certain that conditions in humans are exactly the same. However, it is known that blocking one eye, even for as little as one week some time early in infancy, can result in permanently reduced vision, despite complete access to visual stimuli. Such deprivation of eyesight may occur as a result of lens opacities due to congenital German measles (see chapter 2).

More comprehensive stimulus deprivation may delay or inhibit brain development in a more general sense. The most dramatic example was a study in Romania of impoverished children, who had been abandoned at or shortly after birth and then placed either in foster care or in institutional care. The cognitive capacities of children who remained in an institution were remarkably less advanced than those never institutionalized and those taken out of institutional care and moved to foster care at an early age. So while a deficient environment may hamper early brain development, an intervention at the right time can be successful.[16] Other findings also document that children can suffer serious brain damage and still demonstrate the ability to catch up and approach normal development, a feat that would not be possible for adults.

Our auditory system is also shaped by the spoken language that we are exposed to as infants and perhaps even prenatally. Bilinguals seem to have better attention functions than monolinguals, perhaps because learning a second language helps the brain to become capable of resolving internal conflicts. Subjects who have learned a second language before the age of 5 years and practiced it regularly since then have an increased cell density in a specific part of the parietal cortex, when compared to subjects, who learned the second language at age 10–15 years.[17]

Taking advantage of the continued plasticity, a group of young adults learned a juggling routine. Brain scans revealed that, at the height of training, there was a small increase in cell density in parts of the brain, especially those involved in the perception and spatial anticipation of moving objects, but the increase seemed to be only transient and began to fade three months after giving up the juggling.[18] So the brain's plasticity results in a propensity to adapt to changing needs. These changes are not restricted to the gray matter of the brain. The white matter, responsible for electrical impulse conduction, also shows plasticity, perhaps related to the increased extent of myelination of the axons, so that they can conduct electrical signals more efficiently.[19] Accordingly, the beneficial effects may also extend to other brain functions. Thus, the improved aerobic fitness in schoolchildren with an active lifestyle was associated with better memory and a larger volume of the hippocampus, the part of the brain responsible for this function.[20]

More specific changes in brain organization are known to happen in braille readers, musicians, and upper limb amputees. Magnetic resonance imaging of adults who had their right arm immobilized for only a few weeks showed a decreased thickness of the cortical areas that represent motor control and sensitivity for the right side of the body. At the same time, motor skills were transferred to the other arm, with increases in cortical thickness on that side.[21] Similar changes in the opposite directions occur when the cast is removed. Most if not all of these modifications are probably due to greatly expanded nerve cell connections, rather than formation of new cells. Such plasticity will be greatly helpful to patients with brain trauma or other damage, but it does rely on the presence of functional nerve cells in the right locations. That may not necessarily be true after chemical brain drain. Although the mechanisms involved in local remapping and myelination are poorly understood, they likely depend on transmitter substances and may be negatively affected by toxic chemicals.

Generation of new nerve cells is known to occur in the hippocampus, the part of the brain that is responsible for learning and memory. Local precursor cells are capable of producing new neurons, which are more responsive to incoming information than older brain cells.[22] We don't know yet to which extent this occurs in humans, but this capability is most likely formed during early development. However, some neuron loss does occur with age, and that seems to be compensated mainly by an increase in the number of synapses. Decay is therefore offset by improved connections. But the synapse rewiring depends on the needs and continues to a lesser extent as we age. The successful rehabilitation of patients with a stroke or other cerebral damage is an indication that new synapses can indeed take over functions that have been lost.

In neuropsychology, different brain functions are linked to specific brain structures. The prefrontal cortex is crucial for executive functions, such as judging, choosing, and planning, while nearby parts are responsible for moral judgments and choices in regard to social behavior. Motor function depends on particular areas in the temporal cortex but also relies on the cerebellum and basal nuclei. Regulation of the heart beat and wakefulness is located in the brainstem, and visual perception depends on the occipital cortex. Each of these areas has a particular course of maturation that is distinct from other brain structures, with early sensory cortex development and fairly late development of the prefrontal cortex and cerebellum in comparison with other brain structures. The timing of an adverse chemical exposure may therefore determine the type of resulting damage.

After the brain size has peaked at age 20 years, it shrinks during adulthood by as much as 15%, possibly involving some loss of neurons, loss of myelination, and some synapse pruning. Reaction times become longer, we slow down somewhat, and memories fade, while IQ (intelligence quotient) and language remain virtually unchanged, unless neurological disease sets in. It seems that some people— especially those with a high IQ—are better able to withstand and compensate for neurotoxic damage, perhaps also in adulthood, also when degenerative diseases may develop. As a compensation mechanism, other regions of the brain can take over tasks from damaged areas. When radiology professor Kim Cecil from the Cincinnati Children's Hospital was interviewed by a newspaper about the compensation when other neurons take over for damaged cells, she said: "It's like when you need a hammer to do a job and you're tapping away at it with a screwdriver. You can still complete the task, but you're not using the right tool, and you're not going to get as good a result."[23] So plasticity is not an automatic mechanism we can rely on to counter chemical brain drain.

In short, the brain depends on external stimuli for its optimal development, as its plasticity allows it to respond favorably to beneficial circumstances. These positive challenges are necessary to stimulate brain development. Some reserve capacity is present, as we generate more nerve cells than we need and too many connections between the cells. But the full buffer ability is present only when brain development has worked out according to the genetic blueprint. Experiments have demonstrated that serious adverse effects occur when the young animal is deprived of essential stimuli at specific windows of time. By way of parallel reasoning, it seems likely that environmental chemicals may influence the electric activity of nerve cells or some other crucial processes at sensitive stages and thereby hinder their optimal programming.

The complexity and vast number of processes that take place during central nervous system development provide multiple opportunities for differential effects of chemical exposures.[24] Perturbations during the first trimester result in faulty proliferation of brain cells and malformations, such as microcephaly (small brain and small skull with mental retardation). The importance of genes to steer the developmental processes is evidenced by the multitude of genetic disorders of brain development that often result in mental retardation. Information from many genes is needed for brain development to occur flawlessly.

One possible mechanism for brain-toxic chemicals is therefore to affect the expression of the genes, by methylation or other modification of the DNA (so-called epigenetic effects that do not involve genotoxicity or mutations). Also, we now know that acetylcholine is involved in controlling the expression of genes in the brain. Interference with transmitter substances may therefore also have consequences for the genetic control of brain development.[25] Such effects can likely happen very early in development. We can detect electrical activity of the fetal brain by modern neurophysiology instruments, and responses can be elicited by means of external light and sound. Perhaps the sensory stimuli are affecting gene expression in the brain, and perhaps chemical stimuli can obscure them or damage the way the genes are transcribed.

While my focus is on environmental factors, genes are of course crucial for optimal brain development. After all, the design of the brain is laid out in the genes that we inherited from our parents. Identical twins have the same genome and also share their intrauterine existence. Identical twins separated after birth show remarkable similarities in attitudes and behaviors, although also many dissimilarities.[26] A large-scale study that compared genetic differences with various aspects of intelligence recently concluded that about half of the variation can be attributed to inheritance.[27] However, in experiments where a mouse embryo was implanted into the uterus of a dam of a different strain, the pups developed behaviors that were more similar to the adopted mother's than to mice of its own strain.[28] Thus, both the prenatal and the postnatal environment play a role in shaping the brain, along with the genes. The final product is a result of a complex interplay between genetic and environmental influences.

Protection of Developing Brains

The brain is sheltered inside the skull and floats in cerebrospinal fluid that provides a cushion against punches to the head. Against environmental chemicals, the brain is protected by a blood-brain barrier that is meant to keep unwanted toxicants and pathogens from entering the brain. The barrier is made up of a wall of tightly packed cells, which line the tiny blood vessels that permeate the brain. Between each of the cells is a kind of mortar called "tight junctions," which prevent foreign molecules in the blood from slipping through. Protein pumps act as sentinels, expelling waste and other substances that don't belong, and the brain's supporting cells play a key role in maintaining the barrier. The blood-brain barrier is of course not a solid wall—it does let in oxygen and nutrients, for example. It was quite sufficient during millions of years to safeguard mammalian brains. But new harmful chemicals emerged and manage to pass through the barrier. Thus, the protection is no longer complete.

Despite the blood-brain barrier—and the placental barrier, which I will discuss in the next chapter—the fetus and the infant are not safeguarded against industrial chemicals. Perhaps a more efficient barrier was not necessary during evolution when industrial chemicals did not exist, but our dissemination of toxicants is now putting any innate protection to its most severe test so far. Moreover, while the fetus would in particular need this protection, the barrier is not fully functional until late in pregnancy when some of the most sensitive processes in brain development have already been completed.

When sufficient evidence had cumulated that children should not necessarily be considered little adults in regard to environmental chemical risks, the US Environmental Protection Agency (EPA) in collaboration with a private research company, the International Life Sciences Institute (ILSI), called a conference to discuss the implications for regulation of chemicals. It was clear to everybody that children may deserve special consideration in the assessment of chemical risks. However, some speakers at the conference emphasized examples of children occasionally being *less* vulnerable than adults due to immature metabolism of chemicals that need to be activated to become toxic. One commonly quoted example is acetaminophen (a.k.a. paracetamol), a common painkiller. An overdose is less damaging to a child's liver than to an adult's, because the immature liver produces a toxic breakdown product of the drug at a much lower rate. Based on the presentations at the conference, the organizers offered the following very restrained conclusion: "Differences in sensitivity between children and adults are chemical specific and must be studied and evaluated on a case-by-case basis."[29]

This conclusion has been repeated many times to support the notion that children should not be regarded as more vulnerable unless proven on each occasion. In other words, let's continue exposing the next generation and their developing brains until we are certain that damage has occurred. This conclusion has framed prevention strategies ever since. However, the characteristics of human brain development that I have outlined in this chapter would argue for a very different conclusion. From the evidence on brain development that I have summarized, I would argue that complex brain development is so vulnerable to damage from potential brain drainers that protection against chemical exposures should be a top priority. Any exception to this default rule should be accepted only on the basis of convincing documentation. In other words, chemicals should be considered a threat to brain development until proven otherwise (not the reverse as things stand now, and as argued by the EPA-ILSI conference). I shall return to the policy issues and decision making in chapters 9 and 10.

There are additional factors that add to the vulnerability during early life. The exposure pathways, the uptake, metabolism, and general sensitivity place infants and children in a uniquely high-risk group in regard to industrial chemicals.[30] During pregnancy, a mother shares with her child the chemicals that she herself has accumulated in her body thus far, and some of them are passed on in her milk (more about that in chapter 2). Infants explore toys and other parts of their environment by licking and chewing, and they therefore ingest paints, soil, and dust that may contain toxic chemicals. Warning labels are of no use unless parents read them and act accordingly to protect their child. In respect to their body size, infants breathe more, drink, and eat more than adults, and the immature gut is more easily penetrated by metals and other compounds that adults barely absorb. For example, a toddler can absorb between 40% and 70% of the lead present in flakes of paint, while the adult's gut will allow only a few percent to be taken up. Once inside the body, the child's liver is not as efficient at breaking down many industrial chemicals, and the kidneys are not mature enough to meet the needs of excreting such compounds. In addition, children potentially have a much longer life in front of them and will depend on their organ functions, and they will also experience a full range of age-dependent disease risks that may materialize over time.[31]

The appreciation of children's vulnerability is very recent and even the realization that children may require different diagnostics, therapy, and care is also fairly new. Scandinavian specialists in pediatrics were recognized in the early 20th century, and the American Academy of Pediatrics (AAP) was founded in 1930. In the United Kingdom, the British Paediatric Association was established about the same time, but only in 1996 were the pediatricians granted a royal charter to form their own college, the Royal College of Paediatrics and Child Health (until then they were part of the Royal College of Physicians). It took even longer to appreciate that toxicology as well ought to be split into pediatric (or developmental) toxicology and adult (or general) toxicology. This split is still under way and is gaining recognition, although it seems excruciatingly slow. The time is overdue. Our reluctant appreciation of brain-draining hazards is also the theme of the next chapter, where I shall focus on our overoptimistic reliance on the placenta to protect the fetus against environmental hazards, and how we only at a frustratingly slow pace began to realize that we cannot count on the placenta to provide developing brains with the protection they need.

CHAPTER 2

Toxic Invasion

THE PLACENTA IS NOT A PROTECTIVE ARMOR

When you go the pharmacy to pick up a prescription, you regularly see a warning that some drug or other should not be used during pregnancy. This concern has a long history in the United States. Famously, Dr. Frances Kelsey, of the Food and Drug Administration (FDA), was responsible for the fortuitous decision not to allow the drug thalidomide on the market. In her opinion, the drug had not been adequately tested, as the immature enzymes of the fetus might be unable to break down any of the drug that might pass the placenta.[1] Her worry turned out to be justified, and thalidomide imprudently used elsewhere was soon linked to serious congenital malformations. As with many other warnings against chemicals, the initial safety concerns were criticized as an overreaction. In the words of a company president as the first cases of thalidomide malformations were published: "There is still no positive proof of a causal relationship between the use of thalidomide during pregnancy and malformations in the newborn".[2] Clearly, the industrialist and the doctor had very different views on the amount of information needed to reach a conclusion regarding safety. But perspectives change with time, and important controversies are often due to the persistence of long-held views that are no longer tenable, sometimes combined with the longevity of influential and inflexible scientists, who risk losing face. A key example is the placenta, in which thin cell layers separate the pregnant woman's blood circulation from the fetus.

Up to 30 or 40 years ago, the placental barrier was thought to allow efficient delivery of the necessary nutrients and oxygen from the mother, while waste products were returned for elimination. Inside the womb, the fetus was kept safe from external hazards—the placenta and the uterus provided near-perfect armor for protection. So was the belief, and medical students were taught that the placenta was virtually impervious to toxic substances, perhaps except in doses large enough to kill off the mother.[3]

The known physiology of the placenta seemed to be in agreement with this view. The basal part of the human placenta develops from maternal cells. An additional layer in touch with the maternal cells derives from the cells that form the fetus. Oxygen, nutrients, and some antibodies and hormones pass through the double-cell layer from the mother's circulation into the fetal blood. The placenta does not allow the blood from the two circulations to mix, thereby avoiding immunological reactions of the mother toward the baby's blood (like the blood of Rhesus negative mothers that would react against a Rhesus positive fetus, with detrimental consequences). Likewise, the logic went, adverse influences from the outside would be unable to bypass the filtering function represented by the "placental barrier."

Research in this field is complicated, as the human placenta differs from the placenta of most animal species that are commonly used in laboratory studies.[4] Some mammals, such as the duck-billed platypus and the spiny anteater, have no placentas at all and those that do vary substantially in regard to placenta development and function. Only recently have researchers begun to study the transfer of drugs and foreign chemicals through human placentas obtained at childbirth.

The idealized picture of the placenta—like the blood-brain barrier—blocking the entry of toxic chemicals may have been true in a distant past, before new industrial compounds were invented. But the beautiful hypothesis was slain by an ugly fact, or a couple of eye-opening facts, rather, that emerged in the second half of the 20th century. One of these new insights was about alcohol, and another was about a tiny virus thought to cause only a mild childhood disease. Then came along an even uglier fact—a host of man-made chemicals that would threaten the fetal brain development.

Alcohol Passed on to the Fetus

Alcohol (or ethanol as it is referred to in chemistry) is formed in nature and is definitely not an industrial compound new to human biochemistry. Most people can metabolize alcohol at a rate that prevents small quantities from causing intoxication. So why not assume the same for the fetus? Since ancient times, heavy alcohol drinking was known to cause severe damage to the imbiber's health. But knowledge of the adverse impacts on the next generation began to be compiled only in the 18th century. Still, these historical accounts primarily blamed paternal drinking for faulty development of the child. Men's alcohol abuse was common, it was highly visible, and it was associated with violence and other social disorder. The costs to society were great. Men drank up their wages, beat their wives and children, lost their jobs, and went to the poorhouse for unpaid debts or to jail for stealing. Social theory at the time suggested that the alcoholic male demeanor was transferred with the sperm to the offspring.[5]

Among notable observations, the Royal College of Physicians of London in 1726 noted that alcoholic women gave birth to "weak, feeble, and distempered children." The English author Henry Fielding—best known for the novel Tom Jones—wrote a social pamphlet in 1751 and asked: "What must become of an infant, who is conceived in Gin? With the poisonous Distillations of which it is nurtured, both in the Womb and at the Breast." About 80 years later, his compatriot, Charles Dickens caricatured in his novel, *The Pickwick Papers,* the impacts on children caused by maternal drinking. Although health problems at the time were hard to distinguish from those caused by malnutrition and by poverty in general, medical expertise began to recommend temperance to prevent adverse effects in one's children.[6]

Not that it changed much. A prison physician, William Sullivan, in 1899 reported that maternal inebriety had some severe effects on the progeny, leading to stillbirths, miscarriages, and, in the survivors, ailments "such as idiocy, or...those slighter forms of mental inferiority which appear to exist in at least a considerable proportion of habitual criminals and prostitutes." Sullivan did not dispute the adverse influence of the father's disreputable behavior, but he stopped short of concluding that alcohol had direct effects on the fetus, since the damage could also be an indirect effect of the pathology invoked in the pregnant woman's body. So the overall verdict was still to blame the drinker, not the drink. Eventually, the appropriately named *British Journal of Inebriety* in 1923 conjectured that "the placenta acts as a protective filter for many substances, but alcohol is not one of these." Much would have been different today if that early insight had been heeded.[7]

The prediction eventually became common knowledge 50 years later, when American pediatrics researchers Kenneth L. Jones and David W. Smith coined the term "fetal alcohol syndrome" in a paper that described eight cases.[8] The children showed delayed growth, cognitive difficulties, and characteristic facial anomalies—and all had an alcoholic mother. The report was published in the prestigious medical journal *The Lancet.* Since then, the paper has been cited in more than 1,000 scientific articles on the adverse effects of ethanol. A true classic in its field, it heralded a paradigm change.

German Measles Shows the Way

By that time, penetration of the placenta barrier had already been confirmed for another substance that could wreak havoc on the fetus, German measles (a.k.a. rubella). It was once considered the least troublesome of childhood infections. As a highly infectious disease that produced life-long immunity, it came in waves in most parts of the world. One such epidemic started in Australia in 1939 and swept through army camps; many young recruits on leave carried the infection home with them.

An Australian ophthalmologist, who specialized in pediatric surgery, Norman McAlister Gregg, was struck by the surprising number of infants with congenital cataract (clouding of the lens of the eye) in his practice.[9] The cataract usually affected both eyes and allowed virtually no light to reach the retina. The involvement of the central layers of the lens and the fact that the cataract was bilateral, suggested that the damage had already occurred during very early fetal development. The clinical picture was highly unusual. While an ophthalmologist could expect occasional cataract cases among elderly patients in his practice, Gregg's clientele was solely pediatric. His finding was a true surprise, as only few and rare heritable causes of cataract are known.

When Gregg, in early 1941, was pondering his statistics of the unusual diagnosis, he contacted colleagues in New South Wales and Victoria provinces for help. He eventually identified a total of 78 infants with congenital cataract, a truly excessive number. The recommended course of action was to remove the opaque lens, but the ophthalmologists often found that the retina was damaged as well, with an unusual salt-and-pepper pigmentation. Many of the infants also had other abnormalities, including deafness, congenital heart conditions, and abnormally small head (microcephaly). By the time Gregg wrote an account of his findings, 15 had already died.

Since the patients appeared within a limited time period, the mothers had been pregnant at about the same time. Gregg therefore believed that a common cause was likely responsible—a daring conclusion at a time when most physicians believed that birth defects were inherited.[10] The clue did not come from advanced blood tests or clinical examinations. It came from the mothers' pregnancy history. Gregg reportedly heard two mothers with affected children speak in the waiting room—they both had had German measles early in their pregnancies. Upon Gregg's inquiry, a total of 68 of the 78 mothers reported typical rashes at the beginning of the pregnancy, in some cases before they were aware of being pregnant.

So Gregg daringly proposed that the mother's disease had somehow gained access to the fetus and caused damage during the early fetal development. At the time, this seemed radical and far-fetched. First of all, as noted previously, it was a common—though erroneous—belief that the placenta provided an absolute barrier against infectious and toxic agents. And second, the German measles virus was not identified until 20 years later.

Before Gregg released his findings, nobody suspected that this mild infection could be associated with such severe and unusual damage to the fetus. This misinterpretation was fortunate in one respect: The mother's own description of rashes and other symptoms could be considered reliable, as it would be untainted by her own suspicions of possible causes. On the other hand, no objective method existed to confirm her history of an infection, as nobody could even dream up an antibody test at that time.

On 15 October 1941, Gregg delivered his conclusions in a lecture titled "Congenital Cataract Following German Measles in the Mother." He spoke at a meeting of the Ophthalmological Society of Australia in Melbourne, and his manuscript was soon thereafter published in its journal, *Transactions* (now long gone).[11]

These pioneering observations had little immediate impact. A number of Gregg's colleagues were skeptical and felt that he was straying from his field of expertise.[12] In an editorial, the *Medical Journal of Australia* urged caution, stating: "the association is not entirely proven."[13] At the request of the National Health and Medical Research Council of Australia, letters were sent to all general practitioners in the state of South Australia informing them of Gregg's findings and asking them to complete a form for all children born to women who had an acute exanthema (skin rash) during pregnancy. The study showed that there were 49 cases in which the mother had been exposed to German measles during pregnancy, with 31 of the infants having congenital malformations including cataract, deaf-mutism, heart disease, microcephaly, and mental retardation. In all but two of the 31 cases, the mother had contracted the disease in the first three months of pregnancy.[14]

Gregg's 78 patients were probably just a small fraction of the infants who had suffered congenital rubella in connection with this wave of the disease. And it was of course not the first time that Australia had such an epidemic. These illnesses came in waves, often separated by 20 years or so. One major German measles epidemic occurred in 1924–1925 and another one back in 1899.[15] The Australian censuses carried out in 1911, 1921, and 1933 included a question on blindness and deaf-mutism, and these demographic data confirmed a relation to the German measles epidemics in terms of season and year. Thus, hundreds, perhaps thousands of cases of congenital rubella infection had happened during past epidemics, each time several months after an epidemic that affected newly pregnant women. Not only did the time interval from infection to childbirth impede the recognition of the cause, but the level of medical specialization at the time did not call for specialist referrals to identify disease etiologies. Eventually, the observant eye doctor in Sydney made the connection.

Still, the link between maternal rubella infection and birth defects was not universally accepted. Gregg had the fortune of being a highly competent pediatric ophthalmologist, to whom infants were referred for possible treatment of their bilateral cataracts, and the sudden surge in occurrence of the unusual diagnosis could be linked to the peak of the German measles epidemic several months previously. But later studies that attempted to verify Gregg's hypothesis were less informative, in part because German measles was sometimes difficult to diagnose in adults, who do not necessarily develop the typical rash.

Three years after Gregg's publication, one of the world's oldest and most highly respected medical journals, *The Lancet,* commented in an editorial that "though the possibility remains he cannot yet be said to have proved his case."[16] Further, the editorial stated that "the lay public have always held that congenital malformations have an extrinsic explanation—from being frightened by a dog to falling down stairs—and it will be strange if the influence of a mild illness in the first months of pregnancy, accompanied by a rash, has escaped attention." The author did not comment on the opposite medical prejudice at the time that birth defects were allegedly inherited, that is, they were thought to be of a genetic origin. Similarly, the *British Medical Journal* expressed doubt that the birth defects could be a new manifestation of German measles, on the assumption that such a dramatic sequence could not have been overlooked in the past. This author concluded "we cannot exclude the possibility of a chance association between congenital defects and true maternal rubella."[17] We shall see later how similar, overskeptical arguments have been used to calm concerns about chemical hazards.

One important concern was that Gregg had only studied children with cataract. He had not looked for children without congenital defects, whose mothers had German measles during pregnancy. The same applied to the extended studies carried out by Gregg's colleagues in Australia. However, given the dramatic association of a rare congenital defect with an infection during pregnancy and the unlikely information bias, this critique would not invalidate the findings. Still, because World War II was ongoing, Gregg's hypothesis received little attention outside of Australia, and the editorials in major medical journals helped silence the little there was. Even after the war, congenital rubella infection was virtually ignored for over 20 years.

Alcohol as Brain Drainer

Important progress in understanding the degree to which the placenta protects the fetus happened in the 1960s. Observant doctors were noticing adverse effects on the fetus as an apparent result of maternal drinking. Seattle pediatrician Christy Ulleland raised awareness of the risks after examining 12 infants born to alcoholic mothers in 1968–1969; all had low birth weights and low postnatal growth. Ten infants were examined with developmental tests—five were clearly delayed in development, three more had a borderline delay.[18]

Soon thereafter, her colleagues Kenneth Jones and David Smith coined the term "fetal alcohol syndrome." Unbeknownst to the American doctors, the condition had been described several years earlier by a French pediatrician, Paul Lemoine. He had assembled records on 69 families with 127 affected children.[19] As the only attending pediatrician at a local nursery in Brittany, Lemoine saw a large number of infants, and he began to observe some striking similarities between those with delayed development.

Particularly noticeable were the similar facial abnormalities in children in the clinic, even though few of them were siblings. After having excluded syphilis and all possible causes he could think of, Lemoine found that the infants had only one characteristic in common: They all had an alcoholic mother. He was soon able to make the diagnosis solely on the basis of the child's facial features. (However, his later studies showed that children without the typical facial features could be as mentally retarded as those with.)

Five mothers who had given birth to adversely affected children later became teetotalers and had one or more healthy babies.

Lemoine first reported his findings in a presentation at the Medico-Surgical Society of Nantes in 1964—several years before the reports from Seattle. He received little attention, although at least some medical colleagues seemed to accept that alcohol could damage fetal development. Lemoine happened to practice in northwestern France (Brittany and Normandy) which at the time was known for the highest national death rates from alcoholism and liver cirrhosis. Louis Pasteur's dictum that "Wine is the most hygienic of all beverages" was evidently taken to heart, although perhaps more than Pasteur had anticipated. In the 1950s, the maximum safe amount of daily wine consumption was considered to be 1.8 liter—half a gallon—for French manual workers.[20] Women could safely drink one-third as much—about four glasses per day. The same survey study also found that about 50% of practicing physicians in France agreed that wine was useful or even indispensable for manual laborers. And the 120-page report, published in 1965, did not even mention any concerns in regard to alcohol drinking during pregnancy.

Undeterred by the lack of support, Lemoine three years later made a similar presentation at the Society of Pediatrics of Western France and published the manuscript in 1968 in the (now-defunct) French regional journal *Ouest-médical*. "Most pediatricians, rather astonished, did not consider this to be serious," Lemoine later wrote about the response from his colleagues. As late as in 1984, his offer to present a lecture at a pediatrics congress in Paris was turned down.[21]

Published in French, Lemoine's account also escaped the radar of article retrieval in the United States and elsewhere. As Lemoine later commented, "This is an amusing fact: the 127 cases of a modest pediatrician from Brittany did not create any interest, whereas 8 American cases became immediately convincing." Perhaps as an indication of scientific inertia, Lemoine's original paper was cited only 22 times in the scientific literature during the following 40 years. Two Canadian scientists noted: "This strongly suggests that we have all missed an incredible body of evidence published in languages other than English."[22] Still, as we shall see from several other examples, inertia is not just a question of scientists not having access to non-English publications.

Once Jones and Smith eventually heard of Lemoine's findings, for obvious reasons they believed him and recognized his work, but they had their own troubles. Several readers wrote to *The Lancet* to suggest other possible explanations of the medical reports on the Seattle children. One suggestion was that alcohol itself did not cause the damage in the developing brains, but it was due to lead from contaminated moonshine alcohol. At that point, lead was still not confirmed as a definite brain drainer, but that was apparently not a problem when the intention was to explain away the effects of alcohol. Later on, the opposite happened—alcohol was suggested as the real cause of neurotoxicity linked to developmental lead exposure.[23] Also, many obstetricians at the time still believed in the beneficial effects of alcohol in halting premature labor.

Medical alcohol research colleagues mostly studied the impact of liquor on the livers of heavy-drinking men. As psychiatry professor Ann Streissguth writes: "In the early 1970s when risks to the fetus were described as being associated with 1–2 ounces of absolute alcohol per day, some male researchers were incredulous. "You'd call that heavy drinking?" they used to ask of me in disbelief." At the time, many of Streissguth's colleagues studied the adverse effects of alcohol on the liver, often at daily intakes at least five times greater.[24] Although it now seemed clear that ethanol easily penetrated the placenta, the fetal alcohol syndrome was still not universally accepted.

Long-Term Consequences

The German measles (rubella) virus was isolated in tissue culture in 1962. Soon after this scientific achievement, a new and serious epidemic emerged. In the United States alone, over 12 million were infected, including about 1% of all pregnant women. As a result, more than 20,000 American children were born with congenital rubella syndrome of varying severity, and 30,000 stillbirths occurred. Investigations were now greatly aided by the new tool available from a serum test that could confirm the diagnosis. Given the number of cases, congenital rubella infection finally became a priority public health issue, more than 20 years after Gregg's discovery. A vaccine was developed in record time.

Among important observations, the likelihood of infection and the severity of the damage to the fetus were found to depend on the actual time of maternal infection. Damage to eye and heart development occurred when the mother was infected during the beginning of the first trimester of pregnancy, while mental deficiency was usually linked to maternal disease somewhat later. The transplacental infection by rubella virus could lead to postnatal persistence of the virus within the brain. Autopsy data showed localized loss of brain tissue and decreased numbers of neurons. In surviving children, the full syndrome seemed to develop over time, with impairment of hearing and vision, and various degrees of brain dysfunction, some of the children later being diagnosed as mentally retarded. Many children had short attention span, inability to concentrate, deficient motor coordination, poor balance, and problems with social skills. Further characteristics, such as enlarged liver, cerebral calcifications, and several other pathologies were also recorded.[25] However, virtually no follow-up was conducted in the United States, perhaps because the vaccine now promised to prevent future epidemics.

Fifty of Gregg's first subjects with congenital German measles were reexamined as 25-year-olds. The results showed that the health of the patients most seriously affected did not improve. Mental deficiency was present in 10%, but the follow-up examinations may have included only the healthiest cases, certainly only the survivors. About one-third led relatively normal lives. One-third still lived with their parents, some patients being employed, though mainly in noncompetitive jobs. The remaining third was profoundly handicapped and required institutional care.[26]

Further follow-up was conducted again at ages 50 and 60 years, most recently in 2001, where the overall picture had not improved. Over time, some had died, most often of cardiovascular disease, and their neurological symptoms seemed to worsen with time. At the 60-year visit, only eight subjects (including one blind woman) were still working. Many had retired early, or received a disability pension.[27]

In Canada, a survey documented the late emerging medical conditions associated with the congenital rubella syndrome.[28] Among affected patients ranging from 5 to 62 years of age, visual loss and hearing loss were highly prevalent, one-third had microcephaly, and almost as many had developed glaucoma, that is, visual damage associated with increased pressure in the eye. One-fourth had received treatment for mental health due to behavioral abnormalities, seizures, and fatigue. These findings agreed with a study of deaf-blind patients in New York City. Thirty percent of the patients surveyed had developed glaucoma, a frequency much higher than the expected 0.5% for the general US population. Other problems were also recorded, including a growing incidence of degenerative neurological conditions.[29] So the complete range of outcomes of the congenital infection did not become clear until decades later.

The severe effects of prenatal German measles spurred action within the public health agencies, and vaccination of children has been recommended since 1969. Soon, the incidence of reported German measles cases declined dramatically and epidemics were effectively prevented. Later on, the recommendation was extended to include vaccination of adolescents and adult women. Since the late 1980s, children in most Western countries have received mumps-measles-rubella (MMR) vaccine during infancy. In the United States, more than 93% of children are vaccinated, and the few cases diagnosed are all imported. In 2004, the Centers for Disease Control and Prevention (CDC) declared that the disease had been eliminated in the United States. By now, about 125 countries vaccinate against rubella, although large populations, for example, in Africa, India, and Indonesia, are not covered.[30] So Gregg's discovery eventually led to a public health intervention that saved thousands of lives and protected an even greater number of brains from rubella-mediated damage.

Worsening IQ Deficits

Follow-up studies of fetal alcohol exposure showed that these adverse effects, too, tended to be permanent, if not to worsen as the affected children grew up. Thirty years after Lemoine's original studies, he and his son contacted 105 of the original study subjects, now young adults. While some of the abnormal facial features had become less prominent, microcephaly was now more pronounced. The most serious problem remained the mental retardation and severe learning disabilities, coupled with behavioral disturbances and emotional instability. Of 63 subjects with severe fetal alcohol syndrome, eight were without language, and another eight were severely debilitated with an IQ below 50. Thirty-two had an IQ between 50 and 65. Fifteen in this group along with six of the 28 with mild fetal alcohol syndrome had an IQ of 60–75, with some reading, writing, and counting skills. Seven in this group had attempted suicide.[31]

Ann Streissguth conducted her own large study and followed 473 adolescents with fetal alcohol syndrome. She found an average IQ of 79, as compared to the expected average score of 100. Although these adolescents were not as incapacitated as Lemoine's cases, alcohol clearly had a devastating effect on the brain development of these adolescents. There seemed to be a graded response, with less alcohol exposure resulting in less damage.[32]

Later studies documented additional abnormalities, such as irritability, tremors, in some cases seizures. Visual problems and hearing loss are common. Often language development is delayed, and motor skills develop more slowly than normal. Even when children with fetal alcohol syndrome have a normal IQ, they typically have low scores on visual-motor tasks. Their short memory span, impulsivity, and emotional instability also contribute to their low scores. Not only that, but 60% of the adolescents (and even 14% of the group already during childhood) had trouble with the law, most frequently in the form of shoplifting or theft, along with disrupted school experiences.[33]

The growth problems, mental retardation, motor dysfunctions, and sensory disturbances seen in the fetal alcohol syndrome show some similarity to the congenital rubella syndrome. These children are not just cases of mental retardation or patients with congenital abnormalities. They often have multiple handicaps, with several types of sensory deficits and organ dysfunctions, including congenital heart disease. In both cases, the characteristics vary among patients, possibly because of differences in the timing of the exposure.

Today, the diagnosis of fetal alcohol syndrome requires growth deficiency pre- and/or postnatally; a distinct pattern of specific malformations including characteristic facial features; and brain dysfunction, such as developmental delay, hyperactivity, and intellectual deficits. Less severe damage is now referred to as fetal alcohol effects, and the overall perspective of damage is called fetal alcohol spectrum disorder.[34]

Following the general acceptance that alcohol can harm not only one's own health but also the next generation's, many countries have chosen to run public education campaigns and to require warning messages on alcoholic beverages. While the beverage industry at first intensely fought these proposals, the strategy changed in response to the possible advantage of indemnifying the industry from lawsuits. Now the alcoholic beverage industry just insists that warnings do not need to appear on the fronts of bottles and likewise not in advertisements. Still, chronic alcoholics and heavy binge drinkers may not stop drinking because of a warning label. So while the risks associated with alcohol drinking during pregnancy have become widely accepted, much remains to be done in regard to providing better services to treat alcoholics.

It is now recognized that even if a pregnant woman drinks only one unit of alcoholic beverage (a beer, or a glass of wine) per day, she could cause neurological disturbances to the child she is carrying. Children exposed to alcohol from the mother's drinking will experience problems with arithmetic, language, abstract problem solving, working memory, attention, and executive function. Attention span appears to be particularly sensitive to alcohol.[35] Children with a history of prenatal alcohol exposure tend to lack the ability to stay focused and attentive over time and have difficulty analyzing problems and forming effective response strategies. Also, vision may be affected.[36] As children mature, deficits in social behavior become more pronounced and are often expressed as classroom aggression, impaired social judgment, and delinquency, thereby leading to school dropout and arrest.[37]

With modern scanning techniques, we are also beginning to understand how prenatal alcohol can affect brain development, mainly through damage to the white matter, through which connections between nerve cells are passing. One study looked at the white matter microstructure in 15 adolescents with heavy prenatal alcohol exposure and compared the findings to a control group. The subjects with prenatal alcohol exposure showed many abnormalities of the white matter, including the parts that conduct signals to the medial frontal and occipital lobes—exactly the areas involved in executive function and visual processing, functions that are known to be sensitive to prenatal alcohol exposure.[38]

Belated Recognition

Thus, with time, the importance of the early discoveries was recognized. Norman McAllister Gregg was eventually knighted and received several awards, including an honorary Doctor of Science degree from the University of Sydney. In 1962, Sir Norman was given the Australian Father of the Year award. An auditorium at the University of Sydney's School of Public Health has been named after him.

The discovery of the congenital German measles (rubella) syndrome was fortuitous. In remote Australia, German measles was not sustainable as an epidemic, as you can catch the disease only once in a lifetime. The specific antibodies generated by the white blood cells in response to the first infection provide lifelong protection against the disease. Epidemics therefore tended to happen at intervals of 20 years or more, when a sufficient number of susceptible individuals, mainly children and adolescents, had accumulated, between whom the virus could be transmitted to maintain an epidemic. Thus, the disease arrived from outside multiple times, over wide intervals of time, sometimes long enough, so that the unprotected population included young women in fertile age groups.

This was the situation in Australia in 1940, when a German measles epidemic hit. Young mothers became sick with the virus from infected army personnel coming home on leave. About 25% to 50% of infections are now thought to be silent, without any symptoms, which may explain why Gregg was unable to elicit a history of rubella infection from some of the mothers he interviewed. Still, the cataract—opacity of the lens normally seen only in elderly people—was a striking abnormality in the infants who were referred to his eye surgery practice. The previous rubella epidemic had reached Australia in 1923. As infants were protected by maternal antibodies and therefore did not develop antibodies themselves, in 1940 the youngest mothers had no protection against the disease. These circumstances gave rise to what, for Gregg, was a lucky situation indeed. This observant specialist, confronted with surprising evidence, drew a courageous and auspicious conclusion.

Gregg's discovery also inspired investigations of whether other infectious diseases may also be dangerous to the developing fetus and the nervous system, but circumstances similar to those in Australia in 1940 have not occurred, and the potential consequences of other microorganisms have been much harder to document. However, much new information is being learned due to the modern availability of serum tests for antibodies specific to individual infections.

One example is toxoplasmosis, a parasitic disease known to be common in cats. Previously suspected of causing serious birth defects, proof was found in 1939 when a baby girl was infected by *Toxoplasma*. Three days after birth, she developed convulsive seizures. Lesions of the retina were found by ophthalmoscopy (and there was no cataract). Her condition worsened, and she died when a month old. Three New York City pathologists, Abner Wolf, David Cowen, and Beryl Paige, examined the damaged brain and were able to isolate the *Toxoplasma* parasite, and they were even able to transfer the disease to rabbits and mice.[39] Later reports suggested that the full clinical picture could vary but usually included blindness and other visual abnormalities, epilepsy, psychomotor or mental retardation, microcephaly or hydrocephalus, and intracranial calcifications.

Toxoplasma is distributed worldwide and has perhaps the widest host range of any parasite. Attitudes toward prevention vary. While France and Austria see it as a significant threat, the United States and United Kingdom are unconvinced of any major public health problem; the low vigilance may result in an underestimation of the prevalence.[40] The congenital infection occurs only when the mother becomes infected by *Toxoplasma* during pregnancy. Transmission can occur from cat feces, consumption of undercooked pork and lamb, and contaminated drinking water. The organism causes lesions in the placenta, passes into the fetal blood supply, and tends to localize in the developing brain. The disease may remain dormant for 20 to 30 years and then become active, with brain damage and blindness as a result. A serum test was developed in 1948 and helped document the occurrence of the disease. *Toxoplasma* in adults has recently been recognized as a serious neurological complication of AIDS but is now largely under control due to combination therapy.[41]

Many other microorganisms undoubtedly play a role in cases of brain disease in infants. Typically, research in this field has focused on mentally retarded children and associations with specific antibodies in the mother.[42] Most studies examined the possible consequences of congenital syphilis and *Haemophilus influenzae* infection, along with rubella. These diseases currently seem to be reasonably curtailed in most industrialized countries. Other organisms may yet be waiting to be discovered. For example, infection with cytomegalovirus (related to herpes virus) is also known to be an occasional cause of mental retardation if the mother contracted the disease during early pregnancy.[43] We know virtually nothing about the less dramatic consequences of maternal infections during pregnancy. Fortunately, the maternal immune system will provide some protection, and most infections last for only a short duration. For some diseases, a previous encounter will have resulted in life-long immunity that prevents subsequent infection.

Nonetheless, infectious diseases during early development may form part of a wider environmental causation complex. Common psychiatric diseases show some features, such as seasonality of birth and urban birthplace suggesting that an infection may have contributed to the development of the disease. Indeed, unspecified maternal infection or fever during pregnancy are associated with an increased risk for the child's developing schizophrenia or bipolar disorder. Both diseases also show abnormalities in certain transmitter substances, such as dopamine and glutamate. Both cytomegalovirus and its close relative, the herpes simplex virus, and perhaps also toxoplasmosis are suspected of being important causative agents, but it is unclear when and to what extent the infection is transferred to the progeny and how the disease develops.[44]

A New Paradigm

With the discoveries by Gregg, Lemoine, and their colleagues, a paradigm shift in science had begun. We established that the placenta is not an armor that is impervious to hazardous agents, and when infectious agents and toxicants permeate it, the effects on the nervous system can be devastating. Tens of thousands of children were severely damaged by prenatal German measles infection, but eventually proper responses were identified, and, as a result, the disease is now close to being eradicated in the Western world. Alcohol is now considered by many to be a leading preventable cause of mental retardation in the United States if not the world. Despite opposition from the alcohol industry, alcoholic beverages must carry warnings against consumption during pregnancy, and the frequency of severe forms of fetal alcohol syndrome has decreased.

Rubella differs in important respects from the industrial chemicals discussed in following chapters. Nobody markets or recommends protection of German measles virus or other microorganism species that may damage the developing brain.

(The largest wildlife conservation charity in Europe is the Royal Society for the Protection of Birds, but there is none for the Bugs.) In contrast, there is a strong commercial interest in developing antibody tests and vaccines. The discovery of the German measles virus and its detrimental effects on the fetus has led to very substantial gains to society and to some industry sectors. Public health and private enterprise both benefited. There was just a tiny stumbling block on the way. The rubella vaccine contained mercury as an additive—this brain drainer is the topic of chapter 4. In regard to alcohol, there are strong industry interests in the marketing of alcoholic beverages, but at least it is clear to the user when she is imbibing the substance (except when the fruit punch has been spiked).

Another element of this changing paradigm was added when a new drug that was safe for adults was found to damage the fetus.[45] In the United States, Vick Chemical Company distributed samples of thalidomide to physicians for recommended use against morning sickness during pregnancy, although supported by little information and also lacking in safety testing. Soon, serious adverse effects were heralded by unique phocomelia malformations, where children were born with severely shortened arms and legs, sometimes also nervous system disorders and other congenital diseases. The number of known thalidomide babies in the United States was only about 40 or so, because the drug was never approved by the FDA, due to the vigilance of Frances Kelsey. Worldwide, the number of cases exceeded 10,000, with the largest numbers in Australia and Germany where the drug had been formally approved.

The scandal had a positive consequence. The UK Medicines Act from 1968 and similar legislation worldwide now call for specific safety tests of all drugs to assess the possible risks associated with pregnancy and breast-feeding. Doctors nowadays have much better information available as to whether a drug is safe to use during pregnancy. Perhaps due to the decreased commercial interest in this drug, it was only in 2010 that researchers identified the biochemical mechanism by which thalidomide can damage brain development.[46] The thalidomiders, as the victims call themselves, campaigned for many years for recognition of their very obvious plight. With a delay of 50 years, the British government eventually in 2009 issued an apology and provided monetary compensation.[47] As late as 2012, German drug producer Gruenenthal issued an apology when the company unveiled a bronze statue as a tribute to the victims.

Thalidomide raised attention worldwide to the risks to the fetus from foreign chemicals. The ground had been fertilized by the earlier observations on German measles infection. Together, alcohol and thalidomide widened the scope and demonstrated that the fetus can be seriously harmed by the mother's exposure to chemicals. It is perhaps surprising that the thalidomide cases raised so much attention. In comparison, congenital rubella disease never seemed to be as fascinating, although a single epidemic of the disease caused more birth defects in one year than thalidomide did during its entire time on the world market.[48] Of course the commercial interests differed markedly. And then again, we have paid very little attention to the much greater problem of brain drain from the multitude of chemicals in the environment.

Chemical Permeability

Today's chemical universe includes a host of placental perpetrators, some of which most people have never heard of (and the proper spelling of which can be a head-ache even to chemists). Worse, you may not know that you are exposed to them. There is no immune system that will neutralize the industrial chemicals, as they are new to evolution and may be resistant to our biochemical breakdown mechanisms. They may remain in the body for years. In fact, a main elimination route for a woman is to transfer part of her own chemical exposures to her child.

Unintentionally, a mother will therefore share her burden of chemicals with her child. Loads of environmental chemicals have been documented in placenta, cord blood, and other fetal tissues. In 2004, the Environmental Working Group collected 10 umbilical cord blood samples from American hospitals and analyzed them for 287 chemicals, including a variety of pesticides, consumer product ingredients, and wastes from burning coal, gasoline, and garbage.[49] The vast majority was present in detectable quantities, and had they tested for an even larger number of chemicals, the authors believed that they would also have found many more.

In collaboration with colleagues at the CDC, we recently carried out a similar study of 12 childbirths in the Faroe Islands, a remote fishing community in the North Atlantic, where we looked for 87 different chemicals in maternal blood, placenta, cord tissue, and cord blood.[50] The substances that were present in the maternal blood were almost invariably also present in the fetal samples. As we had carefully dissected the placenta to remove the maternal tissue and flushed out the maternal blood, the analyses confirmed that these chemicals had reached the child before he or she physically emerged into the outside world. So what the mother is exposed to, she shares with her baby.

In the United States, information on population exposure is available from the National Health and Nutrition Examination Survey (NHANES). The CDC most recently determined the presence of 212 industrial chemicals in blood and urine samples from approximately 2,400 participants. The report[51] includes extensive data for such chemicals as mercury, lead, cadmium, and other metals; phthalates; organochlorine pesticides; organophosphate pesticides; pyrethroid insecticides; herbicides; polycyclic aromatic hydrocarbons; dioxins and furans; polychlorinated biphenyls; and phytoestrogens. The great majority of these chemicals were detected in most samples analyzed. Although this feat is a result of the advanced chemistry methods used at CDC, this documentation reveals that a large number of chemicals have made their way into our bodies, into us, from the very beginning.

Smaller-scale efforts show the same results in a variety of countries like Belgium, Canada, France, Germany, Japan, and Sweden, and results are being assembled from initiatives throughout the European Union (EU) and a global pollution study initiated by the World Health Organization (WHO). An environmental group conducted a *Bad Blood Study* of 14 environment and health ministers from EU countries.[52] These politicians are responsible for regulating environmental chemicals and for preventing them from harming human health and the environment. The ministers' blood samples were analyzed for a total of 103 different man-made chemicals. All of the ministers were contaminated with polychlorinated biphenyls (PCBs), pesticide residues, brominated flame retardants, perfluorinated chemicals, and most with phthalates and synthetic musk. Some of these chemicals have already been banned, but they are so slowly eliminated from the body that they remain for decades as a toxic reminder of past follies. Accordingly, even politicians carry these substances in their blood as an unexpected condition of life that they share with their voters. Pardon me, but I am not worried about the ministers' health as such. Many of them were women, and I worry more about the chemical burdens that the ministers would pass on to their children and their children's brains.

These studies document that industrial chemicals are already present in our bodies and that they penetrate the placenta, formerly—and erroneously—thought of as an armor. Some of the environmental chemicals are persistent and accumulate with time in our bodies. That is true for compounds, such as PCBs, dioxins, and certain pesticides. There is little that we can do to prevent these substances from moving from the pregnant woman's blood circulation into the fetus and the developing brain. In addition, after childbirth, the mother produces milk with a healthy concentration of nutrients. However, along with essential lipids, many pollutants, too, get transferred to the infant. After several months of breast-feeding, the child may have accumulated higher concentrations of these substances in the blood than their mothers.[53]

This situation has been referred to as the *weanling's dilemma*.[54] Is it better to rely on the mother's nutritious milk along with her accumulated concentrations of persistent pollutants than on milk substitute or baby food that may differ both in respect to nutrients and to contaminants? In most circumstances, there can be little doubt that breast-feeding for some months is generally beneficial to the infant. But scientific studies of these benefits have shown much variability in relation to the duration of breast-feeding.[55] Although usually not discussed, perhaps some of the differences in benefits (especially when there appears to be none) may be explained by variations in milk contamination with toxic substances like pesticides and other industrial chemicals. Thus, prolonged breast-feeding in exposed populations could potentially tip the balance and lead to adverse effects.

While we support breast-feeding, it would be a serious mistake to overlook the presence of environmental pollutants in human milk. Why not call attention to the fact that industrial chemicals have made their way into the most important source of nutrition that humans can create? Although seemingly intuitive, this perspective was completely missing when WHO asked its World Health Assembly to support an international recommendation of exclusive breast-feeding for six months.[56] Not a single mention of pollutants was made, even though concentrations in human milk often considerably exceed those normally occurring in food, sometimes also topping legal limits. Just as the placenta does not offer the desired protection against pollutants, human milk is not as pure as nature (and the mother) intended. Both pathways may result in exposures of the developing brain to toxic substances.

These facts were hidden or misinterpreted, a theme that seems to repeat itself, as we shall soon see. We shall now look at the consequences in regard to some of the main problem compounds. Lead pollution offers the best examples of misinterpretation and deception.

CHAPTER 3

Invisible Lead

HEALTH HAZARDS FROM DEMANDING SCIENTIFIC PROOF

People often see only what they want to see. Famously, Vice-Admiral Horatio Nelson in 1801 led a fleet of British warships into Copenhagen harbor to battle the Danish Navy. Although his commander signaled him to withdraw, Nelson ignored the signal. He placed his telescope before his blind eye, not his good eye, then remarked: "I have the right to be blind sometimes. I really do not see the signal."

There have been lots of signals and early warnings about chemical brain drain, but even scientists studying chemical effects on children's brains often saw only what they—or their funders—wanted to see. They "turned a blind eye" by making wrong assumptions, collecting irrelevant information, using inappropriate methods, and evaluating insensitive data. This chapter shows how and why we have overlooked obvious damage when examining the chemical brain drain due to lead—a prime brain drainer.

Lead poisoning was at first thought of as a potentially life-threatening disease, which, in survivors, left no trace. Further, the fairy tale went, as lead is a "natural" ingredient of this planet, lead exposure is a normal and harmless condition, except when clinical signs of poisoning developed. It took decades to realize how wrong these assumptions were. We now recognize lead as brain drainer number one. It has damaged brain cells in an entire generation of children, at least, worldwide. This metal has inflicted more deficits to human intelligence than any other pollutant. Using the metal for water pipes, as a gasoline additive, as pigment in paints, and hundreds of other purposes was a mistake that seems incomprehensible today. We realized the danger at an inexcusable delay that has resulted in enormous costs in terms of brain toxicity. How we got lured into accepting gigantic amounts of lead pollution reveals naiveté and negligence, at least in retrospect, along with devious misinformation. At the heart of the matter were some enduring myths.

Since ancient times, lead was looked upon as a useful metal. Given its increased economic value in the 20th century, any claims that it might be toxic were not taken at face value. They had to be substantiated. When lead additives were introduced as effective octane-boosters for gasoline in the 1920s, spokesman for the lead industry, Dr. Robert A. Kehoe, explained that industry leaders would make responsible decisions, but only when justified: "They have expressed themselves repeatedly not so much as being interested in opinions as being interested in facts, and if it can be shown ... that an actual danger to the public [occurs] as a result of the treatment of the gasoline with lead, the distribution of gasoline with lead in it will be discontinued from that moment." Summing up the argument, he added: "It is a thing which should be treated solely on the basis of facts."[1]

Later referred to as Kehoe's *show-me rule*, his view may seem fair and rather innocent. We should of course not disregard a useful invention based on unsupported concerns. But the way this stance was adhered to during subsequent decades was that very little would be accepted as a "fact" unless it was in favor of the continued use of lead additives. In other words, since there was no immediate identifiable danger that could call for discontinuation of this toxic chemical, industry used Kehoe's rationale to justify 60 years of leaded gasoline usage. The burden of proof fell on public health advocates, not on industry—in this case, the lead industry, the automobile industry, and the oil companies, all of whom had stakes in the use of the octane boosting. Thus, industry's narrow financial interests resulted in a demand of proof before agreeing to restrict a lucrative market product. They argued that tetraethyllead (TEL) was "a gift of God" that was essential to the progress of industry. Alcohol (ethanol) was also known to have octane-boosting properties and would likely be much safer, but the health authorities eventually went along with the arguments posed by industry.[2]

In the early years of the automobile, a common problem during acceleration was that the engine "knocked" due to premature ignition of the gasoline. This could be prevented by adding TEL to the gasoline as an octane booster. The discovery was made by chemical engineer Thomas Midgley, Jr., in 1921. He also discovered that fluorocarbon compounds (freons) could be used as propellants in spray cans. Unfortunately, these compounds later turned out to deplete the stratospheric ozone layer. For these two discoveries, Midgley has earned the unusual distinction of being the single organism in Earth history with far the greatest adverse impact on the atmosphere.[3]

Despite its obvious usefulness, early warnings abounded that TEL was a serious hazard. During the beginning of TEL manufacture in the mid-1920s, several serious poisonings occurred in production workers. The US Public Health Service began to look into the safety of the lead additive, which was already known for its neurotoxicity as a proposed battlefield weapon during World War I. After some improvement of the production methods, public health experts in the United States and the United Kingdom concluded that there was no threat to the public, and that even more widespread use of TEL in gasoline would not increase the pollution of the atmosphere with lead. At that time, it was probably difficult to imagine that the use of TEL in gasoline would, at its peak, result in the release of one kilogram per year for each American. The total air pollution worldwide amounted to 1,000 tons worldwide. Per day. That is a huge amount. As a crude comparison, it takes only a few thousandths of a gram to poison a child.

The post–World War II automobile industry heavily pushed gas-guzzling engines that required high-octane gasoline for acceleration and avoidance of engine knocking. Under pressure from the automobile industry, the US Public Health Service agreed to change the limit for TEL in gasoline from 3 to 5 cubic centimeters per gallon. The authorities were aware that no good environmental lead pollution study had been conducted and that it was therefore difficult to determine a safe upper limit for the lead content. On the other hand, no proof was at hand to support a decision to restrict the TEL use. The facts requested by Kehoe were still missing.[4]

Show Me the Evidence

An important reason for the absence of proof was the medical expertise that claimed that lead poisoning could only develop as a serious and distinctive clinical condition that was usually rather short-lasting, although severe cases could be fatal. As late as the 1960s, when doctors began to look more systematically for poisoning cases, about one in four children admitted to an American hospital for lead poisoning died.[5] Although the condition was potentially life-threatening, there were no intermediate stages of concern, the doctors thought. So if the child did not develop frank lead poisoning, there was no reason to worry. The child would completely recover from the clinical manifestations. Doctors also believed that high lead exposure that caused increased lead concentrations in blood would not result in any permanent damage. So was the general opinion, and this myth was also promoted by the influential Kehoe.

The assumption that surviving children recovered completely was parallel to the belief about most childhood diseases: the disease would just go away after having completed the normal clinical course ending with recovery (unless the patient died, which was by no means rare). This belief of successful recuperation prevailed, even though no attempt was done for systematic examination of children who had been lead poisoned in the past. Medical science may, by nature, be conservative and reluctant to change. And to make it even harder to challenge this myth that children would simply recover from lead poisoning, a high level of proof was demanded by Dr. Kehoe and his associates. In addition, some cases of lead poisoning could resemble other common diseases, such as meningitis, and only in the 1940s did testing for the blood-lead concentration become commonly available as an important diagnostic tool. Accordingly, the frequency of lead poisoning was probably grossly underestimated.

The first attempt to explore the possible long-term consequences of childhood lead poisoning was done by two Boston pediatricians, Randolph Byers and Elisabeth Lord.[6] They traced 20 lead-poisoned children who had at first been discharged from hospital as "recovered." The doctors found that 19 of the children had severe learning or behavioral problems and were school failures, and only five had an IQ in the normal range. During the following years, research began to accumulate suggesting that children with high lead exposure also suffered deficits on intelligence testing and other cognitive performance tests. Lead did not just cause a short-lasting poisoning but the toxicity to the developing brain resulted in permanent damage. So much for that myth.

Byers also concluded that lead could cause toxic effects, even though a child did not have any of the dramatic symptoms of classical lead poisoning. He stated that a group of children that he had studied "deteriorates gradually without ever having had any acute lead encephalopathy.... I think that lead does something to the growing brain which is different from what it does to the adult brain." In other words, children are much more vulnerable to lead toxicity than their parents are. His views were supported by occupational medicine specialist Harriet L. Hardy at a conference in 1965: "If ... growing tissue is more vulnerable to lead than adult tissue, far smaller doses than those required to produce diagnosable lead poisoning in a healthy adult worker become important."[7]

Although these conclusions were highly controversial at the time, the US Surgeon General acknowledged at a Senate hearing the following year that "some studies have suggested an association between lead exposure and the occurrence of mental retardation among children."[8] Again, lead was considered a contributory cause of a medical diagnosis (mental retardation), though no mention was made of less severe cognitive damage. Meanwhile, Kehoe kept arguing that "apparently there is no risk at present in any part of the country outside of occupational conditions."[9]

At a scientific conference called 10 years later by the International Lead Zinc Research Organization (ILZRO), an industry-supported foundation, UK pediatrician Donald Barltrop was asked whether children constitute a more vulnerable group and said: "This might merely reflect the very heavy local exposures which they meet. I am not happy that the child's brain or the developing brain, has been shown to be any more vulnerable to lead than at any later time in life."[10] Barltrop received research support from ILZRO, where his conclusions must have been highly popular.

At the hearings on the use of lead additives in the US Senate in 1984, Jerome Cole from ILZRO relied on the research by Barltrop and others that he sponsored when he said: "There is no evidence that anyone in the general public has been harmed by this usage."[11] In other words, no recognized "fact" was available, and therefore the problem did not exist. This sounds very much like Admiral Nelson putting the telescope to his blind eye. However, by the 1980s, the problem had begun to show its ugly face and soon appeared much greater than most would have anticipated.

Lead Exposure Is Natural

As data emerged that lead exposure occurred everywhere, and that lead was invariably found in blood samples from children, another myth was emphasized. Lead is a natural component of life on this planet.[12] Lead concentrations widely occurring were said to be natural and therefore innocuous, although researchers had little way of separating natural from industrial sources. For example, remote populations were also exposed to lead, and it was not realized at the time that lead particles from car exhausts could travel widely and contaminate even distant food chains. A brochure circulated by the Lead Industries Association (recently declared bankrupt) in 1968 said: "Lead is everywhere. In the soil, in the air, in the sea. It is in the bodies of city dwellers and in the bodies of natives deep in New Guinea's wilds, one of the most remote areas in the world, thousands of miles from modern civilization."[13] The statement of course did not consider how much of that lead came from car exhaust and other sources of lead pollution. In hindsight, I suspect that the blood samples from New Guinea were contaminated in the United States during handling and pretreatment before the chemical analysis.

If lead was indeed present as a natural component of life on this planet, as the industry lobbyists claimed, we probably evolved in the presence of this metal. Classical toxicology therefore suggested that such exposure would be safe, and that there would be a threshold above which adverse effects can occur. As expressed in the 16th century by Theophrastus Bombastus von Hohenheim—also known as Paracelsus—the dose determines the poison. High doses are invariably toxic, and that is even true for table salt. But a toxicant may not be toxic if given in only "small" amounts. So the crucial question is how low a low (or natural) level of exposure is.

Lead is a unique element, because various radioactive elements eventually end up as nonradioactive lead, and relative amounts of lead isotopes therefore reflect this breakdown over time. Some of these radioactive decay processes can take millions of years, and a geochemist at California Institute of Technology, Clair C. Patterson, used the relative abundance of lead isotopes to determine the age of the Earth. Doing so, however, he encountered serious problems getting precise measurements, even in his dust-free laboratory in Pasadena. He discovered that his isotope analyses were tainted by omnipresent lead contamination, and that he needed to purify the air in his laboratory.

I visited "Pat" at CalTech in 1975 and was allowed—after having properly changed into a special gown, hood, and mask—to enter his ultraclean laboratory through an airlock in which the air was filtered. By these measures he was able to establish the true and uncontaminated lead concentrations. Pat determined lead isotope ratios in a variety of biological samples. They differed substantially from the relative concentrations that would be predicted from the local geology. Looking at relative lead concentrations in food chains, he then calculated that humans contained about 100-fold more lead than their ancient ancestors before the advent of industrial lead pollution and gasoline lead additives.[14] Industrial uses of the metal infused foreign lead isotopes into the food chains. Patterson thereby killed the "natural" lead myth.

This daring conclusion created immediate controversy. Could it be that "natural" lead constituted only 1% of current-day exposures? Some support came from chemical analyses of ancient bone samples that contained very little lead compared to bone tissue from modern humans, but even if a skeleton had apparently remained untouched and dry since burial, it is difficult to tell what the lead content was originally. Part of the support for Pat's findings came from ancient Danish bones that I analyzed in the early 1970s as a medical student at the University of Copenhagen.[15] From Danish museums and anthropological collections, I was able to obtain vertebrae (back bones), some of them from crypts underneath ancient churches, where the human remains had stayed dry and undisturbed for centuries. I was also lucky to get bone samples from the excavations in Sudanese Nubia carried out before the Nile waters rose behind the Aswan Dam, which created Lake Nasser and thereby prevented further excavations in the area. The oldest bones contained non-detectable lead concentrations, while bone specimens from modern forensic autopsies showed at least 10-fold increases above the background.

Clair Patterson's article helped inspire the US Public Health Service to carry out environmental health studies in three American cities in collaboration with industry.[16] The results showed that blood-lead concentrations were indeed higher in major cities than in the countryside, and increased amounts of airborne lead were related to increased lead concentrations in the blood of the residents. So gasoline lead did contribute to exposures in urban areas. This evidence was further expanded during the following years.

The possible human health impact of lead pollution from gasoline was also a controversial issue in Europe. The European Commission therefore initiated a study in northern Italy, where the lead in gasoline was substituted with lead additives from Australia, which had a different lead isotope composition. By following the changes in isotope ratios in air, dust, and blood, the relative contribution of the gasoline additives could be calculated. The conclusions were remarkable: Gasoline additives contributed significantly to human lead exposure, not just via our inhalation of air pollution, but also because of contaminated food.[17]

The United States started marketing lead-free gasoline in the early 1970s, Japan at about the same time, and Germany and other European countries soon followed. In the beginning, the occasion for this change was that new catalytic converters on cars could not operate on leaded gasoline. With time, this decision was recognized as a crucial public health intervention. Still, by early 2013, lead additives had not yet been completely phased out and remained in use in countries like Afghanistan, Iraq, North Korea, Myanmar, and Yemen. Also, some Balkan and North African countries have continued to market both unleaded and leaded gasoline.

After the practice of adding lead to gasoline had been discontinued, the most convincing proof appeared in the decreasing blood-lead concentrations. The result of the lead phase-out was no less than dramatic—and very much in agreement with Pat's predictions: Decreases in blood concentrations in the United States closely followed the downward trend of leaded fuel sales. Between 1976 and 1994, the mean blood-lead concentration in children dropped by over 75% from 137 µg/L (micrograms per liter) to 32µg/L, in direct proportion to the amount of TEL produced.[18] Similar findings have since then been reported from just about every corner on Earth after the removal of lead from gasoline. Some of the decrease in blood-lead concentrations was undoubtedly affected by other preventive efforts, such as improved control of lead release from food containers and ceramics, removal of old lead paints, and emissions control from various polluting industries, but airborne lead from car exhausts was clearly the largest contributor.

Still, a multitude of applications of lead and lead compounds resulted in a great variety of sources that could cause hazardous exposures. When clinical descriptions first entered the medical journals over 100 years ago, several came from Australia, where the main source was identified as the white lead paint used on houses, including outside porches. Many lead compounds taste sweet, and small children are therefore at risk for ingesting peeling flakes with very high lead concentrations. This idea had first been pooh-poohed, but was eventually verified. Childhood lead poisoning began to be reported in the United States more than a decade later. Some city health departments began, in the 1950s, to require warning labels that could identify lead paint as a hazardous material. Although it might seem easy to control the lead content of paints, lead white was not the only lead-containing pigment in extensive use. Eventually, in 1977, the US Consumer Product Safety Commission ruled that paint intended for residential use could contain no more than 0.06% lead by dry weight. Similar actions had been taken about 50 years earlier in several European countries in response to a recommendation from the League of Nations in 1922.[19] However, no longer using lead paint did not eliminate the risk. In fact, childhood lead poisoning has recently resurfaced in France, as poor minority groups moved into dilapidated housing with peeling paint.[20]

Uncertainty Means No Need to Ban Lead

As new insights were announced, industry groups countered. One strategy was to criticize the research as being inconclusive. Lead-poisoned children often came from poor families, who lived in dilapidated apartment buildings on heavily traveled streets. So the question was whether these children were truly lead poisoned or merely socially deprived. Parents, primarily mothers, received much of the blame. They were accused of providing inadequate supervision and nurturing, fostering pathological behaviors such as pica that caused children to ingest lead paint.[21]

Accordingly, lead exposure was a result of the pica habit that was associated with deranged behavior and delayed development. So lead exposure was claimed to be the effect, not the cause.

That was how industry representatives argued. At the time, "blaming the victim" fit well with more general tendencies in public health to emphasize individual behaviors, including alcoholism, rather than a polluted environment. So lead poisoning and its effects were attributed to poor parental supervision, and prevention of lead poisoning therefore required better education of parents (and not of industry).[22]

Such misinterpretations only worked to a certain extent. A more efficient strategy was to criticize scientific methodologies, such as criteria for selecting study participants, exposure assessment, and adjustment for the effects of other factors. A typical critique of 22 studies on brain toxicity was published in a newsletter from ILZRO: "All 22 studies appear contradictory, and do not offer any resolution to the question of moderate lead exposure as a significant health hazard." ILZRO emphasized methodological concerns and claimed that the majority of studies with positive results had "flaws which obscure a clear interpretation of their findings." Only five studies were found to be sound, and they were said to disagree. The ILZRO report also stated: "There is no clear trend indicating that moderate exposure causes abnormalities in behavioral development of children."[23]

To be fair, the early studies of lead poisoning in children were, in present-day perspective, rather crude and only dealt with the most severe and obvious adverse effects of lead poisoning in children. So lead toxicity was likely overlooked or underestimated. Thus, the question that should have been raised is, How much lead toxicity might be present without having been caught by the crude research radar?

The industry strategy—demanding proof while raising doubt about the evidence—worked, and researchers and regulatory agencies came to believe that solid documentation of lead toxicity had to be found as a prerequisite for decisions on any form of pollution abatement. A few years later, an international expert group of the International Programme on Chemical Safety[24] was careful in phrasing their science-based conclusions: "Substantial doubts remain as to the validity of some of the studies because the relationship between the exposure to lead at the time the damage occurs and at the time the effects are first observed is not known." A later expert report from 1988, now under the auspices of the UK Medical Research Council, concluded: "While the observed statistical associations detailed in this review are consistent with the hypothesis that low-level lead exposure has a small negative effect on the performance of children in ability and attainment tests, the limitations of epidemiological studies on drawing causal inferences are such that it is not possible to conclude that exposure to lead at current urban levels is definitely harmful."[25] In other words, we think that lead is toxic to the developing brain in high doses, but we really cannot prove beyond a doubt that lower exposures have any effect, so we need to study this some more. These experts must have had very poor eyesight.

Even seemingly independent researchers joined in and expressed doubt in regard to the scientific documentation. Most recently, highly prominent psychology professor Alan Kaufman from Yale University raised concerns in regard to the confounding effects of other factors, such as parental IQ, and the significance of what he considered small decreases in IQ scores.[26] Colleagues reacted to Kaufman's ill-founded critique and did not fail to notice that he had received support from a lead-producing company.

Paradigm Changes

Renegades appeared on the scene. One was British chemistry professor Derek Bryce-Smith, who called attention to the wealth of evidence on low-dose lead toxicity.[27] Following a review article in 1978 in *Ambio*, a journal published by the Swedish Academy of Sciences, the author was called to Stockholm to defend his views. I was invited as well to present my evidence on "natural" lead exposures (which differed substantially from Kehoe's). The debate at the conference was a clash between traditional scientists, who wanted to await final proof before calling for intervention, and, on the other side, the environmentalists who believed that science has a responsibility to voice alarm when public health is at stake.

The main renegade was of course Clair Patterson. Not only did he insist that his view was correct, although his sophisticated measurements had not been reproduced by others, but he also gathered research evidence showing that natural background lead exposures were even lower than hitherto reported. Among his powerful studies, he and his colleagues analyzed layers of inland ice from Greenland and were able to show the small impact of pollution from Roman lead mines, the more recent pollution by the advent of industrialization and then the enormous contribution from automobile exhausts after World War II.[28] When Pat became a member of an expert committee of the National Academy of Sciences, he insisted on writing a minority report on his views on natural lead exposure and its implications for lead toxicology. Pat believed that the experimental studies were unreliable, as they compared adverse effects at high levels with so-called controls that were orders of magnitude greater than his definition of the natural background.[29]

In the 1970s, pioneer physicians like Julian Chisolm in Baltimore began to document serious health damage in children with increased lead concentrations in their blood.[30] Philip J. Landrigan, at the time an epidemiologist with the Centers for Disease Control and Prevention (CDC), and others, began to study larger groups of children.[31] Thus, established medical experts with impressive credentials began to report, in the scientific literature, the serious adverse effects of lead exposure, also over the long term. Finally, the tide began to change.

In the 1980s, environmental groups had gathered sufficient vigor to generate a counterbalance. One of the most successful ones was the British CLEAR Campaign for Lead Free Air. At its 1982 conference, the campaign leader Des Wilson described the UK producer of lead additives, Associated Octel—at the time owned by Shell, BP, Chevron, Mobil, and Texaco—as "the biggest mass child poisoners in the world today" (the facility later earned UK Friends of the Earth's award as Britain's filthiest factory as it continued to produce toxic lead compounds; see also chapter 9). Clair Patterson was a speaker at the conference, and so was Professor Herbert Needleman, the child psychiatrist, who pioneered studies of brain drain in lead-exposed children. It was the only time that they appeared together at an international event and a thrill for me to be part of. While opinion was divided and more research was called for, child psychiatry professor Michael Rutter in London admitted, "the level of probability is such that I think it is worth acting on."[32] CLEAR was a major factor behind the European decision to promote unleaded gasoline.

Otherwise, few stood up and challenged the prevalent industry-inspired notion that lead was natural and that children were not particularly vulnerable. Scientists participating in expert groups were generally conservative and soft-spoken. Only in 1986 did the World Health Organization (WHO) experts decide that a special exposure limit was necessary for children at 50% of the limit applicable for adults.[33] So, compared to adults, children were now considered twice as sensitive to lead. Later on, in 1999, WHO's experts concluded that the concentrations of lead currently found in food would have negligible effects on the neurobehavioral development of infants and children and therefore retained the exposure limit previously adopted.[34] These reports appear as thorough and well-intended reviews of the evidence. They identified uncertainties and emphasized weaknesses, and drew conclusions only if clearly justified. Basically, the experts wanted proof before action. Kehoe had died long before that, but his spirit continued to confuse the logic, and perhaps the exaggerated skepticism was aided by failing vision among the experts.

In the United States, the CDC had already taken a comparatively strong stand in 1991[35] when it decided to lower the children's "blood lead level of concern" to 100 µg/L, at which level children may begin to display adverse effects. This advisory level did not represent an exact threshold or safe level, but was meant to trigger the implementation of community prevention measures. A further lowering did not happen until 2012 (as I shall discuss shortly and in chapter 9).

Gradually, the general attitude began to change. In 2008, the UK governmental Committee on Toxicology (COT) estimated that in infants and young children, the intake of dietary lead at the WHO limit would result in approximately a 36 µg/L increase in the blood-lead concentration, which in turn would cause a mean IQ deficit of 0.36 –1.8 points.[36] This estimation relied on the association between dietary lead intake and blood concentrations described by WHO, as well as the assumption— supported by the US Agency for Toxic Substances and Disease Registry—that each 100 µg/L increase in blood-lead causes a decrease in IQ by 1–5 points.[37] The COT also concluded that "since it was not possible to identify a threshold for the association between lead exposure and decrements in intelligence quotient, efforts should continue to reduce lead exposure from all sources."

The cumulated evidence was evaluated in 2010 by the European Food Safety Authority (EFSA), at the request of the European Commission.[38] According to the dispassionate conclusion, "it was not possible to exclude a risk to the developing fetus through exposure of some pregnant female consumers." Despite the hedged language, this report represents a radical diversion from classical toxicology: There is no known safe exposure to lead, EFSA said. A so-called benchmark dose used by EFSA as a comparison level, not a threshold, represented a decrease by over 85% from the WHO safe limit. All EU rules for lead concentrations in drinking water, food, and air, which had been based on the previous WHO limit, required downward revision.

Current blood-lead concentrations in the European Union and the United States average about 20 µg/L, but as late as 1970, the CDC considered lead levels up to 30-fold higher fully acceptable. In early 2012, CDC's Advisory Committee on Childhood Lead Poisoning Prevention finally recommended that the action level be decreased from 100 to 50 µg/L (but by that time Congress had all but eliminated the CDC's lead program; see chapter 9). For perspective, some researchers have recommended a decrease of the action level to 20 µg/L, and since 2009, German authorities have considered lead concentrations normal only if below 35 µg/L.

The absence of a safe exposure limit seems to be in conflict with Paracelsus's classical toxicology. Thus, lead is not thought to be toxic if only given in "small" doses. The current average lead intake in the United States and the European Union is approximately 1 microgram (one millionth of a gram) per kg body weight per day. This may sound like a very small amount. But if we assume that lead absorption in the gut is 10% and that the lead is evenly distributed throughout the body, then I calculate that about 100 lead atoms will be absorbed every day for every single cell in the body. Would Paracelsus consider that a small dose? Maybe, but I think that no more than a few lead atoms per day would be accepted by Clair Patterson as "natural."

Multiple Misconceptions and Controversies

One may ask how industry was able to exert such a profound influence on science and successfully delay prevention efforts in regard to lead pollution. In addition to raising doubt, industry nurtured close collaborations with select members of academia who were persuaded by lucrative grants. By funding and otherwise controlling access, industry dominated lead research for several decades, thereby ultimately controlling the interpretation and dissemination of data regarding adverse effects. The key player, Robert A. Kehoe, was first recruited as a consultant in the 1920s and soon became Medical Director for the Ethyl Gasoline Corporation, which produced

TEL in the United States. He was named director of the newly established Kettering Laboratory in 1930, with funding from the Lead Industries Association. For 40 years, he conducted research supported by industry and framed his conclusions in a manner that minimized the health risks.[39] The researchers who acted as corporate consultants likewise expressed industry-friendly opinions, although phrased in scientific terms and disguised under veils of uncertainty. Industry this way suborned science as an instrument of profit.

When Randolph Byers and Elisabeth Lord in 1943 disclosed their follow-up study of children who had been lead poisoned, their findings were even reported in *Time* magazine. However, the lead industry believed that many of the alleged cases of lead poisoning were nothing of the kind. The industry threatened to sue Byers or, alternatively, to buy his time as a scientist on contract with the industry.[40] In the United States, the many cases of childhood lead poisoning had, due to the industry efforts, become a "silenced epidemic." Independent research therefore stalled for 40 years, while industry rolled out its own studies.[41]

An intense fight erupted in 1982, when the US Environmental Protection Agency was charged to update its air standard for lead. Herb Needleman had recently published his findings[42] that lead accumulated in the deciduous teeth (as a marker of long-term exposure) was associated with neuropsychological deficits and poor classroom performance. Hearings were held, where Needleman presented his work, and psychiatry researcher Claire Ernhart criticized the findings saying that other factors would likely be responsible, and that this was a case of reverse causality, that is, that mentally retarded children would expose themselves to more lead. The EPA committee then scrutinized the publications again and—not surprisingly—concluded that no definite conclusions could be drawn from the individual studies.[43] When the EPA's Air Quality Criteria for Lead concluded that brain damage could occur in children in the absence of obvious symptoms and at blood-lead concentrations just above 400 µg/L,[44] the conclusions were of course attacked by industry interests that demanded better proof. More seriously, Needleman was accused of scientific fraud or misconduct, and an investigation took years of productive life from Needleman, who was eventually cleared (see chapter 9).

Clair Patterson also ran into trouble. At first, representatives of a TEL producer tried to offer him research support with the purpose of generating results favorable to their cause. Soon after this failed meeting, Pat lost his long-standing research support from both the Public Health Service and the American Petroleum Institute, and he almost got fired.[45]

The industry opposition was misguided for at least two reasons: It raised doubt without reason, and even when appropriate, the uncertainties that it highlighted would generally cause an underestimation of the true effects of lead, rather than the opposite. Thus, most studies had not documented the children's past lead exposures in sufficient detail, and the follow-up was too short, so that they could not document convincingly the doses that were associated with deficient brain development.

Another problem was the lack of proper control groups,[46] as Pat had first highlighted in his National Academy report. Ideally, the studies should include true control groups with minimal lead exposure, but there are simply no children around on this planet who have not been exposed at all to industrial lead. In one early study from 1972, the health outcomes of children in the exposed group (mean blood-lead level of 580 µg/L) did not differ from those of the "control" children, but in the latter group, the mean blood-lead level was 380 µg/L and ranged as high as 550 µg/L. The hapless author concluded that the developmental problems observed in the exposed group were due not to lead toxicity, but rather, like the developmental problems observed in the controls, to poor parenting and environmental deprivation.[47] In today's pediatric practice, some of these "controls" would be admitted to the hospital for possible chelation therapy.

Gradually, adverse effects were documented at lower and lower lead concentrations in the blood, as studies began to use more sophisticated epidemiological designs, larger groups of children, and more sensitive tests of brain functions, with more refined statistical methods.[48] Brain toxicity was also replicated in a wide variety of ethnic and socioeconomic strata in many different countries. As gasoline lead was being phased out, mean blood-lead levels dropped, thereby allowing comparisons with control subjects with concentrations below 50 µg/L. Although follow-up is expensive and takes a long time, often beyond what funding agencies are willing to support, such follow-up studies with repeated exposure assessment began to appear. They tended to show adverse effects at lower levels than had been realized previously, even below 100 µg/L.

A large pooled analysis of seven prospective studies of low-dose lead exposure in children found that the slope of the lead/IQ regression line was steeper below 100 µg/L than above this level.[49] In other words, once better research methods were applied, then adverse effects at very low exposure levels were documented. This is no reason for complacency, however: Even our control groups today have lead exposures far above the "natural" level calculated by Patterson. For this reason, we may continue to underestimate the adverse effects of lead exposures prevalent today. This concern is highly important to the parents of the 500,000 American children that CDC estimates had blood-lead concentrations in excess of the 50 µg/L limit in 2012, and especially the 150,000 above 100 µg/L.

Not all studies show the same effects, and the appearance of lead toxicity depends on the age of the child. Most studies confirm that IQ is strongly affected, even in children as young as 4 years. More complex tasks like reading, doing arithmetic, and using verbal memory seem to be impaired only in older children at school age. This difference is not an indication that lead has different effects in schoolchildren, but rather that the more advanced functions only become accessible for testing when children reach more mature developmental stages. The younger kids could not be meaningfully tested on the more difficult tasks. So the child's age at examination is important, and the full spectrum of developmental neurotoxicity may not be apparent in preschool children.[50]

International studies of fairly low exposures have documented that lead-related brain drain is real and that it persists at least through late adolescence.[51] In all likelihood, the damage is permanent. Recently, colleagues of Herb Needleman contacted subjects that he had first examined in Boston around 1980 and invited them for a reexamination. Although only 43 adults—now in their late 20s—could be located and recruited for the study, their present IQ scores showed a clear negative association with their prenatal and childhood lead exposure.[52] This finding echoes what Byers and Lord said more than 50 years ago: Lead toxicity does not fade away.

On a population basis, these tendencies were even more impressive. Economist Rick Nevin has linked the decreasing lead levels in the United States to rising scores on the Scholastic Assessment Test or SAT. According to his findings, the 1936–1990 preschool blood-lead trends explained 65% of the 1948–2001 variation in US mental retardation prevalence, 45% of the 1953–2003 variation in the average SAT verbal score, and 65% of the 1953–2003 variation in the average SAT math score. Drops in preschool blood levels correlated the best with increases in SAT scores 17 years later.[53]

And the effects of lead toxicity are not limited to cognitive deficits. A study by Needleman and his colleagues suggested that the lead-associated behavioral abnormalities in children would also make them prone to delinquent behaviors.[54] More definite evidence came from prospective data from Cincinnati, where increases in prenatal and postnatal blood-lead concentrations were associated with a greater risk of arrest, specifically for offenses involving violence.[55] Although research in this field is fraught with difficulties, the behavioral consequences of lead toxicity are part of the range of effects caused by lead, and they contribute to the societal costs (see chapter 8).

Modern imaging techniques, such as magnetic resonance scanning, may allow us to see the physical brain damage. Adults with increased lead exposure during childhood have reductions in gray matter (cortex) volume, especially in the prefrontal cortex that is responsible for executive functions, mood regulation, and decision making.[56] So there is even anatomical evidence of brain drain that is obvious to the nonexpert (assuming at least minimal vision). The anti-knock agent used in gasoline successfully protected the automobile engine but knocked out brain cells.

The Historical and Global Perspective

It seems like a contradiction. Lead was employed as a useful metal thousands of years ago, workers and citizens were exposed as a result, and the first records of lead toxicity were published in the Antiquity. Not much was written about childhood lead poisoning, though. In 1848, an extensive monograph by French physician Louis Tanquerel des Planches described that children who put lead soldiers in their mouths were getting colic as a clear sign of lead poisoning. From then on, more detailed information on lead's damaging effects on brain development kept surfacing, with over 10,000 scientific articles published already by the mid-1970s. History seems to repeat itself, again, yet we continue to dismiss the evidence before our eyes.

Spring water and well water rarely contain more than traces of lead, but one of the early uses of lead was in water pipes. We still call the "plumber" to fix the drain, using a term that originates from the Latin *plumbum,* the word for lead. During Roman times, lead became abundantly available from the mining of silver from mixed ores. During the first century BC, Vitruvius was aware of the danger that toxic amounts of lead could be released into the drinking water.

Similar observations were made repeatedly later on. In 1724, the German engineer Jacob Leupold concluded that water running through lead pipes released lead, "which is a dangerous poison to the human body." This conclusion caused the Count of Württemberg in 1778 to prohibit the use of lead pipes for water ducts, thereby protecting the southern part of Germany from exposure to lead in drinking water.[57] Even before that, a decree was issued in Württemberg to prohibit the traditional practice of adding lead to sour wine—under the penalty of death!

Other regions did not fare as well, and lead pipes were widely used in countries like the United Kingdom and France. Following several epidemics of cholera due to unsafe drinking water, the city of Glasgow, in 1859, installed piped water from the pristine Loch Katrine to serve the city residents. Building the 34-mile long aqueduct was quite a feat, and the work was greatly facilitated by using malleable lead pipes. However, the soft mountain water was corrosive and dissolved lead from the pipes and cisterns in the city, thereby exposing the residents to toxic amounts of the metal. Due to superb microbiological quality of the water, mortality rates from diarrhea and other infectious disease plummeted. Evidence of lead exposure and adverse effects were long ignored. Only in the 1970s, when Professor Michael R. Moore and his colleagues started researching these issues did it become clear that an increased risk of mental retardation, delayed neurodevelopment, and other ailments among the Glaswegian children could be linked to the polluted water.[58] The city began adding lime to Loch Katrine water in 1979.

Even worse was the situation in parts of the United States, where the combination of widespread use of lead pipes from water conduits and soft water made lead poisoning rampant. University of Pittsburgh historian Werner Troesken refers to the use of lead for water pipes as an environmental disaster.[59] His extensive studies concluded that child mortality about 100 years ago was closely associated with the usage of lead for water pipes. During much of the history of lead water pipes, the main attention was focused on infectious diseases as a much greater health problem. But adding to the confusion, not everybody consuming the tainted water became sick, the symptoms of lead poisoning were insidious and nonspecific, and the diagnostic criteria were somewhat vague. At the same time, the Lead Industries Association maintained that lead was a safe and cost-effective material for water pipes, and only during the late decades of the 20th century were plumbing codes in the United States changed to require water pipes made of materials other than lead. As a result, a very substantial number of service lines, distribution lines, and household water pipes present today in American communities are made of lead and continue to cause lead exposure.[60] While current rules can force utilities to install copper pipes and brass fittings to keep lead concentrations in community water low, the water pipes on private land are often not replaced, and the galvanic corrosion induced by the new pipes may greatly increase the lead levels in the water coming out of the faucet.

The centuries-old problem of lead exposure from water pipes can suddenly turn into an acute hazard when the water quality is changing. In 2001, the disinfection chemical used for the municipal water supply in Washington, DC, was changed to chloramine instead of chlorine. This switch made the water more aggressive and caused lead to leach from the water pipes and fittings. To make matters worse, the problem was not recognized and corrected until three years later. In Durham, North Carolina, a similar problem occurred when a change in water treatment from alum to ferric chloride caused increased corrosion, and in Maine, where the corrosion was due to a new anion exchange system used for water treatment.[61]

In addition to the sources already discussed, lead exposure may come from cosmetics, improperly fired ceramic tableware, and industrial emissions. Across the country, numerous lead smelters and other lead-polluting industries have been closed down, usually as a result of modern requirements for pollution control. A recent survey by the newspaper *USA Today* identified 230 forgotten factories with contaminated neighborhoods in need of clean-up, because high lead concentrations in dust and soil continue to expose children to the toxic metal.[62] Traditional medicines, whether herbal or Ayurveda, are sometimes found to contain shocking amounts of lead that may be acutely toxic to children.

Most of these additional sources need tightened control in the United States and the European Union, but even more so in developing countries. As lead is being phased out of most industrial uses in northern countries, dangerous uses continue or expand in the south. One of the most serious incidents that has come to light occurred in Senegal, where 18 children died from a rapidly progressive central nervous system disease of unexplained origin. The local community was involved in the recycling of used lead-acid batteries. Because autopsies were not possible, blood samples were taken from siblings and other family members. The highest blood-lead concentration in a child was 6,139 μg/L—more than 60 times higher than the safe level used by the CDC at the time. The researchers studying this incident concluded that most if not all of the 18 deaths were due to severe brain toxicity (encephalopathy) caused by lead exposures from metal recycling.[63]

High exposure levels keep being reported from many other countries, such as China, the Dominican Republic, Jamaica, Kosovo, Mexico, and Nigeria, but most cases are probably not even identified and not likely to be mentioned in scientific journals.

The Blacksmith Institute reported in 2012 that over 500 sites in low- to middle-income countries are seriously polluted with lead due to industrial operations, such as smelting, mining, lead battery recycling, and manufacturing.[64] An estimated 16 million people are at risk of lead poisoning at or near these sites, including several million children and pregnant women. Continued brain drain from lead toxicity will without question make it even more difficult for developing countries to emerge from poverty. But social injustice and naiveté (or "blind" eyes) have subjected us to other major brain drainers in addition to lead. As we will explore in the next four chapters, we relied on optimistic assumptions and breezy dismissals of scientific evidence in plain sight, thereby paving the way for more brain toxicity.

CHAPTER 4

Poisoned Science

MERCURY DAMAGES THE CHILD'S BRAIN
BUT DOES NOT HARM THE MOTHER

A victim of mercury poisoning, Shinobu Sakamoto, has had a profound impact on my career. When she was a young teenager in 1972, Shinobu traveled with her mother from Minamata, Japan, to the first UN environment conference in Stockholm, to protest against the human toll of industrial pollution. I was in medical school then, and my older brother was in Stockholm as the press secretary of the Danish minister of the environment, the very first in the world. The TV news showed poisoning victims at a demonstration, including this girl with spastic paresis carrying a poster. I was shocked that environmental chemicals could have such severe effects. At my medical school, health hazards like that were ignored. Shinobu's fate inspired me to learn more.

The pollution problems in Minamata started in the early 1950s, when residents in the Japanese fishing village began to show symptoms of a mysterious disease: sensory disturbance of lower legs, lower arms, and face, tunnel vision, deafness, ataxia (difficulty in coordinating movements), and dysarthria (difficulty in speech). Although a similar clinical picture had been described earlier (more about that shortly), it was not recognized as methylmercury poisoning. In fact, several years elapsed before it was finally agreed that the source of the toxic releases was wastewater from the local Chisso factory.[1]

Poisoning could occur even in the mother's womb, and more than 100 Minamata children born in 1955 and later suffered from serious developmental disturbance and diffuse brain dysfunction. The children would not reach normal developmental milestones and would not sit up, crawl, or start speaking single words like other children their age. More seriously affected children would suffer seizures, and some would have spastic paresis. Most of the poisoned children were not immediately diagnosed, because their generalized symptoms were less distinctive than the clinical picture of the adult poisoning cases.[2] Although children appeared to be particularly numerous already on the first list of patients, the mothers seemed completely healthy, despite having been carrying a baby who developed congenital methylmercury poisoning.

The key to the poisoning diagnosis rested on a documented exposure to the toxic substance. After the suspicion of methylmercury had been aired by some researchers, local chemists developed analytical methods to detect this substance, so that fish and other biological samples could be analyzed. Luckily, Japanese parents often keep a piece of the umbilical cord from their children as a traditional token of luck. A young physician, Masazumi Harada, went from house to house to collect pieces of umbilical cords for analysis so that he could relate the results to the children's medical diagnoses.[3] His findings left little doubt. Those with recognized congenital Minamata disease showed the highest mercury concentrations in their cords, while those with "ordinary" mental retardation generally had levels intermediate between the poisoned subjects and healthy children. However, beyond narrow scientific circles, recognition of methylmercury as a cause of poisonings took a long time, and the pollution continued for many years.

In early 2009, I attended a conference in Minamata to discuss the scientific insights since the world's first environmental poisoning incident was discovered 50 years earlier. At the same time, a meeting of the United Nations member countries was convened, and a long-negotiated agreement was finally reached to control global mercury pollution.[4] The breakthrough happened after a change in the US administration, which no longer blocked a proposed treaty. The delegates were gathering at the UN Environment Programme headquarters in Nairobi, Kenya. On the very day that the news from Nairobi reached us, I visited Shinobu and her mother with Japanese colleagues as I had done several times before. But that day we had reason to celebrate, as the Minamata poisonings featured prominently in the UN document, and my own mercury studies were also quoted. When told what had happened, Shinobu mumbled something. "We won," a colleague translated. Four years later, the agreement was completed and named the Minamata Convention.

At the Minamata conference, we recalled the early findings, which had so profoundly shaped our thinking in regard to chemical brain drain. Adults dying from Minamata disease suffered uniquely localized lesions in specific brain areas, corresponding to their vision, hearing, and motor coordination symptoms. Poisoning in children and adolescents showed more widely distributed damage in the brain. The most severe and diffuse pattern of damage was seen in infants and children who had been poisoned prenatally from the mother's diet. They had serious disruption of normal brain structures with nerve cells lying helter-skelter rather than in organized columns.[5] All of these findings agreed with the clinical picture showing rather specific signs and symptoms in adults and more generalized syndromes in the children.

Accordingly, exposures during early development produced a more serious and pervasive disease. As a Japanese pathologist summarized in 1977, "It may thus be supposed that the fetal brain is more fragile and susceptible to toxic agents, since it is immature and still undergoing development … and the greatest care should be taken by pregnant women since the fetus has a higher sensitivity."[6] These were visionary conclusions, which only few colleagues were brave enough to follow.

The Forgotten Poisonings

Although Minamata marked the first environmental poisoning disaster, methylmercury was by no means a new or unknown poison. Early warning signals abounded, some of them as far back as the 19th century.

A laboratory technician at St. Bartholomew's Hospital in London was hospitalized on 3 February 1865. The physician in charge, George N. Edwards, noted that the 30-year-old man was unable to stand without support, suffered speech problems, impairment of sight and hearing, and had numbness of his hands. These symptoms were similar to those that much later beset the residents of Minamata. As was commonplace at the time, the treatment consisted of Spanish fly plasters, herb medicines, castor oil, beef tea, and brandy. When this treatment did not work, the physician decided to add a pharmaceutical commonly used at the time—mercury chloride (then called calomel). Neither did that remedy help, of course, and the patient's condition worsened. According to the patient chart for 9 February:

> he became so restless and noisy during the night that his hands had to be strapped to the bedstead. This morning his countenance is pale and sunken; lips covered with sores, and breath very foetid; tongue dry, and covered with a yellowish fur; bowels not open since the seventh; urine passed in bed, and very offensive. He lies muttering incoherently, refuses to take his nourishment, and struggles and becomes furious upon any attempt being made to force him to drink.—Ordered enema of beef-tea.[7]

Five days later, the technician expired. The following month, a 23-year-old laboratory colleague was admitted with similar symptoms. The younger colleague apparently escaped being treated with mercury, but that did not save him. The two men had worked together to synthesize methylmercury, an organic mercury compound, and both died eventually from the same clinical ailments. As noted by Dr. Edwards, "these two cases are of extreme interest, as well from the unique character of their symptoms, which do not resemble those produced by any known disease, or by the action of any hitherto known poison."

In operation since 1123, Saint Bartholomew's is London's oldest surviving hospital and now is part of the Royal London Hospitals collaboration. Many medical discoveries were first published in the hospital's *Reports*, and George Edwards served as editor for several years. Although this pioneering description of methylmercury poisoning is not easily available today, and a photocopy has to be ordered from the British Library in London, it was widely known in the 19th century. The cases described were certainly familiar to occupational physicians and the story of these terrifying deaths was handed down orally from one generation of chemists to another.

Nonetheless, foolhardy attempts were made in the 1880s to use organic mercury compounds as treatment against syphilis and other diseases.[8] Many toxic remedies were tried out at the time when patients and their doctors were desperate to find some cure for serious infections. The patients did not benefit from this treatment, as the remedy seemed more dangerous than the disease. Animal experiments carried out in parallel showed serious toxicity causing incoordination of movements, blindness, deafness, and attacks of wrath at the slightest provocation. After some hesitation, the pharmaceutical use of methylmercury was abandoned, but its known biocidal properties inspired attempts to prevent the growth of fungus on seed grain and wood. Methylmercury and some related mercury compounds were therefore produced for fungicide use at the beginning of the 1900s. Of course this endeavor was not risk-free.

Four men were poisoned during their work in the production of methylmercury fungicides and were described by the British occupational physician Donald Hunter. On one of the patients, he wrote:

> After about three months of the work, he complained that his whole body was going numb and tingling. He began to notice weakness of his arms and legs, and unsteadiness in his gait. His condition became worse.... He became clumsy, dropped trays, began to stagger about, and collapsed on the floor on several occasions. His speech became difficult and slurred, and it was noticed that he sometimes could not see objects held in front of his face.[9]

Despite objective confirmation of neurologic abnormalities, the condition was thought to be "hysterical" until other similar cases occurred at the same factory. At an examination three years later, the constricted visual fields remained grossly abnormal, as did the ataxia. Examining poisoned patients could be a challenge, Swedish physicians agreed: "it may be extremely difficult to communicate with these patients, as the difficulties of speech may increase to a point at which the speech is completely incomprehensible, and as the patient is, moreover, unable to write on account of the ataxia. There is frequently considerable emotional instability."[10] The last sentence is probably medical slang for a patient being in obvious despair. That would seem quite understandable, especially when considering the inadequate aid physicians at the time could offer. As part of the therapeutic regimen, one of the "hysterical" patients was prescribed electroshock treatment (which did not help).[11]

Fifteen years after the first poisonings at the factory, one of Hunter's patients died. This patient had been quite helpless, being severely ataxic, and suffering blindness in one eye and severe constriction of the visual field in the other. He also had high blood pressure and eventually died from heart failure and pneumonia at age 38. Hunter noted at the autopsy that he had cerebellar atrophy, which also occurs in certain rare, inherited diseases, though methylmercury was the first recognized exogenous cause.[12]

Decades before that, chemical engineers discovered that methylmercury could spontaneously form from inorganic mercury employed as a catalyst in acetaldehyde production. In fact, cases of methylmercury poisoning occurred in German acetaldehyde production workers. Two factories in Minamata and Niigata, Japan, had copied the German production process, but the European toxicity reports were apparently ignored and not translated until rediscovered more than 50 years later.[13]

Toxicity in One Monkey and Other Animals

Impressed by the peculiar form of toxicity, characterized by tunnel vision, sensory disturbance, and movement problems, Hunter carried out studies in groups of rats and one macaque monkey to determine if the effects seen in the patients could be reproduced. Nothing was observed after dosing the animals during the first few weeks, but then symptoms appeared with a vengeance. The monkey seemed to be much more sensitive to the devastating effects of methylmercury, and "the cerebral cortex showed an encephalitis resembling that of general paralysis of the insane." So the pathology was as remarkable as the clinical symptoms.[14]

Although Hunter's studies did not document the dose-dependence of the toxicity, his findings went unrecognized in Japan. The Minamata researchers searched for possible clues; disagreed about various candidates, some of them far-fetched; and questioned each other's motives for favoring a particular toxicant. However, it was a very simple experiment by a company doctor at the Chisso factory that clinched the proof that the Minamata residents were being poisoned by methylmercury.

Dr. Hajime Hosokawa mixed cat food with effluent from the acetaldehyde plant, where mercury was used as a catalyst. Nobody knew at the time that the effluent contained methylmercury. The cats that had eaten the contaminated cat food developed severe movement disorders that were dubbed "dancing disease"—a mysterious ailment that was already killing most of the cats in the area. However, once Chisso's management learned of the results, Dr. Hosokawa was told to stop his experiments and not to reveal the results to anyone. He admitted in 1969, shortly before his death, that the results and tissue blocks existed. A full report with microcopy slides of the damaged brains was finally published in 2001.[15]

In a seminal article by leading American neurotoxicologists in 1972, methylmercury was shown in a rat model to be much more toxic to the brain during development than adulthood. Of note, the signs of brain damage emerged only as the animals matured.[16] This discovery spurred many new studies. After the term "methylmercury compounds" was introduced as a medical subject heading in 1980, the National Library of Medicine in the United States has listed far more than 1,000 publications on animal toxicology of this substance. Thus, methylmercury became a paradigm of a brain drainer and also one of the best documented.

Poisoning from Porridge and Bread

If a substance is as toxic to the brain as methylmercury, then you would expect it to constitute a hazard also to the developing nervous system. Evidence already surfaced in the mid-20th century, a few years before the Minamata epidemic was discovered. Again, this case was soon forgotten, or ignored.

A Swedish farming family accidentally made porridge using flour made from seed grain treated with mercury fungicide. An infant apparently ate the porridge almost daily after weaning at about nine months of age. Approximately four months later, the mother noticed that the boy showed no inclination to sit up and crawl, and he became increasingly listless and clumsy. Upon admission to a pediatric hospital ward, the child was unable to say a single word and appeared to be seriously behind in developmental milestones. Eight months later, the child, still at the hospital, was not yet able to sit up or get up on his own, and seemed to be mentally retarded. The mother was unaffected, although she, too, had eaten the porridge. She had been pregnant again at the time and delivered a girl, who seemed healthy during the first two months after birth. Later on, she too lagged severely behind in development and was then found to be mentally retarded. The condition was unchanged, in both children, when seen by the doctors two years later.[17]

The Swedish physicians stressed that this clinical picture was clearly different from poisoning with inorganic mercury compounds, which can cause kidney damage and other adverse effects. They also emphasized that the adults had appeared comparatively unaffected by the poison. Although the exact doses were unknown, they were nonetheless not high enough to affect the mother outwardly, while her children carried the brunt of the damage. Because the second child, as a fetus, had shared the mother's exposure from the mercury-contaminated porridge, this case suggested both that the poison could pass through the placenta (see chapter 2) and that the brain is excessively sensitive to methylmercury toxicity during early development. Clearly, this case report should have put the Minamata researchers on the right track, and it should have inspired serious restrictions of any use of methylmercury for seed dressing.

But fate would have it otherwise. Adverse weather conditions with severe drought caused agricultural catastrophes. When famines occur, necessary safety precautions tend to be forgotten or ignored, unfortunately. In the 1950s and 1960s, mercury-treated seed was used for bread-making in Iraq, Pakistan, and Guatemala, and the largest poisoning incident occurred during another severe drought in

1970–1971, again in Iraq.[18] Warning labels on the seed bags were in English or Spanish, so it was no wonder that the rural population had no or little idea that the pink-dyed seed was toxic, especially because the pink colorant could be washed off, while the mercury remained. Due to the difficult circumstances, clinical data were collected for only 93 patients out of over 6,000 known cases. These data were later used by the US Environmental Protection Agency (EPA) to calculate an exposure limit for methylmercury. However, the Iraqi data have recently been called into doubt, and they may not have revealed the true extent of this poisoning tragedy. Most of the patients poisoned were from Kurdistan, and the poisonings seemed to fit into the designs of then-President Saddam Hussein. Moreover, the data that were shared with Western researchers were controlled by a doctor, who turned out to be the dictator's personal physician.[19]

Soon thereafter, Iraqi pediatrician Laman Amin-Zaki teamed up with colleagues from the United States to study 49 of the exposed children. She documented delayed development of language and motor function in children exposed prenatally to methylmercury.[20] A later report used advanced analytical technology to determine mercury concentration profiles in single hair strands from the mother, so that the researchers could get a calendar record of methylmercury exposure during the entire duration of the pregnancy.[21] These dose measures suggested that adverse effects on brain development occurred at an exposure that was only one-fifth of the dose that would cause symptoms in adults.

Mercury in the Food Chains

In Minamata, the methylmercury was formed as part of the chemical processes in the acetaldehyde production, as had previously happened in the German factories. The mercury compound found its way into the sewage water and then accumulated in the fish in Minamata Bay and beyond. In Iraq, Sweden, and other countries, methylmercury had been used to treat seed grain. But methylmercury seemed to be present in fish everywhere and far from any known sources. Where did that methylmercury come from?

In 1967, this mystery was resolved by a simple experiment. Methylmercury can be formed naturally in the environment. Using sediment from an aquarium, two researchers in Stockholm showed that inorganic mercury could be converted into methylmercury. If the sediment was sterilized by steam in an autoclave, none was formed, thus suggesting that micro-organisms played a role.[22] Further studies in the United States showed that vitamin B-12 could transfer a methyl group to the mercury without the action of bacterial enzymes.[23] As a consequence, any type of mercury pollution could eventually turn into methylmercury in the environment.

After its formation, methylmercury accumulates in the food chains, since fish are generally unable to break down and eliminate this substance. High concentrations therefore build up in large, slow-growing, piscivorous fish (like swordfish and large tuna), though much less so in smaller species at the bottom of the food chains.

In North America, the discovery of methylmercury formation went unnoticed, until Norvald Fimreite, a Norwegian graduate student at the University of Western Ontario, started analyzing fish for mercury. He alerted officials in 1969 that fish in Lake St. Clair had unacceptably high mercury levels, sometimes as much as 40 times the standard of 0.5 ppm set for human consumption.[24] In western Ontario, mercury pollution was particularly heavy near paper mills and chlor-alkali plants that had used mercury in the production since 1962 (slimicide in paper mills and catalyst in chlorine production). Factories in Dryden released about one ton of mercury per year. Sports fish were absent the first 50 miles downriver, but farther away, species like pike, burbot, and walleye survived with mercury concentrations similar to those found in fish from Minamata Bay.[25] After much debate, the Ontario government in 1970 banned commercial fishing on all lakes and tributaries of the English-Wabigoon River system. Despite controversies, Fimreite managed to complete his thesis, but he was so frustrated by intimidations and abuse that he soon thereafter returned to Norway (where he continues to teach biology).

These Ontario waterways included some First Nation people's ancient fishing districts. The Ojibway inhabitants of the Grassy Narrows (Asubpeechoseewagong) Reserve depended on local fish as a staple in their diet, and many of the men earned a living as fishing guides. When the factories upstream leached mercury into the waterway, the main food source of the Ojibway band became highly polluted, and the men were deprived of their occupation. As the band's Chief Simon Fobister said in 1978, "We are now a people with a broken culture."[26]

Several Ojibway children were born retarded, blind, and deformed, but Canadian government researchers were very cautious and did not reach a diagnosis of methyl-mercury poisoning.[27] Health Canada continued the studies to assess possible nervous system damage in Grassy children with exposure to methylmercury during early development,[28] though without reaching any clear-cut conclusions. However, the Ojibway already knew—they called the pollution *pijibowin*, poison: "You can't see it or smell it, you can't taste it or feel it, but you know it's there. You know it can hurt you, make your spirit sick."[29] So the victims disagreed with the experts.

I was invited to visit Grassy Narrows in 1997. As the tribe's consultant, I reviewed the most recent medical reports and met with the new chief, William Fobister, Sr., and members of the community. We discussed the difficulties in reaching conclusions from this type of study, where the exposure is measured many years after the fact and the children's cognitive functions are assessed at various ages.[30] There was not much I could tell them about the *pijibowin* that they did not already know. I felt sad that even the best medical science could do so little to help provide decisive evidence. The band eventually decided to sue the Canadian government for logging as the major disruption of their ancient trapping and fishing rights. Eventually, a compensation of $8,000 was paid to each resident on the reserves, and those with methylmercury poisoning that had been acknowledged by the disability board received between $250 and $800 per month. In 2007, a Grassy Narrows fisherman was charged and pleaded guilty to one count of unlawfully selling mercury-tainted fish. About 25% of fish from the local water bodies still exceed the Canadian mercury limit (0.5 μg/g).[31]

Very high exposures also occurred among other indigenous people. A study of 234 Cree children in northern Quebec showed abnormal tendon reflexes associated with elevated mercury concentrations in the maternal hair that was formed during the pregnancy.[32] Thus, this study supported the notion that, even far from polluting industries, exposure to methylmercury from fish could lead to adverse effects on nervous system development. Similar evidence came from Greenland Inuit with an even higher exposure from eating seals and other marine mammals.[33]

But does methylmercury only cause brain drain within localized populations with unusual excesses of exposure? Or, as industry physician Robert A. Kehoe might have preferred to phrase the question, Is our methylmercury exposure natural and therefore innocuous? No, the exposure is not natural, for at least two reasons. First, modern industrial fishing methods now make it feasible (and economically attractive) to catch large tonnages of species at the top of marine food chains, such as tuna and swordfish, that have never before been a regular component of human diets. So part of our increased exposure to methylmercury is undoubtedly due to our taste for these large fish and the popularity of sushi. Second, food chains in the oceans are burdened by mercury from industrial sources, including releases from coal-fired power plants worldwide. The difficult question is, how much?

To determine how much mercury concentrations in food chains can be considered normal for this planet, a group of zoologists collated mercury analyses from tissues of Arctic indicator species, including samples that had been preserved in the permafrost for hundreds of years. Some of the analyses of polar bear hair were done in my Danish laboratory, so I participated in the data analysis. The trends for the various animal species were roughly parallel and showed that present-day levels are increased by a factor of at least 10 above those present in preindustrial times.[34] Some geographical difference exists, but a slight decrease is apparent during the most recent decade or two. Overall, environmental concentrations seem to average about 10-fold above levels that could reasonably be called natural. Perhaps this study is not quite as elegant as Clair Patterson's analyses of lead isotopes (chapter 3), but the conclusion is just as clear. Industrial pollution with mercury is the major source of our daily exposure from contaminated seafood.

Children Examined for Mercury

Inspired by the studies by Herb Needleman and other researchers on brain toxicity caused by lead, the question emerged whether environmental exposure to methylmercury could cause similar effects on the developing brain. Could habitual seafood consumption in a pregnant woman entail enough methylmercury exposure to cause congenital neurotoxicity? A Swedish-born professor, Tord Kjellström, took action based on what he had learned about methylmercury toxicity as a visiting scientist in Japan. Having moved to New Zealand, he initiated a large-scale population study there. Here the popular meal of fish-and-chips usually does not contain regular fish, only shark, which contains comparatively more mercury. Kjellström's project was sponsored by the Swedish EPA, which also organized peer review before publishing the results. Kjellström's findings documented adverse health effects on development and intelligence in the children when the mother's hair-mercury concentrations during pregnancy exceeded 6 μg/g (sometimes referred to as parts per million, or ppm).[35] This level is about 6-fold higher than the exposure limit used by the US EPA today. However, his results from the late 1980s were ignored by regulatory agencies for a long time, allegedly because they had not been published in a recognized scientific journal.[36]

I learned about the New Zealand findings around the same time as a Faroese physician, Pál Weihe, started working at the occupational health clinic in Odense, Denmark, where I had just been appointed professor. Pál and I decided to measure the exposures to methylmercury at the Faroe Islands, where mercury-polluted pilot whale was part of the traditional diet. We managed to get a sample of maternal hair and a vial of cord blood from over 1,000 consecutive births at the three Faroese hospitals during 1986–1987. We also collected obstetric information and interviewed the mothers about their past medical history and diet. The samples were analyzed for mercury in my Danish laboratory. Then we waited. We knew that we could not expect to find much, if we conducted examinations of the children as infants or toddlers. We would have to wait until the children's brains had developed enough that they could participate in the kind of sophisticated testing that had been done to disclose lead toxicity to brain development.

Thus, seven years later, we invited all the Faroese children for clinical examinations. This was made possible by my first grant from the National Institutes of Health. For the examinations, we relied on advice from the most competent colleagues we could find in America, Europe, and Japan. In fact, all of the neurophysiological examinations were carried out by a team of specialists from Tokyo University. One of them, Professor Katsuyuki Murata, has been back several times to supervise clinical testing and help analyze data.

Based on our examinations of 90% of the children whose mothers we had recruited seven years earlier, the results revealed that the methylmercury exposure was associated with deficits in several brain functions.[37] We even saw clear associations below a maternal hair-mercury concentration of 10 μg/g, a level that World Health Organization (WHO) experts had previously thought to be safe (although 10 times higher than the current EPA limit).

When the first results from the Faroes were ready for publication in 1996, journal after journal refused to publish them, decisions that were undoubtedly inspired by harsh reviewer comments. All of these reviews were anonymous, but I suspect that some of the executioners served more than once. A prominent journal that, perhaps expectedly, rejected the manuscript was *Science*. But when our results became known through presentations at scientific meetings, a writer from *Science* called and asked for permission to post a summary of our findings as a news story. So this prominent journal was willing to highlight our conclusions, but could not afford space for the documentation. I did not accept the invitation.

Eventually, we published our results in 1997. A few weeks after our article had appeared, a commentary was published in *Science* that criticized our conclusions.[38] At a time when the Internet was still in its infancy, such a speedy reaction was highly surprising. How could the critique be written, editorially processed, and then printed almost simultaneously with our own article? There was an important lead. The authors appropriately referred to our work as having been printed in the correct specialty journal, but they indicated that the article started on page 1. Our journal article started on page 417 in the November issue. However, the pagination of the proofs began with page 1. So somehow the proofs with the preliminary page numbers (which were later changed when the journal issue was put together) had reached the authors of the commentary. How did that happen? I may never find out. Evidently, it certainly seemed that a great effort was being made to counter our conclusions as speedily as possible.

Colleagues from Rochester University initiated a similar study in the mid-1980s to examine children prenatally exposed to methylmercury from their mother's fish diet during pregnancy. Their study was conducted in the Seychelles, a developing nation in the Indian Ocean. Largely nonpositive findings were at first reported in these children.[39] The methods were fairly similar to those that we used in the Faroes, but many small differences could have introduced noise or uncertainties that could have masked the mercury toxicity. The apparent disagreement between two studies inspired controversies and fueled a debate on uncertainty and lack of proof (more about this in chapter 9). So history was repeating itself, although the circumstances differed.

One difficulty in interpreting the research results was that methylmercury occurred as a seafood contaminant together with essential nutrients, such as omega-3 fatty acids, that could have the opposite effect of promoting brain development. So a pregnant woman eating contaminated fish would pass on to her fetus both the nutritious fish oil and the mercury. Perhaps mercury and nutrients might cancel out one another's effects. If the nutrient benefits were not taken into account in the data analysis, then mercury would not seem as toxic as it really is, simply because the adverse effects were dulled by the positive influence from nutrients.[40] Thus, the myth was created that mercury is not toxic if you eat fish, but only if you eat whale meat as the Faroese did. So not to worry if you like fish, hailed the tuna canners. However, an important part of the story was that even if exposure-related toxicity was not apparent, then the mercury would be blocking the benefits from the omega-3 fatty acids in seafood. In my mind, that is an adverse effect as well.

But could mercury toxicity not be compensated by other means? Indeed, there are innate coping mechanisms to help the brain recover from trauma and induce nerve cells to take over functions that have been damaged. For example, the BDNF molecule acts as a hormone in the brain and stimulates plasticity (see chapter 1). But neurotoxicologist Sandra Ceccatelli and her colleagues in Stockholm had shown in the laboratory that expression of the *BDNF gene* is inhibited by methylmercury exposure. In a joint study, we measured BDNF in cord blood from Faroese children: BDNF concentrations decreased at higher mercury exposures.[41] Thus, even the repair mechanism can be damaged by mercury.

As more research was carried out, some of the uncertainties were further explored and settled. After introduction of more refined methods, the new research documented adverse effects with greater certainty and at lower and lower levels. When we recalculated the EPA limit using the newest data, we found that the limit should be decreased by 50%.[42] The uncertainties had therefore been hiding important toxicity, not exacerbating it.

Experts and Uncertainty

Given the growing scientific documentation on toxic risks from mercury-contaminated fish and seafood, regulatory agencies began to evaluate the information and consider appropriate safeguards to protect consumers. Expert committees were appointed, and, as competent academics, they emphasized uncertainties and weaknesses of the available data. It seems like an obligatory requirement that experts must express reservations and question the quality of their colleagues' work. Still, virtually no attention was paid to the question of what *could* be known, given the research methods, resources, and possibilities available, and at what level of methylmercury exposure developmental neurotoxicity could be reliably excluded. The reports also generally ignored that measurement imprecision most likely resulted in an underestimation of the true effects. Instead, more research was recommended (another obligatory element, when experts speak).

Inevitably, the researchers' desire to expand scientific activities agreed with the insistence on the need for solid evidence promoted by polluters and also to some degree by the preference of the regulatory agencies. However, the wish to obtain more complete proof always has the untoward effect of delaying corrective action. A few highlights from some expert reports will illustrate what I mean.

The first international risk assessment of methylmercury was carried out by an expert committee under WHO and the UN Food and Agriculture Organization (FAO) in 1972.[43] "The occurrence of prenatal intoxication also calls for caution," the experts said at the time. A few years later, they added that "clinical data from Japan indicate that the fetus is more sensitive than the mother," but the committee refrained from recommending any special protection of children or pregnant women.[44] The international risk assessment was therefore based on toxicity in adults and remained that way until 2003, 50 years after the report on the two Swedish children who became mentally retarded due to methylmercury. These WHO reports may represent a high level of scientific thinking, but certainly a catastrophe in regard to public health.

Meanwhile, mercury was being merrily disseminated into the environment worldwide. In countries where methylmercury was popular for seed dressing, such as Canada and Sweden, unexpected mortality was being registered among wild birds. As the cause of mortality was not firmly established, it was the use of mercury-treated seed grain for chicken feed that eventually drew attention. In 1964, mercury analyses of two hens and a total of six eggs laid by these hens, showed an unusually high mercury content of 5 mg/kg in one of the eggs.[45] This report rapidly spurred a ban in several countries against the import of Swedish eggs. As methylmercury transmission in food chains had suddenly become crucial to commercial interests, seed treatment with methylmercury was swiftly banned. Subsequently, based on extensive fish analyses, fishing had to be banned in countless Swedish lakes and rivers, and similar warnings were also issued in North America. The most recent statistic from the US EPA (2010) lists fishing advisories due to mercury pollution for over 16 million acres of lakes and over 1 million river miles.[46]

Now back to our 1997 article. It inspired wide discussion, not just in *Science*. As most of the US mercury pollution comes from coal-fired power plants, abatement could be costly. Thus, at the request of the White House, an international workshop was called in 1998 with 30 invited experts. They were asked to critically examine the scientific evidence on mercury and its health effects. The organizers chose to invite authors involved in the Faroes and the Seychelles studies, but the New Zealand researchers were not present. The experts reviewed the evidence and highlighted a variety of possible uncertainties.[47] As the conclusions said, "In spite of the stated weaknesses and uncertainties, the finding of adverse effects in the Faroes study...raises some concern that risks of lower exposure to methylmercury may exist. Of particular concern are exposures to women of childbearing age or pregnant women." And then they added: "there are inadequate data on this to draw meaningful conclusions at this time." In other words, more research is needed. Does this sound like a broken record to you?

The experts barely considered the possibility that they had missed or underestimated the toxicity to brain development. In this regard, the workshop experts were quite optimistic: "Measurement error can impact significantly on both the estimated levels of effect and the decision on the level of exposure at which an effect is detected because of potential for misclassification." I certainly agree with this wording, but then the committee added: "The data presented at the workshop suggest that precision of measurements of methylmercury in hair or cord blood is very good." Maybe I should take this as a compliment that the committee members thought that we were good at measuring mercury. But even if we are, we know very little about the exact amount that reaches the brain during early development.

Given the lack of clear conclusions from this panel, the US Congress soon thereafter requested another expert panel to be convened by the US National Research Council (part of the National Academy of Sciences) to determine whether the US EPA's methylmercury exposure limit of 0.1 µg/kg body weight per day was appropriate.[48] This so-called reference dose had been developed on the basis of the Iraq data. An exposure at this level corresponds to a hair-mercury concentration of about 1 µg/g (or 1 ppm). In its report from 2000, the committee supported the EPA limit, but recommended that it should be based on the data from the Faroes examinations as the largest and most detailed study. Overall, the committee also found that the dose-response data from various other sources reasonably agreed with the findings from the Faroes.

By 2003, a WHO-FAO expert committee finally reviewed the evidence on methylmercury again.[49] The experts decided to disregard the New Zealand data and then settled on an exposure limit more than twice the American limit. In reaching this conclusion, the experts said that they took into account the health significance of seafood diets. In order not to scare people from eating seafood, they chose a higher mercury exposure limit than did the National Academy committee. Such a decision is completely counter to our tradition in risk assessment that we focus on the toxicology of the substance only and do not allow any interference from information on nutrients and other associated factors. Otherwise, we would have to accept, for example, higher pesticide residues in such important food items as fruit and vegetables—although our current pesticide exposures are already too high (see chapter 7).

The European Union did not handle the problem with any more elegance. A common mercury limit of 0.5 µg/g had been applied to fish in general since 1993. A few species, notably tuna and swordfish, were allowed to contain up to 1 µg/g. However, this regulation proved problematic because member states reported mercury concentrations exceeding the 0.5 µg/g limit in many other species. The fisheries directorate of the European Commission therefore decided in 2001 to solve the problem by adding all of these contaminated species to the list of those that had to comply only with the 1 µg/g limit. In its decision, the Commission referred to the need for "transparency" and the need to maintain mercury levels as low as reasonably achievable, while taking into account "physiological reasons" that mercury concentrates in the tissues of certain species more easily than others. However, the Commission produced no assessment of the associated health risks and offered no advice to the public. Indeed, apart from the legal notice, no public announcement was made.

When I calculate a safe limit that would allow all of us to eat seafood for dinner twice or more per week, I end up with a limit of 0.1 µg/g. That is one-tenth of the highest limit in current use. It may be a coincidence, but my ecology colleagues say that it fits exactly with their calculations that industrial pollution has increased contamination levels by 10-fold. Thus, before the advent of mercury pollution, most types of available seafood probably contained only traces of mercury and would not cause toxic levels of exposure. But also back then there was no tuna industry.

Fortunately, many ocean fish and shellfish species remain below my 0.1 limit and can be safely eaten. Still, neither the fishing industry nor the regulatory agencies are eager to share the detailed information with the consumers. But you can safely eat shrimp, mussels, and other shellfish, and fish such as cod, haddock, and small flat-fish species. Highly recommendable are salmon and sardines, as they contain lots of omega-3 fatty acids while being low in mercury (as mercury levels vary regionally, only a summary is given here).[50]

Fueling a Controversy

As could have been predicted, industry representatives wanted to draw their own conclusions from the science available. In Minamata, an executive from the pollut-ing factory insisted that the disease was due to rotten fish and not mercury contami-nation from the factory.[51] Asked if he thought there was a danger in using mercury, the company representative replied: "No, we never tested the mercury to find out if it was poisonous." Apparently he had forgotten Hosokawa's cats. When asked about the continued release of effluents after 1957, he said: "There was no solid proof." Only after legal defeat many years later did Chisso agree to pay compensation to the victims. Similarly, the Japan Chemical Industry Association attempted to explain away the source of the problem by claiming that the disease could be due to leakage of explosives dumped during World War II.

The executives of Dryden Chemicals and Reed Paper Ltd. in Canada repeatedly insisted that mercury occurred naturally in the environment and that their efflu-ents were not the only source of mercury in the Wabigoon-English River system. Dr. Kehoe and his followers would have agreed. They also pleaded ignorance of the process of mercury methylation and argued that the mercury that they released was less harmful than the mercury discharged into the Minamata Bay. They insisted that they had no records of how much mercury was purchased, used, or discharged into the environment. The company representatives believed that they had respected all environmental regulations and standards and that they could therefore not be held exclusively liable for any adverse effects.[52]

In the United States, vested interests also followed mercury research with great interest—in this case, the fishing industry, especially the tuna canners, and the coal-fired power industry as a major source of mercury pollution. They must have felt elated when an update of the Seychelles study was published in the prestigious medical journal *The Lancet*.[53] Despite detailed clinical examinations, the researchers did not find any evidence that the children had been harmed by mercury from their mother's seafood diet during pregnancy. Careful reading revealed that the research-ers had subtracted the effect that could be ascribed to the children's own exposure to methylmercury from the postnatal diet. In contrast, they chose not to adjust for the benefits conferred by the nutrients in the mother's fish diet. Although these choices raise doubt about the validity of the results, this article was hailed as the final proof that mercury in fish was innocuous.

The scientists carrying out the mercury research at the Seychelles thereby helped fuel a controversy by downplaying methylmercury's brain toxicity. One of their reports said: "No neurodevelopmental effects related to fetal mercury exposure could be demonstrated in this study."[54] In another report, the authors concluded: "Specifically, our data do not compel us to conclude that the many benefits of fish consumption during pregnancy are reduced by adverse fetal effects."[55] In an interview with the *New York Times*, the Seychelles study pediatrician, Professor Gary Myers, "pointed out that the Seychelles population ate fish, whereas the Faroes population got a substantial amount of its mercury exposure from whale meat. Few people in the United States eat whale meat."[56] Basic toxicology indicates that the medium or seafood type as such should not influence the toxic response from the mercury. But Myers and the Seychelles team became spokespersons that mercury from seafood is nothing to worry about.

Their views were shared by others and inspired a caustic commentary by geriatric neuropsychiatry professor Constantine G. Lyketsos. He erroneously referred to the Faroese population as Inuit and identified their source of methylmercury exposure as exotic pilot-whale blubber (which contains almost no mercury, while high concentrations occur in the meat). Professor Lyketsos went on to claim "that no study has demonstrated that prenatal exposure to methylmercury leads to irreversible or serious effects."[57] The definition of "serious" would likely depend on whose kids are being exposed to the toxicity. These remarks provoked rebuttal letters to the editor, and *The Lancet* chose to print an erratum to correct Lyketsos's slur.

Delayed Compensation

What happened to Shinobu Sakamoto and the other Minamata victims? Did they finally receive compensation and an official apology? In 1963, methylmercury was formally accepted by Japanese authorities to be the cause of Minamata disease. However, it took five more years before a detailed statement could be issued by the government. At that time, Minamata disease had also occurred because of pollution from the similar factory in Niigata.[58] A variety of monetary compensation mechanisms were provided, and after lengthy discussions, criteria were approved for the diagnosis of Minamata disease and for eligibility of compensation. These procedures became the object of further legal proceedings, and final resolution of the problems eventually took several decades, during which the victims most severely affected by the poisoning died. Many of those with marginal cases were denied any compensation. Additionally, the families of the children who had been harmed had to cope with supporting them until a settlement was reached, that is, if they were lucky enough to be awarded compensation.

In 1995, a national relief package was decided. This political settlement called on the Chisso factory to provide a lump sum payment of 2.6 million yen (about $26,000) each to about 11,000 Minamata disease patients who had not been officially recognized before. But in 2004, the Supreme Court found the government guilty of neglect by not stopping the pollution in time and also ruled to acknowledge a group of victims as Minamata disease patients based on a range of symptoms that was wider than the government's stricter standards. This ruling was then followed by a series of additional applications and lawsuits.

In 2009, the year that the UN agreed to a global treaty to combat mercury pollution, the members of the Japanese Diet finally passed a new law that offered compensation to victims with sensory impairment, thus dispensing with the original requirement of paresthesias of the distal arms and legs. This group included approximately 20,000 people. Those currently seeking compensation through damages lawsuits would have to withdraw such claims to be eligible to receive financial relief under the new law.

The new maximum compensation was of a similar magnitude as before, about 1.5–3 million yen (about $15,000–$30,000). A series of cases soon thereafter each received a compensation of 2.1 million yen (about $21,000) plus a monthly allowance of up to 17,700 yen to pay for medical expenses (Japan has no universal health insurance). As a rough estimate, the compensations total approximately $1 billion. Although the overall costs to society have been enormous, they are trivial compared to the suffering through more than 50 years by the brave Shinobu Sakamoto and at least 50,000 other victims. I shall discuss further the costs of brain drain in chapter 8.

The political decisions were certainly made at a very slow pace, and even corrective action was delayed due to legal issues and objections raised by the responsible industry. The procrastinations in dealing with methylmercury poisoning in Minamata provoked Professor Jun Ui to say:

> It might be a coincidence, but a strange, parallel relationship was observed between the actual symptoms of Minamata Disease and the reactions of these formal organizations. A constriction of the visual field was common among all organizations. Ataxia, a loss of coordination between various parts of the body, was often exhibited in contradictions between the measures taken by various parts of the government. There was also a loss of sensation as the appeal of the victims went unheard and there was little effort to grasp the situation as a whole. Many organizations also reacted with spasmic convulsions when they faced the problem. This was followed by mental retardation and forgetfulness.[59]

Along with three prominent mercury researchers from Japan, I recently reviewed the mercury research carried out since the first poisoning cases. We documented how evidence had been forgotten, relevant information from other countries or other fields of research was ignored, and researchers focused on narrow issues that detracted from the issues of main concern for the poisoning victims. At the same time, legal and political rigidity demanded convincing documentation before prevention and compensation would be considered. Scientific consensus was therefore delayed and was used as an excuse for further deferring corrective action. We therefore agreed that the science, too, suffered from symptoms typical of methylmercury toxicity, such as tunnel vision, forgetfulness, and lack of coordination.[60] Knowing that these ailments also affected lead research, maybe I should worry that they may be infectious! Now, we must turn to another brain drainer—arsenic.

CHAPTER 5

Substituted Milk

POISONING DURING INFANCY CAUSES
PERMANENT BRAIN DAMAGE

Chemical brain drain is not just a matter of biochemistry and statistics. Real people, children, victims, are affected. People like Shinobu Sakamoto. Their lives are changed forever. My mentor at Mount Sinai Hospital in New York, Professor Irving J. Selikoff, taught me to remember that the numbers in my tables represent human destinies, although the tears have been wiped away. I therefore wanted to hear and see the testimonies from patients about the burdens of chemical brain damage. Not lead, not mercury—I wanted to understand the effects of a brain drainer that was much less known. What about arsenic? Anecdotes abound on homicidal uses and about Napoleon possibly being poisoned by arsenic.[1] Known only to a few specialists in the West, thousands of children had been arsenic poisoned from powdered milk in Japan. That triggered my curiosity.

It was a huge epidemic, but the details had not been published in English. I first turned to my Japanese colleague, Professor Katsuyuki Murata, and asked for his help in collating and translating scattered information on the dramatic mass poisoning event that happened during the fateful summer of 1955.[2] Many people had died, but I wanted to understand what happened to their brains, and I wanted to meet some of the victims.

This is how the epidemic began. Medical doctors in the western part of Japan became worried about an outbreak of an unusual disease with anorexia, diarrhea, vomiting, abdominal distention, fever, and skin pigmentation among hundreds of infants. At first, the epidemic appeared to be like some kind of infection, and the doctors prescribed antibiotics. The first patient seems to have gotten sick in April 1955, and the incidence reached its peak in July and August. The majority of the sick infants were bottle-fed, and those who were breast-fed also received a milk supplement. A link to the Morinaga company's MF-marked milk powder was established in early August. Then pediatrics professor Eiji Hamamoto from Okayama voiced the suspicion that the particular clinical picture could be due to arsenic. Soon, arsenic was identified in the Morinaga dried milk. On the following day, the results were publicly released, and the sale of this brand of milk powder was banned.

The MF-marked dried milk was manufactured at the Morinaga F-plant in Tokushima. The contamination was traced to the disodium phosphate added as a stabilizer to the powdered cow's milk with the aim of preserving constant acidity. In April of 1955, the F-plant had switched to a much cheaper industrial-grade disodium phosphate of low purity. It turned out to contain 5% to 8% of arsenic. In the dried milk, the arsenic concentration was about 20–30 mg/kg, though some differences occurred between lot numbers. From the instructions on the can, the arsenic level in the prepared milk can be calculated to be about 5 mg/L, an enormous concentration, 500 times higher than the limit applicable to drinking water. Acute poisoning is known to develop when the daily dose is about 1 mg per kg of body weight. An infant weighing 5 kg could get this dose by drinking one liter of contaminated milk per day, which would seem quite possible.

The poisoning symptoms first appeared in late spring and early summer and would have resulted from just a few weeks of exposure. Information from the patient charts suggested that poisoning symptoms developed after milk intake corresponding to about five one-pound cans. If the instructions on the can were followed, a bottle-fed 2-month-old infant would consume this amount in two to three weeks at a daily dose of a couple of milligrams, twice the amount needed to cause poisoning. The total dose would be a massive 60 mg, clearly sufficient to cause a life-threatening intoxication.

The scope of this epidemic can be easily appreciated from the known monthly production of about 200,000 one-pound cans of dried milk. Fortunately, about two-thirds of these cans were recalled in time. But the consumption arising from three months of production with the unsafe stabilizer could have potentially poisoned tens of thousands of infants. However, the official number of poisoning cases is much less than suggested by the production numbers. One reason for underestimating the true number of victims was the stringent diagnostic criteria for a recognized poisoning. I analyzed these numbers in greater detail, but let me return to this later.

In October of 1955, a committee under the Ministry of Health and Welfare, decided that the diagnosis of arsenic poisoning had to include skin pigmentation, although this sign is not typical and may not occur in all patients. Alternatively, a high level of arsenic had to be documented in urine or hair from the case, despite the fact that this analysis in 1955 was cumbersome and imprecise, even assuming that samples were available. In the end, the Ministry reported a total of 12,131 victims, including 130 certified fatalities.

We don't know how many poisoned patients went unregistered, not satisfying the strict criteria. The number could be very large. In the beginning, doctors did not suspect that the infant food was contaminated and did not collect any detailed exposure information. They could have missed many cases. In addition, virtually no arsenic analyses were carried out hair or urine samples from hospitalized infants. As a result, barely any documentation exists of arsenic dose levels.

Further, the ministerial committee assumed that disappearance of acute symptoms was a sign of complete cure. This is surprising, because brain edema, hemorrhage in the cerebellum, and myelin sheath degeneration of the optic nerves had been observed at autopsies of deceased patients. Why would survivors completely escape from having some form of lasting brain damage? Would the children not suffer lowered IQ and some neurological problems? We already met the myth about total recovery in regard to lead poisoned children (see chapter 3). So here we go again.

Neurotoxicity is a well-established effect of arsenic and its compounds, since arsenic can pass the blood-brain barrier, and the toxic effects include cell cycle inhibition and increased cell death (apoptosis). Perhaps the most convincing evidence comes from studies of nerve cells in culture, where arsenic causes reduced outgrowth of the nerve cells, with reduced branching of the dendrites.[3] Such changes in the brain circuitry are also seen in the brains of subjects with certain kinds of mental retardation.

Detailed medical checkups of patients with continued signs of Morinaga dried milk poisoning and on "cured" infants were eventually required by the Ministry of Health due to pressure from worried parents. At the examination, the patients were judged according to the continued presence of acute arsenic toxicity, and most were therefore considered cases without sequelae. After that, no further follow-up was performed until two doctors examined a group of 14-year-old survivors of the Morinaga poisoning.[4] Further surveys then followed, but most of the 20 or so reports are of limited value, as they relied on small numbers and did not include any control groups or data on exposure levels.

Among the largest studies, examination of 415 patients in Kyoto showed a high rate of physical and mental complaints as well as an increased prevalence of central nervous disorders, such as epilepsy or mental retardation. The authors concluded that these physical and mental defects originated from the arsenic-tainted dried milk.[5] In another study in Hiroshima prefecture, all children born between 1 January 1954 and 31 December 1955 were examined at age 14 years. The victim group had a higher rate of severe retardation with an IQ below 50. On an IQ scale, 100 is considered normal average, and scores below 70 would suggest mental retardation. The IQ was found to be lower in exposed adolescents than in their unexposed brothers and sisters.[6]

Although these findings revealed serious abnormalities that were obviously associated with the poisoning in infancy many years ago, little was published about the fate of these patients later on, and nothing on their suffering. How did they manage at school? Did their symptoms fade, or did they become worse as the subjects aged? Could a poisoning during infancy cause permanent damage to the brain? How did they cope? I wanted to find out, so I went to Japan to meet the patients and their doctors.

Learning from a Victim

I decided to travel to Okayama, a city in western Japan. The Okayama prefecture seemed to have been particularly badly hurt by arsenic poisonings. In August 1955, 24 fatal cases were recorded, along with 2,005 surviving poisoning patients. Infants aged 6–10 months predominated, but the age distribution ranged from 1 month all the way up to 61 years. I arranged to meet with two physicians at Okayama University, professor Toshihide Tsuda and his younger colleague Takashi Yorifuji. They agreed to contact some of their patients and help in interviewing them.

The first patient I saw was Yoko, born in May of 1954. She was a lively woman, eager to share her life experience. She said that she was initially breast-fed, but then received milk supplement as her main nutrition after she was approximately 1 year old. That was when the Morinaga milk powder had just become contaminated. She apparently recovered from the poisoning, went to school, and by age 15 managed to complete mandatory junior high school. Afterward Yoko worked in a supermarket storage area, checking inventory and pricing for five years. While taking time off to care for her mother, she held a variety of jobs before becoming a room-maid at a hotel. There she met a waiter, who became her husband and the father of her son, born in 1984. Yoko then stayed home to take care of her child. Not a remarkable job history, but for a victim of childhood arsenic poisoning, I later realized, that was a grand achievement. In school, Yoko had great difficulties because of her dysarthria (difficulty in speech). But she was good at writing, although that has recently become much harder. As a kid, she could do handstands, though that feat has been long lost.

About 20 years ago, she began losing sensation in her toes, and the paresthesias then progressed up her right leg, and later to her left. The same problem started in her hands about five years ago. She stumbled often, and she began to have difficulty lifting her feet. More recently, she developed a stiff right knee and pain in her hip and knee joints. On the suspicion of spinal compression syndrome, she was operated on for arthritis in her neck four years ago and this seemed to have provided some relief.

When we met, her handshake was barely noticeable, though her left hand was stronger. Yoko complained that she could not move her right arm very much and had almost no strength. Other than that, she had photophobia, and she easily got nauseated when scrolling a computer screen. Nonetheless, she read the newspaper, watched TV, and engaged in discussions. Our conversation was pleasant; she was agile, focused, and smiled, mostly with the left side of her face. She was much aware of her incapacities and felt relief being able to talk to us about her experiences.

Although Yoko's husband still worked as waiter at large parties, they relied on a monthly pension. Yoko was receiving 70,000 yen per month, about $700, as compensation for the poisoning. But the company fund had recently announced a plan to reduce the pension to about 20% of the current level, insisting that the difference should be paid by the government. Yoko questioned why the taxpayers should pick up the tab from a foundation created by an industry that had willfully adulterated the milk powder with poison? I saw sadness in her eyes, but no tears. What a brave woman.

Yoko had come all the way from Osaka (about an hour by the Shinkansen express train), and she arrived early to listen to a seminar that I gave for the epidemiology students at the medical school. One of the students sat in the back with her and translated into Japanese. She did not seem the least tired from the teaching session or our hour-long conversation. Later that day, she called back to say how much she appreciated that we were willing to meet with her and listen to her story. I for one learned a lot from Yoko. She was about a year old when the poisoning began, and perhaps her developmental stage determined the type of neurotoxicity: damage to the peripheral nerves, no indication of later improvement, and symptoms becoming more prominent with age.

Meager Patient Support

Yoko's monthly pension came from a fund that was established to support the victims. That happened after 19 years of negotiations and after countrywide boycotts of Morinaga products. Thus, the Hikari Association was formed in 1974, as agreed between the victim group, the Morinaga Milk Company, and the Ministry of Health and Welfare. Hikari was to be a public-interest foundation for permanently relieving the victims of the Morinaga dried milk poisoning incident. The purpose was to support the victims' independence, by covering health care, education, counseling, occupational therapy, and basic compensation. The Association reported that by 2002, the total number of victims recorded was 13,420, of whom about 6,000 had established contact with Hikari. Yoko was one of the 798 victims receiving welfare allowances as of 2001. A total of 337 reportedly suffered from mental retardation; 129 suffered from various disabilities, 103 from mental disorders, and 33 from epilepsy. These numbers did not make sense to me. They seemed way too low—I shall soon get back to my own calculations.

Hikari means light and is also the name of an express train. It stops at all major stations and lets passengers off and on. It provides its service as stipulated and according to the needs of the passengers. The same name was used in 1969 by a patients' group formed after the first reports about the poor health of the adolescent survivors. Then, the name was taken over by the foundation. Victims' representatives claim that, of the original agreement, Hikari has honored very few of its obligations. The fact that fewer than 800 victims were receiving a pension would seem to support this critique.

Some relatives have tried to fill the hiatus left open by Hikari and the health authorities. The parents of one Morinaga fatality compiled detailed records on the incident along with patient information. They stayed in touch and tried to build a network for mutual support. The victim's younger brother, Hisaya Okazaki, a successful businessman, maintained and expanded the materials after the parents had died. I was invited to see his collection—the Museum of Morinaga Arsenic Milk Poisoning Incident.

I walked with Hisaya through his crowded office, through the residential quarters to a storage room with all the materials packed into locked bookshelves. Hisaya proudly showed me two original Morinaga milk cans, now somewhat rusty. Both were empty, and I resisted the urge to ask him if they were used by his own family and might have caused his older sister's death. But the way he carefully, almost piously, removed the cans from the locked cabinet, it seems likely. Binder upon binder contained detailed records on over 1,000 patients from the Okayama prefecture, with information on the number of milk cans consumed, and obstetric and other clinical data, evidence of despair and disrupted lives on every page. We stayed for almost two hours, and Hisaya wanted us to stay even longer—I was the first foreigner to visit.

At the Nursing Home

I wanted to meet another patient, who had been poisoned as an infant. So we drove off to a small town in a pastoral setting about an hour from Okayama. Outside the nursing home, the parents were already waiting for us. My two medical colleagues from Okayama introduced and again helped with the translation. We took off our shoes, changed to slippers, and were shown into a small meeting room with uncomfortable stacking chairs. Hideaki was already there. His mother was very talkative and eager to share her history. Her husband was distant and seemed to find the whole situation somewhat tiresome. Hideaki was mostly looking at the floor and did not reveal any desire to take part in the conversation. He was the oldest son, born in early May 1955. The mother recalled the details, 41 weeks of gestation and a birth weight of 3,800 grams, an excellent beginning. She breast-fed for one month, but a public health nurse recommended supplementing with milk powder to ensure that the baby got enough calories. Hideaki soon developed diarrhea and eczema, and his skin color darkened after one week on the milk powder. He also developed some black spots, but they later disappeared. These were the typical skin pigmentations that the Ministry considered a necessary sign to diagnose arsenic poisoning. Living on a farm in the countryside, the parents took the child to a local health clinic. After the poisoning link had been discovered, Hideaki was treated with an antidote. The treatment did not make much of a difference. He was not able to lift his head like other babies his age, and only by age 3 years was he able to stand. Hideaki was thin, he looked sickly, and his dark skin color did not fade.

Although clearly behind in development, Hideaki went to kindergarten, then school. No special education was available, so the mother helped him with his homework. Hideaki had great problems learning the Japanese letters. After his completion of mandatory schooling, he started working in a printing office, though that lasted only for a year. He had a gall bladder stone removed, quite an unusual operation for a teenage boy. He also developed epilepsy with occasional grand mal seizures. Afterward, he just helped around on the farm, the mother said. The father frowned and remained silent.

Eight years ago, Hideaki came to the day-care center, mostly for social reasons, the mother explained. Here he helped with various types of light work, like sweeping the parking area outside. He had good muscular strength, but his coordination was poor. He enjoyed reading the sports pages in the newspaper, watching TV, and listening to music. But Hideaki had trouble concentrating, often forgetting what he was doing, and he had difficulty making plans and handling money when shopping as well as separating right from left. When I asked him to move his hands back and forth, he clearly had the type of muscular incoordination referred to as dysdiado-chokinesia. There appeared to be no hearing and vision problems, though, but he easily got nauseated and flushed. Hideaki responded slowly and without enthusiasm when I asked through Takashi about his health and everyday life. His mother paid close attention and offered her perspective, while his father continued to look sad and ill at ease. Their son had suffered much more serious brain damage than Yoko, but he was exposed much sooner after birth.

Back in Okayama, we met with Mr. Enokihara, whose daughter had been poisoned from the milk powder and was later diagnosed with schizophrenia. She was also born in May 1955 and received the milk substitute soon after birth. Although she overcame the poisoning and managed to complete school, she was sleepy during the day and received drug treatment to stay awake and to sleep at night. When she was 15, a psychiatric diagnosis was finally made. Despite her severe mental problems, she had no obvious problems with motor coordination. The father knew several other parents in town in similar desperate situations, trying to care for their brain-damaged children in a country where health care is not free and where support for the handicapped is almost nonexistent. He said that he was shocked by Hikari's inhumane and callous attitude. Toshihide and Takashi both confirmed that they heard such complaints quite often.

The True Numbers

Yoko and Hideaki's stories were heartbreaking, and there were many like them. So I wanted to get back to the statistics to understand the true magnitude of the poisoning incident. I therefore asked Takashi if he could retrieve the detailed data on numbers of contaminated cans that were marketed and their contents consumed, so that we could do some calculations. For each prefecture, the number of cans shipped from the Morinaga plant in Tokushima is known for the period from April to August 1955 (680,000). From this number, we deducted the number of cans recalled (403,000) after the contamination was discovered. The recall was deemed complete, but some older, uncontaminated cans may also have been included in the count. The difference between the two numbers (277,000) would therefore represent the minimum number of cans whose contents were consumed from this production period. Analyses carried out to determine the proportion of recalled cans that were contaminated showed that about 75% contained arsenic. Assuming that three out of every four cans produced during this period were contaminated, we can then estimate that milk from approximately 205,000 contaminated cans were consumed. That is likely a minimum number, as different assumptions would suggest that milk from a higher number of cans was consumed.

The clinical records suggest that it took the contents of an average of 4.7 cans to cause a poisoning. As any remaining milk powder was probably discarded, we assumed that 5 cans were a sufficient amount to result in poisoning. Theoretically, the 205,000 cans could have generated a maximum of 41,000 poisoning cases, assuming that the cans were distributed evenly among households with infants. This number is more than threefold higher than the official number of Morinaga patients. So, our calculation suggests that as many as 29,000 cases may have been missed.

Using the same assumptions, the approximately 12,000 officially recognized cases would represent about 60,000 cans. This would then leave 145,000 cans unaccounted for, as they had not been returned. They could have been shared by a large number of households. But even the consumption of a single can containing 12 mg of arsenic would likely cause some degree of toxicity. If so, the number of less serious cases of arsenic poisoning could be as high as 100,000. True, some of the poisoning cases occurred among adults, but they constituted a minority. The powdered milk was marketed for infant nutrition.

During the 12 months up to August of 1955, the number of babies born in the 14 prefectures of western Japan was just above 400,000. The official numbers suggest that only 3% of these infants were poisoned. But our calculations suggest that as many as 10% could have been poisoned, and that inclusion of milder poisoning cases could bring that number up to 25% of the infants. The latter percentages would better reflect the number of infants, who were bottle-fed or received milk supplement.

These calculations are unlikely to be exact, but there can be little doubt that the official numbers reflect the tip of an iceberg, as I had heard several people suggest. How could such numbers be hidden and remain hidden for so long? Why was there not an in-depth investigation? These questions are difficult to answer but may relate to the time and general attitudes.

Indifference and Oversight

The poisoning incident happened during the early phase of Japan's rapid economic growth during the post–World War II period. The market for powdered milk in Japan was covered by three major enterprises, including the Morinaga Milk Industry Company, that were in fierce competition. Food safety concerns were apparently neglected by the industry, as no quality control or assessment of raw materials was conducted. It boggles the imagination that a production plant would use a crude by-product containing arsenic as an additive. If Morinaga had chosen to use fresh milk for manufacturing the powdered product, a disodium phosphate stabilizer would not have been required. It is easy in hindsight to say that a simple review of the raw materials should have been required, as it would have identified the toxic contaminant of the additive.

Moreover, once the epidemic began, the hospitals and the health authorities were not prepared to tackle the situation. Thousands of cases could probably have been prevented, but the evidence that the bottle-fed infants had a dried milk product as a common source of exposure was slow to emerge. The clinical criteria established by the governmental authorities were rigid and misleading, and chronic toxicity was disregarded. Even after the recognition of the Morinaga product as the source, exposure information was not collected in a systematic fashion, nor was a registry set up, and long-term follow-up of exposed population groups was carried out only sporadically. To make matters even worse, the victims of this unfortunate incident have not received the support and compensation that they deserve.

But the data available certainly document that neurotoxicity occurred. First, neurological symptoms were present as part of the acute poisonings. The follow-up studies showed a preponderance of mental complaints in exposed subjects, who also had an increased prevalence of mental retardation and epilepsy, as compared to unexposed controls. More than 20% of the Kyoto victims examined in 1970–1971 had an IQ below 85, which is clearly an excessive proportion when compared to the average rate of about 2% in Japanese children.[7]

As in Minamata, the epidemic of arsenic poisonings was felt to be embarrassing, research and publicity were frowned upon, and only brief reports in English have been published by Japanese scholars in international scientific journals. Even so, these reports were ignored by scientists abroad and by international agencies. The National Academy of Sciences[8] and the World Health Organization[9] published thorough risk assessment documents on arsenic. None of these extensive reports provides a single sentence on developmental neurotoxicity. Nothing. Somehow, the world seemed to turn a blind eye to this very serious poisoning incident.

And there is much more evidence that could be consulted. That children are highly vulnerable to arsenic poisoning was already suggested by the case of a little girl in Lancashire, England. More than 100 years ago, she was poisoned from a surprising source—arsenic-laced beer, as described by the family physician:

> The patient was a pretty-looking little girl aged 2 years. She had been unwell for some days, suffering from pains in the feet and legs. She wanted her shoes always off; evidently her feet felt hot and uncomfortable. The child was too young to give subjective symptoms....As the child sat in the lap of a relative the feet looked "dropped" as if the extensors were paretic, but there was no distinct paralysis.... The knee-jerks were absent.[10]

The missing patellar reflex is highly abnormal, and the girl was clearly subdued and developmentally delayed. According to the description, the girl's father ran a "public house," or tavern. The guests apparently had given the girl a sip of the local beer, which turned out to be adulterated with arsenic. The arsenic was causing widespread neuritis and paresthesias among beer adult imbibers, symptoms that were much less severe and only affected the peripheral nervous system. The innkeeper's daughter had more serious symptoms. Although the medical practitioner did not present any information on the possible dose, even for her body size, the girl would have swallowed much less of the contaminated beverage than the adult clients.

Other poisonings happened in the 1800s among London children employed to stain paper with arsenic dyes. Many were as young as 8 years and had long working days. As a factory foreman said, "I have to bawl at them to keep them awake," while another recommended "just a lick of the head now and them, perhaps" to make sure the children performed their duties. The kids were not just lazy, but "a boy here and there goes queer with the paint."[11] Medical records from the time are few and without much detail. I am in no doubt that these kids suffered brain drain caused by the arsenic dyes. Ample support comes from modern studies on children exposed to arsenic pollution.

Worldwide Exposures

There are many reasons that we should not act like Admiral Nelson and turn a blind eye to these cases. There are in fact millions of reasons. Arsenic is a common groundwater contaminant that affects large populations in many countries.[12] Well water in the southwest of Taiwan was first found in the early 1960s to contain arsenic concentrations up to 1.82 mg/L—a concentration similar to the one in milk prepared from Morinaga milk powder. The total population affected was about 140,000. At about the same time, a similar number of inhabitants of the Antofagasta region in Chile were drinking water with a concentration of about 0.8 mg/L.

The most serious problem emerged when water wells were dug in Bangladesh and the West Bengal in India to avoid pathogenic bacteria. In the late 1970s, it was discovered that 6 million people in 2,600 villages in the West Bengal were drinking arsenic-laced water. The contamination can exceed concentrations of 1 mg/L of water, about 100 times the limit permitted by the US Environmental Protection Agency. Such serious problems also occur elsewhere in the region, in Pakistan, Nepal, Myanmar, Cambodia, Vietnam, and China, where eroding rocks release arsenic into the groundwater as a result of the oxidation processes.

Why did that ever happen? After severe cholera epidemics, UNICEF and the World Bank sent engineers to Bangladesh and other affected countries in the early 1970s to help combat the infectious diseases by providing clean drinking water. They drilled thousands of tube wells.[13] Little did they know that the underlying geology contained traces of arsenic. Locals warned that it was the *devil's water* they were bringing up from under the earth. Indeed.

High arsenic concentrations in drinking water have been discovered at many other locations, in Argentina, Canada, Hungary, Japan, Mexico, New Zealand, Poland, Spain, Sri Lanka, and in the United States. It is a worldwide problem.

Arsenic researcher Peter Ravenscroft from Cambridge University has estimated that, worldwide, over 137 million people in more than 70 countries are at risk of arsenic poisoning from contaminated drinking water. In the United States, the number is somewhat uncertain, since one-sixth of all American households get their drinking water from private wells, which are usually not monitored. An estimate from the International Agency for Research on Cancer puts the global number at 160 million people.[14]

Children exposed to arsenic from drinking water suffer brain drain, as shown by numerous research studies.[15] In Taiwan, pattern memory and switching attention in adolescents were negatively affected by arsenic in their drinking water. In the Bengal region, children aged 10 years whose drinking water showed increased contamination levels and who had increased urinary arsenic concentrations registered cognitive deficits on an IQ test. In 6-year-olds, the water arsenic concentration at their homes was associated with deficits in their performance and processing speed scores on an IQ scale for young children. Similar results were obtained in children with arsenic exposure from a smelter and children exposed to arsenic from mining tailings. These more recent data fit with the high-exposure findings from Japan. Still, none of these more recent reports refer to the Morinaga evidence, and most authors discuss arsenic neurotoxicity as if these effects were hypothetical. Having met Yoko and Hideaki, I can tell you that arsenic-induced brain drain is real!

In the United States, arsenic-contaminated drinking water was first discovered in Millard County in Utah, but the exposed population in this desert area is very small. Lane County in Oregon and Lessen County in California added greater numbers to the exposed population. Fairbanks, Alaska, was also found to be affected, as were communities in Nevada, New Hampshire, and New Mexico. The most recent data from the US Geological Survey are based on samples from 31,350 wells. Overall, arsenic concentrations in groundwater are highest in the "slate belt" in the southeastern United States; western states such as Nevada, New Mexico, and Alaska; and parts of the Midwest and Northeast, where arsenic concentrations often exceed the EPA limit of 10 μg/L.[16] In the northeastern states, about 13% of wells that reach the crystalline bedrock aquifers exceed the EPA limit, some of them by huge margins.[17]

Most of these communities show arsenic concentrations that would be far too low to cause acute poisoning but which could certainly cause chronic toxicity, increase the cancer risk, and perhaps damage brain development. The Natural Resources Defense Council has calculated that at least 34 million—and more likely 56 million Americans—in 2000 were drinking tap water with average arsenic concentrations that posed unacceptable cancer risks.[18] This estimate was based on available and incomplete information reported to the US Environmental Protection Agency (EPA) by 25 states only.

Arsenic exposures also come from industrial emissions from mining, smelting, or agricultural sources (pesticides or fertilizers). Among industrial sources in the United States, copper smelters in Anaconda, Montana, and Tacoma, Washington, have released arsenic in concentrations sufficient to cause diseases among the workers. Neighborhood exposures have also been documented, posing harm to families who live nearby. Coal-burning power plants also cause large emissions to the environment. The majority of the arsenic used industrially in the United States is as a wood preservative, but smaller amounts are applied in paints, dyes, alloys, drugs, soaps, and semiconductors. Believe it or not, arsenic is an approved dietary supplement to chicken to help kill intestinal parasites that plague fowl raised on big farms. The chicken then excrete the arsenic into the environment. This practise is still legal in most US states. Thus, there are many possible sources of arsenic exposure.

All sources of arsenic exposure are potentially preventable, although the remedy is not necessarily inexpensive. If arsenic-free groundwater is not available, there are several methods of removing the arsenic either at the water treatment plant or at the faucet (about $1,000 for an arsenic filter). Is this cost too steep to protect brain development? I would think not, but the price mattered when politics entered the discussion of the permissible amount of arsenic in the water.

Based on the report from the National Academy of Sciences, the US EPA had reduced the allowable concentration of arsenic in drinking water to 10 μg/L. However, after the change in administration, the EPA in 2001 announced that it was withdrawing this Clinton-era rule. The George W. Bush government asserted that the rule was being dropped because it had been rushed through the rule-making process and was not based on "sound science." This was a surprising decision, as the EPA had been working on this rule for over a decade and the National Academy committee had concluded that the previous, 5-fold higher limit was inadequate to protect health. A hidden agenda later reported was a push to win votes in New Mexico communities where many locals considered new wells or water treatment overly expensive. The limit now stands at 10.

Brain drain due to arsenic is a real risk, regardless of whether neurotoxicity examinations have sufficiently documented the exposure-related brain drain. I have met victims of arsenic poisoning, and I got much more than I bargained for. A few tears in the eyes (including mine), and much despair. The victims of arsenic poisoning in Japan and elsewhere are not receiving the support they deserve. In the United States, it is possible that neurotoxicity is not a serious problem, but the risk has been ignored and it remains unexamined. The expense for drinking water treatment perhaps makes this information undesirable to those who have to pay for the remediation (we will return to the economics in chapter 8). But is it better not to know the enemy? The Morinaga poisoning was due to a thoughtless production process, and the arsenic in drinking water is released due to oxidation of minerals in the underground. The problems could have been prevented, but arsenic is a common geological component and may not be the prototype of a brain drainer. There are thousands of man-made chemicals that may also be toxic to the brain. I shall now turn to an industrial chemical, which certainly occurs on this planet only as a result of human ingenuity, due to synthetic chemistry. More tears to come.

CHAPTER 6

Persistent Problems

CHEMICALS RESISTANT TO BREAKDOWN
CAN BREAK BRAIN CELLS

Anniston, Alabama, is one of the most polluted towns in America. When the citizens looked for help, the notable trial lawyer, Johnnie Cochran became interested and came to meet with local representatives. The meeting turned into a public spectacle, with more than a thousand people trying to catch a glimpse of the famous attorney, who had successfully defended the sports idol O. J. Simpson. After a remarkable career practicing criminal law, Cochran was now concentrating on civil rights and social justice issues. The Anniston case fit into that picture. Cochran told the crowd:

> We have our basic rights in this country, and one of those is that every citizen should live free of pollution, live free of PCBs, live free of mercury, of lead, anything that is deleterious to our health. We've not been told about the dangers here...there is always some study and they'll study it to death and then thirty years later you find out it's bad for you. I'm here to tell you tonight we know it's bad for us right now![1]

I wish the late attorney had been able to put his legal mind to many more cases than the Anniston pollution. Man-made industrial chemicals differ from lead, mercury, and arsenic by being generated entirely due to human ingenuity. They have never occurred naturally on Earth before we started producing them. They are new to our biochemical defense systems. Some of the chemical inventions could easily be toxic to brain cells. But it is hard to say, as such suspicions are generally ignored. The potential for adverse effects is particularly worrisome in regard to man-made substances that do not easily disintegrate, once they reach the environment or get absorbed. So even if we at some point decide to ban the substance after its adverse effects have been discovered, it is likely to remain with us—and inside us—for a very long time. Such is the case with the polychlorinated biphenyls (PCBs) that polluted Anniston, Alabama.

First synthesized in Germany in the late 1800s, PCBs were massively produced soon after World War I. PCBs were stable and turned out to be highly useful in electrical equipment due to their insulating and fire-proofing properties. PCB production first began in Anniston in 1929. Chemical giant Monsanto soon acquired the facility and obtained a monopoly to market the promising product under the name of Aroclor. Various health problems soon emerged among the workers but were not considered serious enough to halt production.

Soon thereafter, Harvard professor Cecil K. Drinker showed that liver toxicity could be induced in rats exposed to doses similar to those encountered at the PCB production facilities.[2] His findings were presented along with other evidence at a one-day meeting at the Harvard School of Public Health in 1937. As industry was unwilling to give up this profitable production, one of the executives stressed to the meeting participants the "necessity of not creating mob hysteria on the part of workmen in the plants."[3] The wait-and-see sentiment prevailed, and production increased during the next decades, with factories in China, France, Germany, Japan, Slovakia, the Soviet Union, and the United Kingdom.

In 1964, an important discovery was accidentally made in Stockholm, Sweden, by Søren Jensen, a Dane, who had moved to Stockholm to study chemistry. After graduation, he was hired by the Swedish Environmental Protection Agency to measure the environmental pollution caused by the pesticide DDT. He used a gas chromatograph for the chemical analyses of samples like pike, feathers from white-tailed sea-eagles, and human blood. But Jensen ran into problems because of mysterious peaks that disturbed his analyses. The instrument noise came from compounds with properties somewhat similar to those of DDT, and they contained only carbon, hydrogen, and chlorine. As the mysterious compounds were also present in museum samples collected before World War II, they were unlikely to be pesticides, Jensen reasoned.

Jensen found that all of Sweden and the adjacent waters were contaminated, even samples taken from his wife and three children showed traces of the compound, with the highest levels in his nursing infant daughter. The mystery pollutant was everywhere he looked, although pike from Lapland contained much less than pike from southern Sweden. When he measured the molecular weights in fat extracts from a dead eagle, the peaks occurred at an interval of 34, and this could only happen if one chlorine atom at a time substituted a hydrogen atom in the molecule. The noise therefore had to come from a family of organic compounds with different numbers of chlorines.[4]

Eventually, as Jensen explained, "I was convinced that what I had to deal with were chlorinated biphenyls, but I didn't have the faintest idea where such compounds were used in the society." Searching the literature, Jensen learned of the industrial uses of PCBs. The German chemical manufacturer, Bayer, provided Jensen with a sample of their Clophen product—similar to Aroclor in America. Jensen analyzed it and found that it matched exactly the "peaks" found in the poisoned eagle. "The circle was closed," Jensen said. "There was no doubt that the unknown peaks came from the use of polychlorinated biphenyls, which I gave the name PCB."[5] By 1968, PCB was also discovered in California wildlife, and further studies soon documented worldwide dissemination. PCB was resistant to breakdown in the environment and had already traveled through the air or marine currents to the remotest corners of the world.

An Industrial Success

At the time of Jensen's discovery, PCB was an industrial success story. The largest amounts were used in transformers, cables, and electrical equipment, where the stability of the chemical was advantageous. PCB was used in paints, caulking products, carbonless copying paper, and many other products. When I started medical school, we used so-called immersion oil on the microscopy slides to obtain better light transmission through the objective. At anatomy classes, I certainly got immersion oil on my hands, and I only recently realized that the thick fluid may have been pure PCB! The total world production of this resistant chemical is unknown but probably exceeds 1 million tons. Some has been broken down by the action of sunlight and enzymes, but much still remains, some of it very far from the production sites, some closer to the source.

The plant in Anniston thrived and its toxic wastes were blissfully discharged into streams and open landfills. The pollution problems first came to light in 1966, the same year that Jensen published his findings. A group of biologists from Mississippi State University arrived in Anniston to conduct studies on fish in Snow Creek downstream from the Monsanto facility. Professor Denzel Ferguson had in fact been hired by the company to conduct a series of confidential tests of the water quality. The researcher's bluegill fish died within minutes when lowered into Snow Creek. Downstream, in Choccolocco Creek, the fish lasted longer due to the dilution. The biologists concluded that the effluents from the facility would probably kill fish even if diluted 1,000 times.[6] The following year, Monsanto nonetheless expanded the PCB production in Anniston and at its second plant in Sauget, Michigan.

In 1970, the Food and Drug Administration carried out analyses of catfish from Choccolocco Creek and found PCB concentrations over 50-fold higher than the legal limit. Downstream in Logan Martin Lake, levels were almost eight times higher than allowed. In Anniston, a Monsanto study had already found PCB concentrations in (surviving) fish that exceeded the limit by 7,500 times. The state authorities got involved, and a corporate memo stated very frankly: "There is extreme reluctance to report even the relatively low emission figures, because the information would be subpoenaed and used against us in litigation. Obviously, having to report these gross losses multiplies, enormously, our problems because figures would appear to indicate lack of control."[7] The Monsanto officials managed to convince the state government to keep quiet about PCB contamination of the waterways.

These records only became public in connection with a legal case 25 years later. During the production years, the Anniston plant was pouring 50,000 pounds of PCBs into Snow Creek per year. The wastewater ran straight into the creek, with no settling ponds or carbon filters to remove the PCBs. In addition, more than 1 million pounds of PCB-laced waste was buried in antiquated landfills.[8] The company claimed that the discharges were negligible, and, anyway, no federal regulations applied specifically to PCB. However, Monsanto headquarters were already aware of serious adverse effects of PCB before the information became publicly known in the 1970s and 1980s. In its marketing of PCBs, the company began to use a so-called responsible approach, which involved acknowledging certain aspects of the problem and tightening restrictions. So Monsanto began to ask customers to sign indemnity forms that they were using PCBs at their own risk. This way, profits were secured while liability problems were minimized.

Denials of the dangers would continue even after PCBs were banned in the United States in 1979. "There has never been a single documented case in this country where PCBs have been shown to cause cancer or any other serious human health problems," a Monsanto toxicologist said in 1981. Their toxicity was similar, he said, to that of table salt.[9] Still, the company's responses to finding PCBs in the environment "were swift and effective," and Monsanto was "committed to stop making PCBs as soon as substitutes were developed."[10] The production peaked in 1970 at 85 million pounds (almost 40,000 tons). However, faced with increasing problems, Monsanto quietly ceased production of PCBs in Anniston the following year. In 1977, PCB production in the United States stopped completely. Near the Anniston facility, 40 stream miles and 6,000 acres of floodplain remain directly affected by PCB contamination, 40 years after the production stopped.

Problems Discovered

Again in this case, attention to possible brain toxicity was triggered by a poisoning episode, in fact two. First, in Japan (the so-called Yusho poisoning) and then in Taiwan (Yucheng). In both cases, rice oil had been contaminated with PCBs used in the refinery distilling machinery. Poisoned children were easily recognized because of so-called coca-cola spots on the skin and abnormalities of nails, gums, and teeth. Later follow-up studies showed that the exposed children also had lower IQs.[11] Along with the PCBs, the cooking oil had been contaminated with similar substances with dioxin-like effects. So we cannot be absolutely sure that any brain toxicity in the children was necessarily due to PCBs as such. But this association is supported by examinations of children exposed prenatally to environmental PCB pollution.

Because PCBs accumulate in fat and are passed through the food chains, we continue to be exposed through the food supply. As PCBs pass through the placenta, a pregnant woman shares her body burden of PCBs with the fetus, and exposure continues during infancy due to PCB elimination in the breast milk. During a six-month duration of breast-feeding, a mother can transfer up to half of her own accumulated burden of PCBs to her child. So the PCB exposure is particularly intense during the most vulnerable period of brain development. The impact of PCB exposure on brain development has been studied in a dozen different populations.

The first pioneering effort was orchestrated by the husband-and-wife team of psychiatry professors Joseph and Sandra Jacobson in Detroit, Michigan.[12] As part of a follow-up study, they examined 236 children, whose mothers had eaten contaminated fish caught in Lake Michigan. The PCB concentration in umbilical cord serum predicted poorer short-term memory function at age 4 years. They also found decreased attention span and, at age 11 years, deficits in IQ. In a study in North Carolina at lower exposure levels, PCB-associated effects were also seen.[13] Similar examinations of children in Germany and the Netherlands support PCB-associated brain drain, in part due to PCBs transferred via human milk.[14] Overall, this evidence suggests that PCB exposure can adversely affect motor skills, concentration, learning, impulsivity, and memory, as also reflected by lower full-scale and verbal IQ scores and reading ability.[15]

However, all of the population groups studied were also exposed to other substances, such as dioxins and metabolites of DDT and other pesticides. So in each case, the PCB concentration was probably an indicator of a more complex exposure, of which PCB was only part. Nonetheless, the overall consistency among studies would suggest that PCB is likely to be a common and at least partial cause of brain drain in these children. (Also, the impact of other environmental chemicals cannot be deduced from the results, and independent toxicology studies are therefore needed to determine their significance.)

There is another difficulty that we need to take into account. PCB is not a well-defined substance but a mixture consisting of many compounds of similar structure. These individual substances vary in their chlorine content, as Søren Jensen had found. In the environment, and in the human body, especially those with less chlorine are fairly rapidly broken down, and most of our exposure now consists of the very persistent highly chlorinated PCBs. But which ones are causing the brain toxicity? We cannot tell from the human studies, since we are all exposed to PCB mixtures, not to single PCBs at a time.

The European Commission in 2006 began to support a series of studies to disentangle the effects of different PCBs, in particular those that act through mechanisms different from dioxin. Surprisingly, different numbers and positions of chlorine atoms in the PCBs result in different mechanisms of action. In particular, several

PCB molecules interfere with the development of receptors in the brain and the amount of transmitter substances.[16] In parallel studies, PCBs were found to interfere with brain cells, in particular the growth and plasticity of their dendrites. The laboratory studies therefore provide a link between developmental PCB exposure and its effects on cognitive development.[17] However, while the experimental studies suggest that effects in humans are plausible, they cannot provide detailed dose-response relationships or thresholds in regard to toxicity in humans.

Once again, science is decades behind in documenting and understanding the toxic effects of an industrial chemical produced since the early 1900s. Given the persistence of PCBs, this chemical has accumulated in the environment for many decades. In addition, PCBs from old transformers and other applications are probably still leaking. So despite the bans on production and use more than 30 years ago, our exposures to this "old" chemical continue and are only slowly decreasing.

We Are All Exposed

About 25 years after the production at the Anniston plant had stopped, the management became interested in properties nearby. In 1995, the company made an offer to purchase a lot owned by the Mars Hill Missionary Baptist Church just across the highway from the plant. That offer triggered curiosity and concern in the church community and beyond. It turned out that Monsanto was buying about 100 nearby properties only to demolish the buildings. It also came to light that PCB was leaking from a nearby dump site, and that the land that Monsanto had already bought might be contaminated. As more and more information surfaced on PCB contamination in the community, people began seeking out lawyers in order to sue for damages. That was how Johnnie Cochran got involved. Meanwhile, Monsanto spun off the division that had produced PCBs into a firm called Solutia, Inc.

The TV program *60 Minutes* aired a story about the community in 2002 and called Anniston one of America's most toxic towns. This broadcast and an interview with environmental health professor David Carpenter provoked a response from Elizabeth Whelan, president of the American Council on Science and Health, a think-tank that often supports industry views on environmental and health issues. In a letter of complaint to the TV station, she said:

> "there is no credible evidence that environmental exposure to PCBs—at levels comparable to the exposure in Anniston—poses any known risk to human health....Not only is there no convincing evidence that background PCB levels in the general population cause ill health of any type, but even the very high levels to which some occupational groups have been exposed have not resulted in...intellectual deterioration in children exposed to PCBs in the womb.[18]

Dr. Whelan may have a point that the evidence is perhaps not "convincing." Industry spokesman, Robert A. Kehoe (see chapter 3), would have agreed with her. But how much documentation does it take to assure us that we can safely allow our children to be exposed to PCBs and similar compounds?

Once the evidence was presented in court, as a result of lawsuits brought by Johnnie Cochran and other lawyers, the jury was not in doubt. The jury members found the industry defendants responsible for the PCB contamination in Anniston, and they stated that Monsanto's conduct was "so outrageous in character and extreme in degree as to go beyond all possible bounds of decency, so as to be regarded as atrocious and utterly intolerable in civilized society."[19] Although this verdict was later annulled, as a joint settlement was reached with all of the plaintiffs, the wording leaves no doubt about what the jury thought of PCB, the company, and the health risks.

The overall settlement for $700 million became the largest amount ever paid in a civil suit. It even exceeded the amount paid by PG&E in the California pollution cases depicted in the movie *Erin Brockovich*. Of this amount, $100 million would be reserved for cleanup operations, education, and a medical clinic. The remaining $600 million would be used to pay damages to the claimants according to a formula that involved the PCB concentration in serum and medical conditions. However, before that happened, the legal expenses had to be covered, including a 30% fee to the lawyers.[20]

Most attention was paid to the adverse health risks that might harm adults exposed to the PCBs in the past, whether from eating local fish or otherwise. But 22% of the plaintiffs were categorized as children. Their serum-PCB concentrations were much lower than those of the adults, who had probably absorbed PCBs during the most intensive production years of the chemical. Disregarding any increased vulnerability, the court decided to award equal compensation for PCB exposures, so that the children received only $8 million out of the $131 million, as calculated from the serum-PCB concentrations. Children whose mothers had an increased serum-PCB concentration received some additional money, and some other adjustments were in the children's favor. Overall, adult claimants received an average of $9,100, while the children received $2,000.

The lawyer in charge of managing the compensation fund contacted me in 2009. He was worried that the PCBs were causing more adverse health effects than recognized by the court. Although the cases had been settled, he thought that the combined health information could be used to extract scientific documentation that might help prevent similar pollution problems in the future. So I traveled to Anniston to meet with the lawyers and plaintiffs' representatives.

The meeting with the Anniston residents was disheartening. The pollution and the legal disputes had hit the town like a spell, just as in Minamata. Residents could not afford to move, as nobody would buy their homes. Some were living in deserted streets, with no neighbors, as all of the properties were known to be contaminated. The compensation was far from sufficient. Many residents had chronic diseases, like diabetes, hypertension, or heart disease, and they could barely afford their prescription medicine. The medical clinic paid for by the settlement was about to close. I heard many sad stories of poverty, disability, and despair. Like one of them said, Monsanto left a community still sick, still dying, and very dissatisfied. All I could do was take notes, but I also thought of the polluting company, which way back in the 1930s attributed symptoms in production workers to the "natural laziness of the black man." But my main surprise was that I heard few concerns about children and adolescents, who must have been exposed to PCB during their most vulnerable ages. An obvious reason is the difficulty of linking poor school performance to PCB exposure in a deprived community, given other competing risks. Of course, no studies had been conducted. And those who knew about developmental neurotoxicity seemed not to care.

But PCBs are not only present in Anniston. About 75% of the PCBs produced were used in capacitors and transformers. In principle, this PCB is enclosed and will be released only as a result of improper maintenance, fires, or unsafe disposal. However, old electrical equipment is an important source of continued releases to the environment. We are talking about huge amounts. While Monsanto's annual production peaked at 40,000 tons, the total world production amounted to about 1.5 million tons.

Another important application was caulking materials used in construction and renovating buildings, including public buildings. Believe it or not, tons of PCBs were actually used in schools across the country and abroad. Some caulks used for sealing windows contained PCB concentrations up to several percent.[21] Much of this PCB is still in place in schools built or renovated before 1978. It evaporates very slowly and maintains PCBs in the indoor air and on indoor surfaces. So school kids with vulnerable brains under rapid development are exposed to a chemical brain drainer in public buildings—the very institutions that are meant to promote brain development. PCBs were also used in light fixtures (so-called ballasts) for fluorescent lights, also popular in public school buildings.

Fortunately, the PCBs that evaporate the easiest and therefore contribute the most to the exposure[22] are not known for sure to cause chemical brain drain, at least not yet. That does not mean that the PCB release is innocuous. Due to the health concerns, parents have complained to public school authorities and demanded PCB abatement, for example, in New York City.[23] Because of the expense involved, pilot studies and removal projects are moving forward only at a snail's pace. Among the findings of ongoing analyses, a government office was shown to have over 35% PCB in its caulking.[24] Although intriguing, I do not dare suggest any causal connection with the lack of strategy for PCB abatement!

The Dirty Dozen

PCBs were not just a problem in connection with its production. One of the companies that purchased Aroclor from Monsanto was General Electric, which used the material to insulate and fireproof cable wires. The company started in 1946 producing capacitors containing PCBs at its Fort Edward plant in New York. Unfortunately, PCBs spilled into the Hudson River, and in 1984, the US Environmental Protection Agency named it the largest chemical waste dump to date. This Superfund site covers a 200-mile stretch of the Hudson River, from New York City and upriver to Hudson Falls. The PCB had to be removed. Several hundred million dollars have already been spent to dredge the river and safely treat and dispose of the PCB from the sludge. Here, PCB's praised stability turned out to be a disadvantage. PCB remains one of the most common contaminants at the hundreds of Superfund sites registered by federal agencies as a danger to public health or the environment. But PCB is not the only industrial chemical causing problems due to its persistence.

In 2000, PCBs were globally banned by the UN Environment Programme's Stockholm convention, along with other members of the so-called dirty dozen that also includes dioxin and similar compounds that are very persistent in the environment. Once released, they all cause long-term problems. PCB is the best documented brain drainer of this group, but dioxin, DDT, and perhaps others on the Stockholm list, are probably as dirty in that regard.

All of these dirty substances remain in the environment even decades after being banned. They are persistent and tend to occur together because they are fat soluble and accumulate in food chains. This happened at many Superfund sites in the United States and in company towns elsewhere, like Flix in Spain, where industry pollution and agricultural pesticide use caused highly increased exposures to several of the dirty substances. In the Arctic, food chains accumulate particularly high concentrations of these substances, and traditional food now contains record-high concentrations of industrial chemicals emitted from far-away sources. Studies in these populations suggest that hexachlorobenzene, DDT, PCB, and their mixtures may cause developmental neurotoxicity.[25] The dirty dozen will remain with us for a long time, and their toxic effects may last even longer.

Other chemicals, initially not listed by the Stockholm Convention, are also persistent and possibly neurotoxic. Brominated flame retardants are somewhat similar to the PCBs in chemical structure, and they have been widely used to fireproof textiles and electrical equipment. Some of them are quite stable in the environment, and accumulated exposures have been reflected in increasing concentrations in human milk. Now they are also suspected of causing brain drain.[26]

A different group of chemicals, the perfluorinated compounds, is also problematic. Best known are PFOA and PFOS, often referred to as C8. Among their useful properties, they are highly stable. For several decades, production and use of these substances caused contamination of the groundwater in the Mid-Ohio Valley (West Virginia and Ohio) and near the Twin Cities in Minnesota. Tens of thousands of people were exposed for many years to C8-polluted water before the companies revealed information that environmental releases had occurred.[27] As these substances are neurotoxic in laboratory models,[28] researchers are now trying to determine the risks to brain development.[29] The jury is still out in regard to C8 as a potential brain drainer.

Although resistance to breakdown was initially thought of as an advantage, we now know that this very property can be highly problematic. If we are unable to metabolize the chemicals and eliminate them, they can build up in the body—including the brain—and cause long-term damage. But persistence is of course not a prerequisite for causing toxicity, and the list of suspected brain drainers is long, as we shall see next.

Unusual Suspects

CHEMICALS THAT PROTECT THE LAWN
MAY DAMAGE THE BRAIN

As a medical expert, I once participated in a consumer program on Swiss television to discuss the health risks from pesticide exposure. I argued that pregnant women and children deserve special protection against these substances and provided advice on how to avoid pesticide exposure. The next day, I received an e-mail from a mother, who worried about pesticide use in a garden shared by many families in an apartment building. The children used the lawn as a playfield.

"Little toddlers learn to walk or crawl on their hands and feet. Logically they also put everything into their mouths. Now all this looks like paradise." But twice a year the lawn was treated to get rid of dandelions, daisies, and clover. She then described an impressive variety of chemicals, including 2,4-D, which became famous as an ingredient of Agent Orange used in Vietnam. She had recently seen the gardener applying pesticides while wearing a face mask and a plastic suit, which even covered his entire head. She added that "normally the gardener tells us in advance. The children are then not allowed to play in the garden for a few hours."

I can understand her worry. Household and garden applications can easily expose us and our children to substantial amounts of toxic agents. But pesticides are also used widely in agriculture to maintain and increase crop yields. Usually, we are exposed to more than one pesticide at a time, and that complicates the situation. Pesticides were on the top of my list of substances I wanted to know more about, for several reasons.

Pesticides are designed to be toxic, and many of them target the nervous system of insect pests. Although directed at other species, the specificity may not work out, as basic neurochemical processes in all living creatures are similar in many ways. Apologies, but the biochemistry between your ears has some similarity with the processes in a cockroach brain. Thus, a pesticide aimed at knocking out an insect is also likely to be toxic to humans. And such pesticide toxicity can be particularly detrimental during brain development.

So brain toxicity is both a purpose and a risk, albeit in regard to different species—pests and humans. You might ask why pesticide producers decided to inflict chemical damage on the brains of insects. Why not choose another target? The answer is that neurotoxic chemicals are extremely efficient, due to the vulnerability of the insect brain. The distressing problem is that the vulnerability that these pesticides target also extends to human brains.

When I reviewed the medical literature on poisonings, I found that pesticides constituted the largest group of substances that had caused neurological signs and symptoms,[1] and I have now collected information on close to 100 neurotoxic pesticides (see Appendix). Most of them are designed to be toxic to insects, usually by targeting their nervous system. It would seem likely that human brains during early development might also be vulnerable to pesticides. Likely, yes, but there was barely any documentation. In my search for answers, I made some surprising discoveries that began when I was tracking down the origin of a flower bouquet.

Thorny Roses

Few people think of pesticides when they buy roses. But perfect, long-stemmed roses without mildew and brown leaves are a specialized industrial product. One of the world centers for floriculture is on the high plateau in the Ecuadorean Andes just north of Quito. The pesticide use is intense. On my way by car from the capital, I noted the white rectangles covering large parts of the mountain valleys. It was not snow. Reflecting the light, these thick plastic sheets protect rose bushes that are seven feet tall, in rows that may be more than 300 feet long. In the Andes close to the Equator, the climate is fairly constant, and under the plastic, humidity and temperature can be easily controlled.

Optimal conditions for rose production are secured with a wide spectrum of pesticides. Spraying is done almost daily—sometimes also with pesticides that are banned elsewhere. Such bans do not affect production and export, so toxic chemicals often originate from companies in the United States or the European Union. Inside one of the greenhouses, I noted the dried-out droplets on the rose leaves from the recent shower of pesticide. I touched the underside of the plastic wall with a finger and felt the gooey layer of chemicals that had built up from frequent sprayings. I hurried out to wash my hands, since many pesticides can easily penetrate the skin. Afterward, I worried that even the water at the floriculture site may be contaminated from effluents.

Each of the flower production facilities generally has over 100 employees, most of whom are young women. They work with their bare hands, for gloves are impractical and the thorns would puncture them anyway. The 50,000 floriculture employees generate one of the largest export items in the country. Most intense is the production just before Christmas, Valentine's Day, and Mother's Day, when millions of roses are flown every day to the United States and other wealthy countries. Still, wages in Ecuador are minuscule. The greenhouse workers earn about $150 per month, and they only have Sunday off. A large bouquet of roses will cost you a few dollars here, but last time I ordered a dozen long-stemmed roses for Valentine's Day in Boston, I paid more than a hundred dollars—close to a month's salary for a greenhouse worker in Ecuador.

Tabacundo is a small town in the Ecuadorean Andes. A brief glimpse of the countryside leaves no doubt about the influence of the chemical industry. The farm houses are painted with colorful advertisements for pesticides, though these are not the usual billboards that change periodically. The commercial murals are a permanent decoration for which the farmer has probably received a small fee. In this region, women have few other job opportunities, so there is a high likelihood that if a woman has a job, she is employed in the greenhouses.

My local colleague Raul Harari initially told me about this community several years ago, and he was my guide when I came to visit the Cayambe-Tabacundo area. Raul was the first specialist in occupational medicine in Ecuador, educated in Argentina and Italy. The level of occupational safety in the greenhouses is rather high, he says. It is very rare that somebody gets poisoned. Men only are responsible for the spraying operations and for mixing the pesticides before application. When doing this work, they wear protective oilskin clothing and a mask that provides clean air.

While all this detail is explained to me, my concerns focus less on the employee safety, which is covered by legal requirements, or the early symptoms of poisoning that may be easily recognized by the workers. Based on my training and research experience, my main worry is, "Are there brain-drain risks that may hurt the next generation?" Most of the women, who prune and cut the roses, are young and definitely within what demographers call fertile age groups. Raul tells me that they normally work throughout their pregnancies. As they cannot afford otherwise, they begin their 12-week maternity leave as late as possible. That means that the baby throughout the gestation shares the pesticides that the mother absorbs during her work. Although we are told that the women very rarely get sick from pesticide exposure, there could be adverse effects on vulnerable processes during brain development of her child, as evidenced by other toxicants.

We ask around in Tabacundo, and a fair number of the local children have a mother who works in the greenhouses. But the kids that we see bicycling and playing at the square outside the school seem perfectly normal. They shout, joke, and kick soccer balls like the kids I know in Boston or Copenhagen. We clearly needed specialized tests to determine whether the kids have more subtle problems in regard to neurological and cognitive functions.

A main reason that we know so little about the long-term effects of pesticides on brain function is that most important exposures occur during the early brain development, while the effects would only be apparent at school age—many years later. So based on what I had heard and seen as well as my impressions and previous years of research experience, Tabacundo appeared an excellent setting to examine the local children's performance in regard to a history of prenatal pesticide exposure. Due to the presence of greenhouses, the long-standing presence of the flower industry, and the well-established experience of the workers, we should easily be able to classify children with high-level exposures for comparison with virtually unexposed children.

Hence, we created a project plan to examine children from the same neighborhood who had different pesticide exposures during early brain development. We decided to use techniques similar to those that we applied in studies of lead and mercury. The ethical review committee in Quito approved the study. In addition, the school principal and the teachers agreed to help, and the local health clinic made their examination rooms available to us.

Next, an informational meeting was held to which the parents of the children in first and second grade (named second and third grade in Ecuador) were invited, where the study was outlined and the need for signatures on the informed consent form explained. Not a single mother declined. So we began making arrangements to pick up four children at a time at the school for escort to the clinic. Also, rides home were provided for those kids who missed the bus because they were examined at the end of the day.

All of the kids underwent a thorough medical examination, neuropsychological testing, and a blood test for cholinesterase, the enzyme that is inhibited by some of the pesticides. Sophisticated testing was performed by my Japanese colleague, Professor Kasuyuki Murata, who had brought his neurophysiology gear. He attached EEG electrodes on each kid's skull, and the screen display of brain waves was a tremendous hit! Carlos, Daisy, Gabriela, Luis, and the others complied with our instructions, and we got complete data from almost everybody.

The exposure history was obtained from the mothers, and Raul Harari organized the systematic review of all of their jobs and checked their social insurance cards to determine the extent of any occupational exposure to pesticides during the pregnancy. He also recorded the information about their families, housing, nutrition, alcohol, smoking, and other relevant facts. In our first study, the mothers of 37 of 72 children had worked in greenhouses during the pregnancy, while for the second study, 35 of 84 had. So overall, almost half the children had been exposed to pesticides prenatally, just as we had anticipated. But none of the mothers had experienced any pesticide-related symptoms from their floriculture work. So we would now be able to check if the children had been harmed by the pesticides that had left the mothers unscathed.

When we analyzed the data, we found some remarkable results.[2] Most impressive was the difference among children in spatial performance. On this task, we asked the children to copy geometric figures of increasing complexity. If the mother worked in a greenhouse during pregnancy, the child averaged about two years behind the unexposed children in spatial development. We saw a similar tendency in finger tapping, a measure of motor speed that depends on muscular coordination. Other differences were not as pronounced, except for blood pressure, where children of the greenhouse women had higher blood pressure, both systolic and diastolic. This change would of course not be due to heart disease or calcified blood vessels at that age, but increased blood pressure sometimes occurs as a result of toxicity to the nervous system, perhaps due to deficient functioning of nerve cells in the brain stem. Incidentally, the nervous system uses acetylcholine to control the contraction of the blood vessels as part of the blood pressure regulation. Some pesticides affect the breakdown of acetylcholine by inhibiting the cholinesterase enzyme.

Our findings fit with the hypothesis of increased vulnerability to brain drainers during early development. But could the findings, although similar in the two studies of Tabacundo school kids, be due to some other factor? There was virtually no association with the children's current exposure, and none with the father's exposure. There are no tropical diseases of importance in the Andes, so DDT and related compounds have not been used much here. However, malnutrition is a widespread problem that results in delayed growth, so-called stunting. We did find that malnutrition was associated with poorer mental development. But malnutrition was less common than expected in the greenhouse women's kids. In fact, in comparison to other households, the households with a mother working in the greenhouses had a higher income, better housing, and better nutrition. However, with one problem on top of the other, the children with the poorest results were those who were malnourished and also had been exposed to pesticides prenatally.

The question is then, are these findings relevant to the pesticide exposures we encounter in the United States and elsewhere today? In a narrow sense, no, they are not. The exposures in greenhouses are invariably higher than levels we would be exposed to from pesticide used in residential buildings and from residues in food. Also, some of the pesticides commonly used in Ecuador have recently been banned in the United States and the European Union (although still produced for export). But these compounds were not banned due to neurotoxicity, and industrialized countries used them for many years without any such concerns. On the other hand, I cannot pinpoint any specific pesticide as the cause of the deficits, as the exposures involve a mixture of pesticides. But the fact that the kids were as much as two years behind in development at an age where brain growth is particularly rapid suggests to me that a pesticide-induced brain drain is indeed present and should be taken seriously.

Lasting Effect of Poisoning

Our findings of lasting pesticide damage to brain development fit in well with several older reports on children who had suffered pesticide poisoning. Nebraska pediatrician Carol Angle wanted to know the long-term fate of children who had been poisoned by a variety of substances during infancy. Of five children with a history of acute pesticide poisoning (four due to chlorinated insecticides and one to diazinon, an organophosphate), only one child had no gross difficulties when examined at follow-up.[3]

More recently, diazinon was involved in a poisoning incident in California, where the pesticide had mistakenly been used for indoor spraying purposes. The family members suffered acute symptoms, and persisting neurological symptoms included memory loss, decreased concentration, irritability, and personality changes. Upon clinical testing three years later, serious consequences, such as impaired balance, reaction time, color vision, and motor coordination, were still present in the three children.[4]

More systematic studies were carried out by Israeli neuropsychologist, Ora Kofman. She examined healthy school-aged children, who had been hospitalized in infancy for suspected poisonings. One group of children had been exposed to organophosphate pesticides, while one comparison group had been exposed to kerosene and other similar chemicals. She also included age- and sex-matched non-exposed children. Most children seemed to have overcome the acute one-time exposure incident, and all of them attended school. However, in regard to their specific cognitive abilities, Kofman found signs of impairment. The children with pesticide exposure showed a deficit in regard to inhibitory motor control. Both children with pesticide exposure and those with kerosene exposure had retrieval deficits on verbal learning, thus suggesting an adverse effect on memory function.[5]

The hypothesis of brain drain due to pesticides is further supported by clinical examinations in the United States after the discovery of widespread usage of neurotoxic pesticides for indoor treatment in both Ohio and Mississippi. Methyl parathion—another organophosphate that inhibits cholinesterase—had been illegally applied. Infants acutely exposed to this pesticide in that connection were later examined for neurobehavioral development. Compared to non-exposed children, they had persistent problems with short-term memory and attention.[6]

Other medical findings on pesticide damage to motor functions are similar to the results from Ecuador. However, the results reported from the various studies do not show the exact same deficits in pesticide-exposed children. These variations can arguably be explained by differences in the pesticides involved and in the timing of exposures that occurred at different stages of brain maturation. Also, severe, acute exposures may show a differing pattern of effects, as compared to more long-lasting exposures.

In concert, these studies strongly suggest that at least some pesticides can cause lasting adverse effects on brain development that emerge as detectable deficits at school age. Although the case reports or case series refer to illegal and excessive exposures, the neurobehavioral findings suggest that children can suffer permanent and more serious brain toxicity than adults who are similarly exposed.

American Children Affected

More solid evidence is being published and will likely continue to emerge from long-term prospective studies of American children followed from birth and onward to decipher the long-term consequences of prenatal exposures.

In a farmworker population from California, researchers first studied reflexes in neonates as a measure of nervous system integrity, as IQ testing is not a realistic option at this age. An increased frequency of abnormal or absent reflexes was associated with higher concentrations of organophosphate metabolites in the mother's urine during pregnancy. In a follow-up of the same children, urinary metabolite levels in the mother during pregnancy were inversely associated with mental development in the children at 24 months of age.[7]

Likewise, in New York City, researchers measured maternal exposure to a common pesticide, chlorpyrifos. Increased exposure, coupled with low maternal levels of paraoxonase activity (an enzyme which helps break down certain organophosphate pesticides, including chlorpyrifos), was associated with reduced head circumference in the infants. In addition, increased pesticide exposure was associated with abnormal reflexes in the babies.[8]

In another group of New York City children, prenatal chlorpyrifos exposure was measured. The children's cognitive and motor development was assessed at age 3 years and showed that highly exposed children lagged behind by 3.0 and 7.1 points on mental and psychomotor scores, respectively, when compared to children with low prenatal exposure to chlorpyrifos. The proportion of delayed children in the high-exposure group, compared with the low-exposure group, was 5 times greater for the psychomotor score and 2.4 times greater for the mental score.[9]

Follow-up studies are ongoing for all three groups of US children just mentioned. The updated reports at age 7 years suggest that the deficits are lasting and in some respects may become more prominent as the children's brain functions develop, particularly in regard to reduced short-term memory and attention and more general cognitive deficits.[10] While these studies focused on pesticides that are highly suspect in regard to neurotoxicity, one of the reports from New York City suggested that permethrine, an insecticide based on pyrethrum chemistry, may also be responsible for developmental delays.[11]

Perhaps the most dramatic follow-up test involved scanning the brains of 40 children, 20 of them with high-level prenatal exposure to chlorpyrifos, and 20 controls. Many differences were apparent, perhaps the most troubling being that high-exposure children had frontal and parietal cortical thinning, with an inverse dose-response relationship between exposure and cortical thickness.[12] This finding suggests that brain cells had not found their way to their proper locations in the cortex, or that cell multiplication or survival was negatively affected. Either way, the scanning results provide an anatomical basis for the cognitive deficits seen in the exposed children.

The urinary pesticide metabolite levels in all of these studies were similar to those that have been recorded from the general population in the United States and the European Union.[13] So these children had not been exposed to levels of pesticides that would be considered hazardous. Although some substances have since then been banned, it is unclear whether the use of modern substitute pesticides provides any better protection.

Pesticide Science

Pesticides—usually referred to as plant protection products by industry—are used in very substantial amounts. In the United States, the Department of Agriculture maintains the Agricultural Chemical Usage Reports (although temporarily eliminated in 2008, allegedly due to lack of funds).[14] These are the only publicly available data on pesticide use in the country, lately somewhat reduced in scope. Based on data collected by the Environmental Protection Agency,[15] the total US use of active ingredients in all pesticides in 2007 was 857 million pounds (about 22% of the world market), which corresponds to almost three pounds or well over one kilogram per US resident annually.

In the European Union, the annual application of synthetic pesticides to food crops alone exceeds 140,000 tons,[16] an amount that corresponds to 280 grams per EU citizen per year. Despite European policies to reduce pesticide use, EU statistics show that the annual pesticide consumption has not decreased for many years.

Pesticides form a very heterogenic group, and not all of the insecticides specifically target the nervous system of pests. For example, herbicides used against weeds have different properties, and they may be safe to brain cells—or they may be toxic. It is hard to predict. Along with two Danish colleagues, I therefore examined the published literature on pesticide effects on brain development.[17]

The group of insecticides called organophosphates inhibits the enzyme cholinesterase, which breaks down the neurotransmitter acetylcholine in both the peripheral and the central nervous system. Inhibition of the enzyme therefore causes accumulation of acetylcholine in the nerve cells that use it as a signal molecule, which then leads to over-stimulation that can be fatal. Acetylcholine is also an important guidance chemical during brain development, where it helps nerve cells locate their proper destination (see chapter 1).

The most extensively studied organophosphate is chlorpyrifos, the common pesticide that I just mentioned. In the laboratory models, prenatal or neonatal exposure can cause behavioral abnormalities in both mice and rats. These effects have been demonstrated at exposures at or below those commonly encountered by human beings and therefore they support the findings from the studies of New York City children exposed to this pesticide. When rat fetuses were exposed to chlorpyrifos, microscopy of the brains showed deficient cell numbers and disturbance in communication systems, but the damage was delayed and only became obvious in adolescence, continuing into adulthood.[18] In rodents, the time of greatest vulnerability to this pesticide extends into relatively late stages of brain development (in humans, these stages occur prenatally).[19] While most nerve cells have been formed at this time, the formation of supporting cells and the generation of synapses between nerve cells appear to be particularly vulnerable to pesticide exposure.

Remarkably, the deficits elicited by developmental exposure to chlorpyrifos are detectable even at exposures that do not cause any inhibition of the cholinesterase enzyme. And they are far, far below the 70% inhibition of the enzyme that leads to poisoning symptoms in adults. Although some local interference with the enzyme may occur within the brain, mechanisms other than enzyme inhibition may, at least in part, be responsible for the developmental neurotoxicity of this pesticide. So our current reliance on enzyme inhibition as a safeguard against organophosphate toxicity may be erroneous, perhaps even dangerous.

Another group of pesticides, the dithiocarbamates, may have similar effects on cholinesterase, although shorter lasting. Thus, several pesticides may affect acetylcholine in the brain, and this transmitter substance is also known to play a role in the development of dementia and other degenerative diseases in the elderly. Also, laboratory animal studies suggest that developmental exposure to a manganese-containing pesticide, maneb, may predispose to the development of Parkinson's disease later in life, and exposure to paraquat seems to escalate this effect.[20] It therefore seems that degenerative diseases of the nervous system, otherwise associated with aging, may be triggered by developmental exposure to pesticides that somehow sensitize the brain to later insults, which could be subsequent pesticide exposure or merely aging. This hypothesis has not yet been confirmed in humans, but some epidemiology studies suggest an increased risk of Parkinson's disease in farmers thought to have a greater exposure to pesticides.

In addition to "direct" neurotoxicity, several pesticides may indirectly cause neurotoxicity, for example, by interfering with the functions of the thyroid gland. The thyroid hormone is crucial for brain development, as is best illustrated by studies of iodine deficiency, where cretinism and mental retardation can occur if the deficiency occurs prenatally. About 60% of all herbicides, including 2,4-D and thiourea compounds, have been reported to hinder thyroid function, and similar effects are suspected for certain ethylenebisdithiocarbamates, organophosphates, and synthetic pyrethroids.[21] The reason that this type of toxicity is important is that impaired thyroid function may alter crucial hormone-mediated events during development, thereby leading to permanent changes in brain morphology and function.[22] Other types of endocrine disruption can conceivably also lead to neurobehavioral deficits, and this concern is now attracting much research attention.

Some discrepancies almost always exist among results of animal studies. That does not mean that the results are uncertain or irreproducible. Thus, the timing of exposure varies between studies. In some studies, animals are exposed prenatally, in other studies neonatally (during the first weeks of life), and in some studies both. The time of exposure can greatly influence the extent and type of neurotoxicity induced. Most animal studies have been performed in rodents, where brain development begins neonatally and continues during the first three to four weeks of postnatal life. Thus, neurotoxic effects may be induced in rodents by prenatal exposure alone, but it is possible that such studies will underestimate the neurotoxic effects that may occur from the full duration of prenatal exposure in humans, where the third trimester of pregnancy is a crucial period of brain development.[23]

Very few laboratory studies have addressed a more pressing problem, the fact that humans are exposed to several pesticides at a time, usually along with other neurotoxic compounds. Because it is possible that some of these may have synergistic or additive effects, exposure to even very low doses during development may cause neurotoxic damage.[24]

The evidence on pesticide brain drain can be summed up as follows. A substantial proportion of pesticides in current use is known or suspected of being neurotoxic. However, pesticides usually have not been examined for potential damage to the developing brain, as legal mandates only require tests for peripheral neurotoxicity in hens exposed to organophosphates. Because developmental neurotoxicity can occur at exposures much below those that cause toxicity to the adult brain, usage restrictions and legal limits for pesticide residues in food may not be sufficiently protective against developmental neurotoxicity. The exposures in three ongoing US studies that documented exposure-related effects are quite typical and not excessive, also compared to levels elsewhere. The brain drain associated with these exposures are therefore of public health relevance, also internationally. In commenting on recent research, the North American Pesticide Action Network in 2012 referred to today's children as "a generation in jeopardy".[25]

Pesticides Are Essential

In 2008, I was invited to meet with members of the European Parliament at a seminar in Brussels to discuss health concerns in regard to pesticides. The parliamentarians were proposing to update and simplify the EU legislation, and the intention was to provide better protection of its citizens—and of the next generation. I therefore emphasized the point that the brain in the information age is our key resource and that we therefore must protect the cognitive skills of the next generation the best way possible. The proof that pesticides adversely affect brain development is somewhat uncertain, in part because proper testing is not required by law, but how much evidence is needed before appropriate prevention is put into place?

Although some of the existing evidence relates to substances that have now been banned or restricted, this information should be utilized to properly protect developing brains in the hope that modern use of pesticides will not cause similar negative effects. Neurotoxic pesticides are likely to induce developmental neurotoxicity at low doses. However, for most pesticides, no data on developmental neurotoxicity are publicly available. Still, the absence of any reports on brain toxicity of any given pesticide is of course no guarantee that the pesticide is not neurotoxic. A prudent evaluation of the evidence would therefore suggest that if individual members of a chemical grouping of pesticides have been documented as neurotoxic, then all parts of that group should be considered neurotoxic as well until proven otherwise. Thus, substances with biochemical mechanisms similar to known brain-damaging pesticides—such as organophosphates, carbamates, pyrethroids, ethylenebisdi-thiocarbamates, or chlorophenoxy herbicides—should all be considered a risk to the developing brain until contrary evidence is available. The parliamentarians agreed and voted that the draft legislation should ban all pesticides that can cause neurotoxicity.

However, the Parliament version was not approved by the council of EU ministers. The member states were concerned that food prices might increase, and EU agriculture would suffer from outside competition. According to the European Crop Protection Association (the pesticide producers), "All crops need protection from disease and pests. If you remove the tools farmers use to protect their crops, yields will go down—and prices will go up."[26] It seemed that organic farming was not an option worth considering (see chapter 9). What the calculations failed to include was the externalized costs caused by pesticides on the environment and human health (more about this in chapter 8).

Although I have focused on pesticides in this chapter, the everyday risks include a much wider span of industrial chemicals. Pesticides constituted the largest group in my search for neurotoxic chemicals, but the second largest was solvents (see Appendix).

Solvents and Other Toxicants

Among the brain-toxic chemicals, I have so far identified more than 40 solvents (see Appendix), one of them being toluene. Because of its anesthetic effects, toluene has been used for sniffing—and that is what the clinical studies address. Case reports describe delayed development, especially of speech and motor function in children of mothers who had sniffed toluene during pregnancy. These effects have been observed not only after abuse of the solvent; mothers who reported occupational exposure to solvents during pregnancy had a greater risk of having a child with neurodevelopmental damage. Seven of eight available studies documented developmental deficits in regard to several sensory, motor and, cognitive tasks, and some also reported attention deficit hyperactivity behavior.[27] Solvents—not just toluene—are suspected of causing brain toxicity, as they are soluble in fats and are therefore likely to pass both the placenta and the blood-brain barrier to reach the fetal brain. Xylene and glycol ethers are among the prime suspects that are produced in very large quantities and commonly used. Another solvent, perchlorethylene (also called tetrachloroethylene) contaminated community drinking water on Cape Cod during the 1960s and 1970s, and follow-up of exposed subjects born during this period suggested an increased risk of bipolar disorder and adverse effects on visuospatial functioning, learning and memory, motor, attention and mood.[28]

Octane-boosting lead additives caused serious air pollution with lead, but the organic lead additives could also cause brain damage by themselves. Gasoline sniffing used to be rampant among children and adolescents on Indian reservations in the United States. As a schoolteacher told the story on a poisoned child to the sociologist Kai Erikson, "Alicia started sniffing gas when she was three years old. She's burnt now, and the brain damage is permanent. In class, she can't concentrate, and she's lost her retention ability. She has lost her sense of balance."[29] While the organic compounds in gasoline are likely also neurotoxic, studies show that the tetraethyllead as such was the main cause of the brain drain in the gasoline sniffers.

Many other industrial chemicals have caused signs of neurological damage. In some cases, poisoning causes narcosis; in others more specific symptoms occur, like tremor or sensory disturbance. Such signs and symptoms indicate that the chemical can pass the blood-brain barrier and exert toxicity to brain cells. Among inorganic substances that are likely brain drainers, manganese[30] is of much concern, as its exposures are so widespread, often from contaminated drinking water. The same applies to fluoride, and I shall return to the inconvenient results on this otherwise useful chemical in chapter 9.

Aniline, carbon monoxide, ethylene, hydrazine, and phenol are also on the list of suspected brain drainers (see Appendix). None of them are exotic chemicals or substances that have long been banned. Almost half of the substances listed in the Appendix are high-volume production chemicals. So they are among the most commonly produced and used in industry, and therefore are understandably among the frequent causes of poisonings. Close to 100 are on the list of chemicals monitored by the Toxic Release Inventory. Twenty-one are on the top-50 list of compounds from chemical waste listed by the Agency for Toxic Substances and Disease Registry. So these potential brain drainers are widely encountered at work and from environmental exposures.

More chemicals of concern can be identified from other sources. For example, the National Institute of Occupational Safety and Health (NIOSH) provides information on exposure limits for workplaces and warns against specific adverse effects if exposure limits are exceeded. A total of 278 substances with an exposure limit are considered to represent a risk of nervous system damage. Most of the chemicals in the Appendix are also listed by NIOSH, which seemed to require less extensive documentation than we did for our *Lancet* article. So substances that are not on my list may also constitute a hazard to human brains.

Drugs and the Chemical Universe

The Appendix list does not include drugs, as these substances are subject to much more rigorous testing. The safety of prescription drugs has been a concern ever since the thalidomide malformations were discovered. Because of intensive pre-market testing and vigilance in regard to usage during pregnancy, only a few drugs seem to have slipped through to cause adverse effects on brain development. About two out of three women take at least one prescription drug during pregnancy, and many women take several. Chronic conditions cannot go untreated for nine months without posing risk to both mother and fetus. Fortunately, drugs that are prescribed must be registered, and adverse effects are required by law to be reported. However, there is no general mechanism for collecting information on possible drug-related damage to the fetus and the fetal brain. After-the-fact studies have been conducted when new animal studies suggested that a particular drug might cause adverse effects on fetal development.

Use of anticonvulsants during pregnancy, especially valproate, seems to cause developmental delays and severe deficits in language acquisition in the child. In addition, several drugs used for psychiatric disease, such as selective serotonin reuptake inhibitors and tricyclic antidepressants, are suspected of having similar effects. Anesthetic agents, due to their intended effects on the brain, are also primary suspects as brain drainers, for example, in regard to pediatric surgery.[31] Psychologists have recently raised concerns about excessive obstetric use of oxytocin to induce labor, as any resulting hypoxia in the fetal brain may cause damage and is suspected of leading to development of attention deficit hyperactivity disorder (ADHD).[32]

Drugs of abuse, such as cocaine, when used by women during pregnancy, are important brain drainers.[33] Ethanol is perhaps the best documented (see chapter 2), but other stimulants, such as tobacco smoke, constitute an additional hazard.[34] Tobacco of course contains nicotine, which has been used as a pesticide, and a multitude of tar chemicals. Even passive tobacco smoke inhalation during childhood has been linked with ADHD and externalizing psychopathology. Carbon monoxide, another major component of general air pollution, car exhausts, and smoke from wood or tobacco, can cause brain lesions in adults and has also been linked to delayed brain development in children.[35]

My list of brain-draining industrial chemicals in the Appendix excludes the drugs as well as snake venoms and other biological toxins. The list is based on published reports in the medical literature and mainly reflects brain toxicity in adults. Thus, more than 200 different chemicals have, one way or another, caused neurological symptoms. If these compounds can enter the brain and cause damage to brain cells in adults, they can certainly also access the brain during development, where damage will likely be more serious.[36]

Although we know a couple of hundred chemicals that are toxic to the brain, we found convincing evidence only for a handful of chemicals that they can also damage the human brain during development: lead, mercury, PCBs, arsenic, and toluene—compounds that we already know very well. The list may be extended by adding a few more substances, such as manganese, fluoride, and some pesticides. We already recognize that most of the chemicals pass the placenta, so that a pregnant woman may share her chemical exposures with her fetus. We also know that the developing brain is highly vulnerable to chemical injury. Then why did we find so few definite brain drainers?

The small number is certainly not due to any special resistance to toxicity within the developing brain—quite the opposite. The problem is lack of opportunities to obtain documentation. Solid evidence would have to include detailed information on exposures happening in early life in relation to the brain development assessed later on during childhood. Such studies are available on only a handful of chemicals—in fact, on the very substances that are known to be toxic to human brain development. The rest of the substances have not been studied. That means that none of the chemicals on the list can be considered safe to developing brains.

But the neurotoxic universe is much greater than the 213 compounds in the Appendix. Perhaps a thousand more brain drainers can be identified from animal experiments conducted so far. They have not caused neurological symptoms in people, at least not yet, or details have not been published. However, no systematic testing has been carried out. Future testing could add many more. Based on current experience, perhaps one chemical out of five will test positive for neurotoxicity. That would mean that the list of potential brain drainers could expand to many thousands. Although the magnitude of the problem will depend on the level of exposure for each compound, we will clearly underestimate the problem by only considering the few examples that we know best. In addition, so far we have looked only at individual substances and not considered mixtures, where the effects of one brain drainer may add to the effects of another.

Air pollution is certainly a mixed exposure and it has also been linked to neurodevelopmental deficits in several reports.[37] A study in Mexico City linked severe air pollution to changes on magnetic resonance imaging of the brain, with lesions and growth abnormalities mainly in the prefrontal cortex. In parallel, these investigators also examined dogs growing up in Mexico City and replicated the finding of lesions of the frontal cortex and related pathologies. Further studies have linked neurodevelopmental delays to exposures to tar chemicals measured on portable particle samplers. The evidence is therefore strengthening that air pollution may harm brain development. However, like tobacco smoke, virtually thousands of chemicals occur in air pollution, and it is not clear if any specific components represent the main culprits. In addition to carbon monoxide, I also suspect that nitrogen oxides may play a role, as even indoor air pollution may represent a brain drain risk. Thus, the use of gas stoves for cooking, known to be an important source of nitrogen oxides indoors, seems to be associated with delays in brain development.[38]

As discussed in chapter 1, multiple processes during brain development are highly susceptible to toxic interference. The perspective for brain drain is therefore wide open. In addition to direct effects on enzymes, transmitter substances, or gene expression, some environmental chemicals (in addition to the pesticides) may negatively affect brain development by interacting with hormones, such as the thyroid hormone, thereby disrupting essential endocrine control functions.[39] Such brain-damaging mechanisms have been ascribed to phthalates from plastics and personal care products.[40] Given these potentials, the universe of chemical brain drainers is therefore much larger than our existing documentation would seem to indicate.

In contrast to the pharmaceuticals, other industrial chemicals are not tested for their effects on brain development before they are marketed; their environmental exposures are generally not monitored, and any adverse effects do not need to be reported. The situation is only slightly better for pesticides. According to current legislation, a neurotoxicity test in hens is required only for organophosphates and some carbamates. However, the sole purpose is only to assess the possible risk of delayed peripheral neurotoxicity following acute exposure. Thus, developmental neurotoxicity is not routinely considered when pesticide safety is determined, nor for any other industrial chemicals.

I should also note that physical factors, as well, may cause risks to brain development. Exposure to ionizing radiation prenatally is known to cause cognitive deficits, especially if the exposure happens during weeks 8 to 25 of gestation.[41] Other types of radiation—for example, from mobile telephony—is not as stringently regulated but has recently been reported to pose a risk to developing brains due to the electromagnetic fields from cell phones held close to the skull.

The new EU pesticides legislation approved in 2009 was a compromise between the elected Parliament and the Council of Ministers from the member states. Certain pesticides were banned, and the risk of neurotoxicity (when available) must be included in future evaluations as to whether a pesticide should be approved. Neurotoxic substances may be approved for up to seven years and must be considered candidates for substitution. These rules are tighter than anywhere else in the world. We can only hope that the EU regulations will affect pesticide use elsewhere, to the benefit of future generations of children. But we should also consider critically our need for pesticides. Like the Swiss mom said in her e-mail, maybe "the whole idea of a beautiful lawn should be abandoned." As a mother, she worried about the costs without having done any formal calculations. We now need to take a closer look at the dollar costs of brain drain.

CHAPTER 8

Mindless Costs

BRAINS ARE INDISPENSABLE TO EACH
INDIVIDUAL AND TO SOCIETY

We normally do not think of brains in terms of their dollar value. The value of a brain is of course infinite, but just how much is it worth? Economists argue that cost estimates are necessary in order to prioritize the allocation of public spending.[1] The point is that it can be expensive to prevent chemical brain drain, so we need to argue that it is worthwhile. Although instinctly repelled by this attitude, I realized that there may be some truth to it when I saw an example from a surprising angle. It came from a market that has recently emerged—human egg donation. Student newspapers at colleges and universities have begun to print advertisements that offer up to $35,000 to egg donors with a Scholastic Assessment Test (SAT) score above 1400 (out of a 1600 maximum).[2] Less is offered at schools where admitted students have lower average SAT scores. A statistical analysis suggests that an increase of 100 SAT points on average fetches about $2,000 and twice that much if the ad is placed on behalf of a specific couple. Money talks: Brainy genes are valuable.

We use "economic" comparisons or cost-benefit analysis every day, though perhaps indirectly and often unconsciously. This happens when we buy the slightly more expensive organic vegetables or when we open the windows wide if we use a paint stripper in the house in the winter. As a Canadian mother expressed to me in an e-mail, talking about indoor fumes, even a small disturbance to her son's nervous system would "greatly outweigh the benefit of beautifying the house with risky chemical products." Wouldn't all parents agree with this view? But how do we argue against the view that the toxic chemicals generate benefits to society and cannot be easily controlled or substituted? These questions are complex. The difficult challenge is to put a dollar value on brain functions.

Although one's own brain, like life itself, has an infinite value, economists express the marginal changes in quality of life or probability of death in terms of monetary equivalents. These calculations on dollar costs due to brain drain are thought to be meaningful for the sake of comparison between different risks and options for prevention. The estimated economic benefits (or avoided costs) are increasingly used to justify, or repeal, public health policies. That is what they do all the time at the White House's Office of Information and Regulatory Affairs to make sure that new regulations are cost efficient. That is what they do in the European Commission and in many other government offices. Economists claim that their tools are helpful to measure the importance of a risk. Large amounts of money draw attention. So we need to express in terms of dollars the importance of optimally functioning brains.

I shall focus on lead, mercury, and a few other specific substances, well-established brain drainers about which we have the most detailed information. This is not to say that these few substances are the only ones we need to control. On the contrary, lead and mercury are just the tip of the iceberg. They appear to be the most serious toxicants, but we do not know.

In my literature survey with Phil Landrigan, I had found more than 200 industrial chemicals that can cause brain toxicity in adults (see the updated list in the Appendix, now numbering 213 known brain drainers). As all of these substances are capable of entering the brain and damaging brain cells, they should be regarded as highly likely brain drainers.[3] Perhaps thousands more can also cause brain drain (see chapter 7). But the information we have on the best-known brain drainers will at least serve as an illustration of how we might calculate the costs and what the magnitude might be.

Brain Values and Disease Costs

To quantify the harm that a disease or health risk poses to people, economists generally use the cost-of-illness approach, which measures the value of resources forgone, including costs of medical treatment, lost earnings, and other output lost. Some costs may be difficult or impossible to assess, such as ethical violations or intangible expenses due to effects on brain functions and livelihoods of future generations (some of which I will address in chapter 10). For now, let us concentrate on the dollar amounts that economists have calculated in regard to the most obvious brain drainers. This way, we will get an idea of the sheer order of magnitude of brain-drain expenses.

The simplest way to analyze the costs from chemical brain drain is to identify one or more specific diseases, in which the chemical exposure contributes to the development of the disease. Estimates of the total cost already exist for many relevant diagnoses, thus all that is needed is an estimate of the fraction that is due to each brain drainer. In Europe, the total annual cost of brain disease has been estimated at €386 billion ($480 billion in the 2012 exchange rate), and brain diseases are responsible for 35% of Europe's total disease burden. Much of that is due to degenerative diseases and the increased size of the aging population. Faced with these enormous costs, a group of neurology experts concluded: "A clear message emerges: unless immediate action is taken globally, the neurological burden is expected to become an even more serious and unmanageable threat to public health."[4] Because the expenses are staggering, even a small fraction of these costs would be a very large amount. But how can we estimate this portion?

Some diseases are primarily determined by genetic factors; other diseases are due to a variety of environmental factors to a smaller or greater extent. As defined by the Institute of Medicine, the "fractional contribution" expresses the extent to which one or more environmental exposures, on average, contribute to the development of a specific illness.[5] It could also be defined as "the percentage of a particular disease category that would be eliminated if environmental risk factors were reduced to their lowest feasible levels."[6] In technical terms, the environmental attributable fraction is the product of the frequency of an environmental risk factor and the relative disease risk associated with the risk factor. If the exposure is rare, the fraction of cases associated with the exposure is low. In contrast, common exposures can contribute significantly to the overall disease risk, especially if the chemical somehow triggers disease development by more than a negligible extent.

Using this approach, calculations of the environmental burden of disease have been carried out by the World Health Organization (WHO).[7] Unfortunately, not enough is known about the exact contribution of environmental chemicals to disease development; certainly we know very little about children's neurological disease and dysfunctions and almost nothing about the contribution to degenerative diseases in the elderly. Lack of information will invariably lead to underestimating the environmental contribution.

Some data are available on mental retardation, where declines in prevalence in the United States have been linked to decreasing lead exposures. Economist Rick Nevin documented that the 1936–1990 preschool blood-lead trends explained 65% of the 1948–2001 variation in mental retardation prevalence. He also found that reductions in preschool blood levels correlated with decreases in mental retardation 12 years later.[8] If true, a large proportion of mental retardation cases would seem to be caused by lead poisoning. The lifetime health care costs for each case of mental retardation have been calculated to be about $1,250,000,[9] so the total expense caused by lead exposure could be substantial.

An increasing number of children and adolescents suffer from learning and behavioral problems in general, and a large proportion of these conditions could be due to exposure to environmental chemicals. A National Research Council committee suggested that 3% of neurobehavioral disorders in American children are caused directly by toxic environmental exposures, while another 25% are caused by interactions between environmental factors and genetic susceptibility of the child.[10] Using an overall fractional contribution of 10%, the monetary costs of chemically induced neurobehavioral disorders in the United States were estimated by a group led by Professor Landrigan to be $9.2 billion annually (1997 costs).[11] As these calculations are based on known diagnoses and assumed contributions by brain drainers, the costs calculated are uncertain. They likely represent a minimum as they are based only on well-documented brain drainers. We need some better estimates.

Lost Income

Expenses due to chemical brain drain may be more reliably estimated in terms of cost of specific illness or dysfunction. This approach assesses the direct costs for treatment and management of chemical exposures and adverse effects, including costs for doctors' visits, hospitalization, medication, and special equipment needed for sick children. Depending on the availability of public and private health insurance and its coverage, these costs may be carried either by the individual or by the taxpayers. Indirect costs include income lost by parents who have to take off time from work to look after their children, and other similar costs. If the disease or dysfunction is long-lasting, the child's own productivity losses must be assessed, the key measure being lost lifetime earnings.

On one of my visits to Minamata, the fishing town that was ravaged by mercury poisoning, Shinobu Sakamoto gave me a hand-woven place mat as a gift. Despite being born with congenital poisoning, she had managed to learn to weave, but her mother admitted that it had taken her several days to make the place mat. While the feat was impressive, it is impossible to judge Shinobu's talents and what she might have achieved had industrial pollution not interfered with her brain development. Aside from economic success, the less tangible costs, such as pain and suffering and loss of quality of life, must be counted as well.

Loss of income alone leads to very large brain-drain costs that can be calculated from known losses associated with decreases in IQ points.[12] IQ impacts on incomes have been studied by political scientists, notably Charles Murray, co-author of *The Bell Curve*. He obtained IQ scores from the Armed Forces Qualification Test and selected sibling pairs, of which one sibling had an IQ in the normal range (between 90 and 109). He also required that the siblings come from homes with an income in the upper 75% range, and that they lived with both parents until they were at least 7 years of age. When their annual incomes as adults were compared, the siblings with an IQ of 120 and above earned $18,000 (or 34%) more than their normal-IQ siblings. The effects were more pronounced in siblings with a lower IQ. Those in the 80–89 range, earned $13,300 (or 25%) less, and those with an IQ below 80 earned $29,100 (55%) less each year compared to their siblings.[13] In general, these estimates suggest that a difference of one IQ point corresponds to a 1% to 2% difference in lifetime earnings. Economist Elise Gould generated overall estimates for each IQ point lost in terms of loss of lifetime earnings, with 2008 estimates of $18,832 (or €17,363, adjusted for relative purchasing power).[14] These estimates are adjusted for discounting (usually 3% per year, as future income is not worth as much as money right now). The calculated amounts should not be misinterpreted as being exact, as each of them is associated with much uncertainty and many caveats. But they represent an order of magnitude.

Are these costs exaggerated? Probably not. I have yet to meet someone who would be willing to part with one or more IQ points for some cash amount like that. We simply value our brain functions too much. We can compare the calculated price for one IQ point with the tuition costs at major universities. Five years of studies might win me a master's degree or even a doctorate, but I would have to sell 10 IQ points or more to pay for it. But that investment would of course be in vain if the IQ loss incurred prevented me from passing my finals and from receiving the degree.

Still, on a national scale, the costs become truly impressive. For all children born within one calendar year, economists have computed the total number of IQ points that these children have lost due to some type of brain drain. That number is then multiplied by the value of each IQ point. For the United States alone, Gould calculated that lead exposure in children below 6 years of age caused a total loss of 9.3–13.1 million IQ points. Give or take, approximately 10 million. Multiplying by the value of each IQ point, the net lifetime earnings lost is about $180 billion for children up to six years. If shared between the annual birth cohorts (total of six in this case), the average cost for the children born during a single year will be $30 billion. These costs will continue as new children are born, until the exposure has been eliminated.

Less information exists on the costs due to other neurotoxic exposures. American pediatrician Leonardo Trasande, in collaboration with Landrigan, estimated mercury-related losses of 0.2 to 5.1 IQ points in several hundred thousand children born every year in the United States.[15] Decreased lifetime economic productivity resulted in an annual cost of $8.7 billion. The downward shift in IQ would also be associated with approximately 1,500 excess cases of mental retardation (with IQ below 70) annually, thereby accounting for about 3% of the annual number of cases, at an expense of about $2 billion. More sophisticated modeling has resulted in more reliable estimates,[16] but the outcome rests in part on assumptions of the degree of IQ losses at increased exposures and the possible presence of a threshold.

French economist Celine Pichery used the most recent data on mercury toxicity and both linear and logarithmic relationships between methylmercury exposure and IQ losses. From analyses of hair-mercury concentrations in French women, and assuming a threshold corresponding to half of the reference dose defined by the US Environmental Protection Agency, she calculated annual benefits of €0.7–2.25 billion from removing excess mercury exposure in France.[17] Considering that the US population is approximately five times greater than the French, and that exposures differ somewhat between the countries, the two sets of calculations are in remarkable accordance, although based on different assumptions. While not as costly as the effects of lead exposure, these amounts are substantial.

My Harvard colleague, David Bellinger, calculated IQ losses from pesticide exposures in the United States.[18] He used the most recent data on dose-related IQ losses in children whose mothers had been exposed to organophosphate pesticides during pregnancy (see chapter 7). He then compared them with the exposure levels reported by the Centers for Disease Control and Prevention (CDC) from analyses of urine samples from women across the country. For children up to 6 years of age, Bellinger calculated a total of 16.9 million IQ points lost due to the mother's pesticide exposure during pregnancy, or about 2.8 million for each annual birth cohort. In terms of lost lifetime earnings ($18,832 per IQ point lost), pesticide exposure would therefore represent an annual loss of over $50 billion—even more than Elise Gould's calculated losses due to lead exposure.

Professor Bellinger also calculated comparable IQ losses associated with a variety of other causes, with preterm birth being the medical condition having the greatest impact (5.7 million IQ points lost annually). Neurodevelopmental disorders, including autism, attention deficit hyperactivity disorder (ADHD), and pediatric bipolar disorder, cause a total loss of about 5 million IQ points, and poverty about 8.4 million (with brain drainers possibly contributing to the causation). Bellinger's total estimate for lead, pesticides, and mercury is 6.7 million lost IQ points per year. If we multiply with the estimated dollar value of one IQ point, the total cost amounts to $120 billion annually, which corresponds to about 3% of the annual budget of the US federal government. Thus, although Bellinger's estimate for pesticides may be too high, and the calculation for mercury too low, the total losses due to these known brain drainers are clearly very, very substantial.

IQ and Cognitive Functions

Thus far the discussion has relied heavily upon IQs, but "intelligence" alone does not necessarily capture all the damage that can result from neurotoxic chemical exposure during brain development. IQ tests are meant to reflect the so-called g factor—the general intelligence—to which all cognitive skills are related. This notion can be traced back to Sir Francis Galton, who in the 19th century initiated the formal study of individual differences in human performance. A better-known proponent is American professor Arthur Jensen, who emphasized that performances on virtually all tasks requiring mental ability are positively correlated, though some scattering occurs. The higher the g factor, the better the school performance, level of education, income, and even physical health and longevity.[19] That may well be true for people on average, and the g alone cannot reflect the diversity in different types of mental abilities or chemical brain drains affecting specific functions.

For reasons that we do not yet understand, some brain-toxic chemicals do not target overall intelligence but preferentially affect specific parts or functions of the brain. Methylmercury may particularly cause memory deficits, lead may primarily decrease attention span, and pesticides may cause damage specifically to spatial perception, although such deficits also depend on the time of exposure. So we should not expect a uniform effect on general intelligence. Thus, when researchers convert specific deficits into losses of IQ points, they likely underestimate the damage to the most vulnerable functions, whether it be attention span or memory, each of them crucial for our overall functioning.

Even what we refer to as "memory" is not just a single well-defined function with a particular location in the brain. Short-term memory (up to a few minutes), also called working memory, is available for ongoing or immediate processing. Long-term memory, on the other hand, consists of "declarative" memory, which holds our language, events, and concepts, while "procedural" memory is not dependent on words, but reflects our remarkably resistant storage for motor skills, such as buttoning a shirt. The bottom line is that we have not resolved the challenge of assigning a particular value to specific functions. Even if we can estimate the value of an IQ point, the challenge is to express the value of a short reaction time, an excellent working memory, and other specific brain functions.

An additional concern is that performance on IQ tests or other aptitude scores is affected by personality traits such as perseverance, or "grit." How well a child performs in school is determined not only by IQ tests but also by self-confidence and self-control. For example, self-discipline was much more important in eighth-grade students than IQ in regard to final grades, high-school selection, school attendance, and hours spent doing homework.[20] Could brain drainers somehow affect our self-determination? It seems possible, but we do not know.

Nonetheless, the decisive advantage of using IQ scores for estimating costs is that data are available to link IQ scores to an average lifetime income. That could not be done on the basis of memory or attention scores alone. So the use of IQ points as an indication of one's future production potential is far from ideal and may underestimate the effects.

Plasticity and Repair

While a toxic chemical may hamper brain development, an early intervention can help it recover. Brain-drain effects are therefore not necessarily permanent. A stimulating environment crucial for a child's development includes access to responsive caregivers and normal language exposure. That some recovery is possible, even in institutionalized children seriously deprived of stimulation and affection, was demonstrated by the Bucharest Early Intervention Study.[21] Children who had been abandoned and placed in the institution at or shortly after birth were put either in foster care or in continued institutional care. The children were tested at the beginning of the study and 54 months later. The cognitive outcome of children who remained in the institution was remarkably lower than children who had never been institutionalized and those taken out of institutional care and moved to foster care. For those in foster care, the younger the children were when placed there, the greater was their improvement. The greatest benefit occurred in children younger than 2 years when removed from the institution.

The positive effects of general educational programs also demonstrate the malleability of the brain. For example, the Head Start program for disadvantaged children is known to be highly beneficial in terms of school performance.[22] Economist and Nobel laureate James Heckman calculated the payback of one such program in terms of the funds invested and the gains from avoidance of special education, repeated grades, and other interventions. He found that the return was eight to one, which could be translated to an annual interest of 17% on the initial investment.[23] Heckman did not include the benefits derived from better quality of life and other less tangible benefits.

These studies and the known plasticity of the brain would suggest that deficits originating from chemical brain drain could at least partially be compensated by social and educational programs. For example, Danish pediatrician Troels Lyngbye found that the need for special education increased in children with higher lead exposures during early childhood.[24] One estimate suggested that 20% of children with a blood-lead concentration above 250 μg/L would need special education.[25] So when we calculate the societal costs due to neurotoxic exposures, we must figure in the costs of special education for affected children. In America, special education services for students with disabilities cost $77.3 billion, or an average of $12,474 per student in 1999–2000, which is almost twice the cost per regular education student, and it adds up to almost 22% of the 1999–2000 total spending on all elementary and secondary educational services.[26] More recent cost estimates from France (2008) are somewhat higher at €39,000 to €48,000 ($42,000 to $52,000, with adjustment for relative purchasing power) per year for each student needing special education.[27] While these expenses are high and special education may be successful, it will not necessarily cancel out the adverse effects of chemical brain drain. Plasticity of the brain also requires that brain cells are functional and available at the right location, which may not be the case in brains exposed during early development to toxic chemicals.

When affected by developmental neurotoxicity, some functions of damaged areas may be taken over by other regions of the brain, but the final outcome is unlikely to provide full compensation for the damage. In collaboration with colleagues in Boston, my Faroese colleague, Pál Weihe, and I attempted to visualize brain-drain abnormalities by using advanced brain scans. We invited 12 Faroese adolescents who had widely different levels of prenatal exposure to methylmercury and polychlorinated biphenyls (PCBs). At McLean Hospital in Boston, we examined the patterns of activity in different brain regions using a magnetic resonance scanner. When the control subjects with low levels of exposure were asked to tap the fingers on their left hand, the right-hand motor cortex lighted up in all of them, as it should do, since the nerves cross to the opposite side in the spinal cord. But those with prenatal brain-drain exposure activated the motor cortex of both sides of the brain, which is highly abnormal. Likewise, when given a light stimulus, all of the subjects activated a small part of their visual cortex in the back of the brain. But the adolescents with brain-drain exposure used an abnormally large area that is normally involved in processing of visual stimulation. To utilize a large number of additional brain cells would seem an inefficient way to analyze a simple light signal. Our results suggest that in the attempt to compensate for the neural deficits, the brain involves other brain areas, some of them far away, although this complicated compensation results in a lower functional quality.[28] Thus, when the compensation mechanisms recruit other brain areas to take over for parts that are damaged, they do not function as well.

Behavioral Effects

So far, we have considered increased risks of neurological disease, IQ deficits, and needs for special education, but what about behavior? Can it, too, be affected by environmental chemicals that damage brain development? The answer is likely yes, as numerous studies have documented that exposure to, for example, lead, mercury, and organochlorine pesticides have been linked to poorer scores on behavioral scales, including those used to identify children with autism-spectrum disorders and ADHD.

This question also relates to an issue of great socioeconomic importance. Some toxicants, like lead and perhaps manganese, may cause an increase in aggressive behavior and loss of control over impulsive behavior. So is it possible that pollution could be part of the reason that some children grow up to become criminals? Elevated concentrations of toxic metals have been found in prisoners, who have committed violent crimes, as compared to nonviolent prisoners. Combined with poverty, social stresses, access to illegal drugs, and other social factors, conceivably neurotoxicity could produce individuals who commit violent crimes.[29]

Psychiatry professor Herbert Needleman first reported a link between delinquent behavior and lead in 1996, and his findings were later supported by larger population data.[30] Herb followed 301 boys in the Pittsburgh public school system over a period of several years. Needleman gathered information on their behaviors from the boys' teachers, their parents, and the boys themselves. He and his colleagues determined past exposures to lead by measuring the concentration accumulated in bone. Boys with the highest lead concentrations were more likely to engage in antisocial activities like bullying, vandalism, and shoplifting. These associations held true, even after adjustment for differences due to race, education, and neighborhood crime rates. Further, their behavior got worse as they grew older, a tendency that was not seen in the boys with low lead concentrations.

These results inspired economist Rick Nevin to examine the correlation between long-term trends in crime levels and changes in environmental concentrations of lead. Beginning in the early 1990s, violent crime, which had risen for decades, showed a sudden decline, according to the Federal Bureau of Investigation's Uniform Crime Reports. By the end of 2004, all violent crimes (murder, robbery, rape, and aggravated assault) had dropped by 32% since 1995, in parallel with the decreased lead exposure. Juvenile violent-crime rates in the United States also declined, and violent crimes in schools fell to about half of what they were in 1992. According to the US Justice Department's 2004 National Crime Victimization Survey, the rate of violent crime was at its lowest point since the survey began in 1973. Although many explanations may be offered, these statistics show a surprising concordance with decreases in childhood lead exposures about two decades before.

A more detailed multiyear study was carried out by law school professor Deborah Denno. She followed a group of 487 young black males from the time their mothers gave birth between 1959 and 1962 at the University of Pennsylvania Hospital in Philadelphia up until the subjects reached age 25. All told, she considered more than 3,000 variables over the 25 years to test differing theories on crime. Denno published her findings in her 1990 book, *Biology and Violence*[31] and included the blood-lead concentrations as a risk factor. Childhood lead poisoning was the single greatest predictor of school disciplinary problems, which in turn were the major predictor for juvenile crime. Lead poisoning was also the fourth-leading predictor of adult crime. (The leading predictor for adult crime was the number and seriousness of juvenile offenses.)

A prospective study of 250 Cincinnati youths with detailed assessment of blood-lead concentrations prenatally and during childhood again showed that increased lead exposure was associated with a greater risk of arrest, specifically arrest for offenses involving violence. In New Zealand, similar findings suggested that lead-associated educational underachievement also increased the risk of criminal behavior.[32] In Deborah Denno's words, lead is, directly or indirectly, the leading predisposing factor for antisocial behavior: "I am very confident in my study, confident that lead predisposes people to act in an impulsive, anti-social way."[33]

If the expenses to society due to delinquency were to be added to the total costs associated with exposure to lead, and perhaps also other environmental chemicals, the amount would definitely increase. From American crime data, lead exposure has been estimated to result in direct annual costs of $1.8 billion and an additional $11.6 billion in indirect costs for psychological and physical damage necessitating medical treatment and for preventive measures.[34] Add these costs to those due to IQ losses, and an economic disaster is taking shape.

The Global Perspective

The costs of IQ deficits are of course even larger on an international scale.[35] However, there is no global database on the distribution of lead exposures or, for that matter, exposures to other brain drainers. We can, however, calculate approximate benefits obtained from controlling brain-draining chemicals by extrapolating US costs to the global level. Economists use the ratio of the world gross domestic product (GDP) to the US GDP, which results in a factor of 4.27. If applied to the increased income derived from the decrease in blood-lead concentrations in the United States since the late 1970s, the estimate of the global benefit from prevention of lead exposure is $2.45 trillion per year. As economists emphasize, many caveats must be recognized, but the magnitude of the estimate is truly mind-boggling.

In their controversial book, *IQ and the Wealth of Nations*, Richard Lynn and Tatu Vanhanen linked the average national IQ and the national income (per capita GDP) and suggested that it is causal in both directions.[36] Thus, poverty can cause low IQ, but the opposite is also true. Although their database is probably inaccurate in several respects, the observed correlation is difficult to explain away. It also fits with the known connection between IQ levels and lifetime incomes.

The same database was recently used to elucidate the possible role of infectious disease.[37] An infection drains away energy, and because the brain is particularly dependent on constant energy supplies (see chapter 1), it is difficult for a child to build a brain and fight off infectious diseases at the same time. The authors found that average IQ in a country was highly related to parasite stress in that country, and that this was even true when adjusting for other factors, such as temperature, per capita GDP, and levels of education. When conducting such studies, one must take into account the so-called Flynn effect, named after New Zealand political scientist James Flynn, who highlighted that IQ results have increased with time.[38] But perhaps part of the Flynn effect could be caused by decreases in the intensity of infectious diseases as nations develop.

A similar link to average IQ in different countries could no doubt be observed if we could generate, for each country, a measure of neurotoxicant exposure from pesticides, metals, solvents, and other substances. These exposures are bound to be much greater in developing countries that have continued to use leaded gasoline until recently, where pollution from hazardous industries flows freely, and where neurotoxic pesticides banned in the North are still widely used. Had the data been available, I would have produced country-based brain-drain scores for comparison with national income data. Unfortunately, this is not possible. However, if my suspicion is correct, the rapid industrialization in developing countries—often involving seriously polluting industries with chemical emissions that are largely unregulated—will have unfavorable consequences in terms of developmental neurotoxicity and subsequent losses in productivity.

The Role of Inheritance

IQ scores are affected by inheritance, and some researchers believe that inheritance primarily determines intelligence. They claim that inherited qualities (nature) play a major role in brain development, much more than does the environment (nurture). When identical twins are more similar than fraternal twins, then that must be due to nature, the argument goes. For IQ, heritability is often said to be around 0.5, that is, that the genes are responsible for about 50%, with most studies ranging between 40% and 80%. In *The Bell Curve*, Herrnstein and Murray claim that inherited traits, rather than advantages associated with wealth or education, explain much of the social class structure and racial divide in the United States.[39] But can genetic background really explain the association of poverty with poorer scores on IQ tests and poorer academic achievement?

An important test of the impact of race was carried out in Germany, where both black and white servicemen fathered children with German women. When examined at young school age, boys did better than the girls, but the overall average IQ for those with a white father was 97, compared to 96.5 for those with a black father.[40] Despite the fact that mixed-race children may have suffered more prejudice, the difference in IQ is negligible.

A strict hereditarian view is unfortunate because it predicts that you cannot do much about your own IQ or your children's, since the outcome is primarily a matter of the genes passed on from the parents. Fortunately, as argued by psychology professor Richard Nisbett and others, education and environment shape our cognitive skills to a great extent. While about 50% of the variation in IQ seems to be strictly heritable, that percentage is an average, although it may not be representative for children of all social backgrounds.[41] An early study compared black and interracial children adopted by middle-class black or white parents. Those raised in white families had average IQs 13 points above those raised by black adoptive parents.[42] The families were probably not entirely comparable, and the results could likely be ascribed to social differences, with some black families providing less stimulation than white homes. More recent studies support the conclusion that a stimulating home environment is crucial for brain development.

Overall, children in the poorest groups of society reveal much lower IQ heritability than children from upper socioeconomic strata. In families at the very bottom of the socioeconomic scale, shared family environment accounted for as much as 60 percent of IQ differences in the statistical analyses, while the contribution by genes was close to zero. Thus, in poor families, the environments were much more varied, and children were often held back in their development by lack of positive stimulation, poor education, and other negative factors that hamper or slow down brain development.[43]

Low birth weight, alcohol use, lack of breast-feeding, infections, other health problems, and insufficient health care are all more frequent among the poor. Add domestic violence, parental divorce, inadequate schools, lack of nutritious food, and the conditions are very far from optimal. So only under the best of circumstances, when a stimulating environment is available and the child is allowed to develop his or her cognitive skills to the greatest possible extent, will inheritance be the main determinant of brain development. The relative impact of inheritance therefore decreases when children are not shielded from adverse factors and deficient stimulation.

A crucial environmental factor associated with poverty is often ignored: exposure to chemical brain drainers. Increased lead exposure among African American children can explain at least part of the achievement gap observed in regard to school performance.[44] In failing schools, lead exposure is a crucial concern. A study of schools in Arizona aptly concluded: "The fact that most "failing schools" are in low-income neighborhoods where children live in housing known to be laced with a brain damaging neurotoxin is not just a coincidence."[45] Ironically, PCBs have been widely used in caulking materials and sealants in many schools in America and elsewhere (see chapter 6).[46] Schoolchildren are therefore exposed to chemical brain drain even at school.

Failing schools would need funding to better satisfy the specific educational needs of exposed children. Additionally, efforts should be made to remove the chemical hazards from the schools, the neighborhoods, and other sources. Given what we know now, it would be seriously improper to refuse support by referring to inherited intelligence or racial differences. The social inheritance injustice that children from poor families fail at school and grow up to become as poor as their parents needs to be combated by addressing the roots of the problem. Forget about deficient genes, but focus on the chemical brain drainers.

Compensation Awards

Dollar amounts that reflect the value of brain functions can also be extracted from legal settlements or compensation awards in court. In the United States, exposures to chemical substances are generally regulated by post-market laws. This means that most substances have entered commerce without any required pre-market testing. If harm occurs, then the victims may sue for compensation. The outcome of such legal cases is highly variable, and many are settled without making the compensation public, assuming that the responsible company still exists. Huge amounts may be won in these cases, but often they must be shared by a large number of affected victims.

The settlement that involved the famous lawyer Johnny Cochran (see chapter 6) forced the producer of PCBs in Anniston, Alabama, to pay a total of $700 million—the largest amount so far paid in a mass tort case. However, after the legal fees and other expenses had been paid, the award had to be shared among over 18,000 claimants. Each received an amount calculated according to the claimant's PCB concentration in serum and medical conditions. Due to their lower serum-PCB concentrations, children received an average of only $2,000 in compensation, while the adult claimants received almost five times as much. These amounts were not based on any assessment of the value of health or brain functions. The total settlement amount was determined from the revenues that could be extracted from the company.

In Japan, close to 50,000 methylmercury poisoning victims have been approved for damage compensation that averages at least $20,000, that is, a total of about $1 billion (chapter 4). Chisso, the company responsible for the pollution in Minamata, eventually had to spin off all its business operations into a new company to secure compensation costs for patients. The parent company allocates all dividends to payment of compensation and debts. Rather than going bankrupt, this scheme allows the company to stay afloat in the hope that the current (mercury-independent) production will be sufficiently profitable to generate the agreed benefits to the patients.

Other monetary compensation paid to subjects exposed to brain drainers also seems minuscule when compared to the estimated losses of income. For example, recognized mercury-exposed victims of the Grassy Narrows tribe in Canada receive a monthly payment between $250 and $800, while a typical compensation that a Japanese victim of the Morinaga milk poisoning receives is $700 per month (chapter 5). This monetary support may barely cover the health care costs. Forget any other damages or loss of income.

Thus, while the total amounts won in lawsuits can be large, individual compensation awards are sometimes trivial and incomparable to the value of an optimally functioning brain. Monetary awards are far less than what victims are due based on the costs calculated by economists.

Costs of Abatement

So far, we have looked at the value of brain functions and not at the costs to protect brain development. As an essential and separate part of the cost-benefit analysis, we must also consider the costs from the prevention of hazardous exposures. So the very substantial benefits associated with maintaining IQs and optimal brain function need to be compared with costs associated with the control or removal of brain-draining chemicals and products. Primary prevention is likely to be much less expensive than the resulting costs of removing those chemicals that have already been discharged into the environment and in consumer products, if at all possible. We could have saved billions and billions had we not given in to company doctor Robert Kehoe and others, who demanded scientific proof before discontinuing a hazardous technology.

In regard to lead from gasoline additives, the octane-boosting itself was associated with economic advantages. But the costs of the ban corresponded to only about one-tenth of the monetized health benefits from removing the toxic exposure.[47] Lead paint remains a major contributor to American children's lead exposure. Assuming an overall national average of $7,000 per unit to make a residence lead-safe, and that at least 1 million homes constitute a lead hazard, the total cost of intervention would be $7 billion.[48] The expense may be greater, as some amount of lead paint is probably present in as many as 25 million US homes. There are also costs associated with the removal of lead pipes from drinking water distribution systems affecting several million residences. All of these expenses are by no means negligible. But they constitute a one-time investment, and IQ-related benefits will accrue with each birth cohort and each generation of children that is protected from the toxic exposure. With that in mind, investing in lead removal would seem highly attractive.

Economists at the Harvard School of Public Health carried out a cost-benefit analysis for mercury. Although they underestimated the IQ effects in their analysis, the net benefits of preventing mercury exposure ranged from $75 million to almost four times as much, when taking into account the costs from controlling mercury releases from the major domestic source, coal-fired power plants.[49] These calculations were of course disputed by the American Enterprise Institute and other industry-related organizations, which prefer alternative (and erroneous) estimates suggesting a benefit of only 0.01 IQ points from eliminating mercury pollution from coal-fired power plants.[50] More recent studies carried out for the United Nations Environment Programme suggest that the benefits from decreasing mercury exposures also justify the introduction of emission reduction measures at a global level.[51]

Costs may be quite substantial also in regard to the "dirty dozen" (chapter 6) that resist breakdown in the environment. Such chemicals do not readily disappear once they have been discharged. Economists calculated that removal of PCB-contaminated sites in Sweden would cost 3–5 billion Swedish kroner (about $400–$650 million). They then extrapolated the costs to all of the European Union and calculated that the expenses during 2011–2018 would be €15 billion (about $23 billion).[52] This amount does not include expenses associated with the PCB-laden salmon from the Baltic Sea (which is illegal to sell), or renovation costs due to PCBs in caulking or other building materials. In the United States, the removal of PCB-contaminated sediments from the Hudson River had by 2010 cost General Electric $830 million, and the project has not even been completed. The owners of a previous electrical component plant in New Bedford, Massachusetts, in 2012 agreed to pay $366 million to help clean up the PCB-polluted harbor, where fishing and lobstering has been banned since 1979. In another settlement, the PCB-polluting industry in Anniston, Alabama, agreed to pay $100 million to cover cleanup and other expenses (see chapter 6).

Similarly, in regard to arsenic in drinking water, unless safer sources of ground water can be found, the 50 million people in the United States whose water supply exceeds the limit determined by the US Environmental Protection Agency (EPA) may have to consider installing a filter at a cost that may exceed $1,000 per household. Unless safer drinking water sources can be found, the total expense is considerable.

In Washington state, the main source of arsenic pollution is a former copper smelter owned by Asarco and in operation from 1905 to 1986, when pollution problems could no longer be ignored. The EPA and state officials documented contamination by arsenic and toxic metals covering as much as 1,000 square miles. Facing a $1 billion lawsuit for environmental damages and cleanup costs, Asarco filed for bankruptcy. In a settlement, Washington state in 2009 received $188 million from the company, half of it earmarked for cleanup near the Tacoma Smelter.[53]

The magnitude of these remediation costs should not be taken as an indication that preventing chemical brain drain is overly expensive and should be called off. Rather, these costs could have been prevented if we had realized early what was at stake. The risks to human brain development, and human health in general, must be identified as early as possible so that prudent or restricted use will avoid later societal costs both in regard to human injury and belated environmental cleanup.

Nonetheless, other viewpoints are frequently voiced. Friedhelm Schmider, director general of the European Crop Protection Association, commented on the proposed EU legislation that would ban the most toxic pesticides: "With huge pressure on agricultural productivity and food prices at an all-time high, pushing through such legislation without thoroughly understanding all of the consequences for the food supply and the cost of living verges on negligence.... Banning pesticides may be a populist measure, but it will not ensure the production of safe, healthy and affordable food."[54] According to an industry calculation, a worst-case scenario would cause prices for cereals and vegetables to rise by 73% and 104%, respectively. These results were widely disseminated to and through the media, but of course the industry spokesmen did not consider the benefits of protecting the consumers—and their children—against substances toxic to brain development. And some say that the industry costs were exaggerated.

Normal brain function is a prerequisite for our daily activities and ability to learn and adapt. When the intricacies of the brain are disturbed, the resulting adverse effects—whether or not they represent medical diagnoses—may be debilitating to a larger or smaller extent, because basic functions such as movement, communication, interaction, and personal feelings can be affected. Optimal brain function is desirable and advantageous—in fact, crucial—both for the individual and for society. The calculations carried out according to standard economic equations suggest that the monetary value of brain power is very considerable in terms of billions of dollars and euros. Beyond that, the value is perhaps so great as to exceed calculations. However, the estimated dollar amounts would at least seem to justify very strong primary prevention and abatement efforts to protect developing brains. But as we shall see next, brain-draining chemicals can generate economic benefits, thereby poisoning both corporate decisions and science.

CHAPTER 9

Inconvenient Truths

VESTED INTERESTS CAN ENDANGER BRAIN DEVELOPMENT

In the summer of 2006, the *New York Times* and other major American newspapers displayed full-page advertisements to convince the readers that mercury in fish was safe. The same ad appeared in magazines like *U.S. News* and *The New Yorker*. A colleague of mine called me and said that similar posters were exhibited in the Washington, DC, Metro. The message was: "Concerned about Mercury? You shouldn't be. Unless you eat this." Then there was a picture of canned whale meat. There was also a reference to a website, which ridiculed three mercury researchers as disreputable advocates. Information combined from different sources clearly showed that the researchers were out of their wits. I discovered that I was listed as #1. The prominence of this campaign suggested that the need to downplay mercury risks was worth a lot of money to somebody, although that somebody was not identified.

I took the ads to the legal office at Harvard University and asked for advice. They promised to look into the case, although only informally, as the university could not offer to provide legal advice to faculty members. Professors are on their own when they deal with contentious issues. (The American Association of University Professors has recommended that universities provide assistance to their scientists who come under attack without regard to the merit of the challenge.)[1] It did not take the lawyers long to figure out what was going on. The website and the ads were set up by an organization called Center for Consumer Freedom, run by lobbyist Richard Berman. According to Wikipedia, he has managed several industry-funded nonprofit organizations and campaigns that downplay the dangers of obesity, smoking, and drunk driving.

In this case, the campaign was apparently paid for by the tuna industry. Their concern was that the sale of canned tuna, which used to be Americans' favorite seafood, had tumbled 10% nationwide and had been bypassed by shrimp (which has less mercury).

With a revenue loss of nearly $150 million, allegedly because of the mercury scare, the tuna canners decided to band together for a $25 million campaign.[2] In one year, they would spend an amount much greater than the total support for mercury research that I had received during 20 years from the National Institutes of Health.

The industry critique of mercury research also infected the media in more indirect ways. In its editorial space, the *Wall Street Journal* called my work "problematic." Nobody seemed to take my side, but the Harvard lawyers advised me to ignore the fuss. Being hauled over the coals on the Internet was more than I had bargained for, so I asked my Harvard colleague, Joel Schwartz, what he thought I should do. He has studied the health effects of lead exposure and air pollution, and he has a history of tense relationships with vested interest groups. Joel listened, and then he asked: "Would you rather that they praised you?"

Burden of Proof

Whole-page ads aside, other less resource-demanding strategies have been used to launch attacks on research with undesirable conclusions. Thus, industry skillfully turns what should be a debate over policy to a debate over science.[3] Best known is the tobacco industry for the strategies used to curb unwanted public policy interventions that threatened company interests,[4] but such tactics are not limited to cigarette companies. At the most subtle level, expertly drafted critique can target the methodology, the data interpretation, or any other aspect considered crucial to the validity of the study. Although the intention to discredit the unwelcome findings is clear, such challenges can be difficult to distinguish from credible collegial comments, especially if authored by multiple sources, a group of respected scientists, or seemingly reputable organizations, while it is often not transparent how the critique was initiated or funded.

These strategies may be mean, narrow-minded, and destructive, but there is one approach that is probably as damaging as the sum of all the others. The industry view is that the burden of proof must fall on public health advocates and not on industry. Thus, a chemical is innocent until proven guilty, just like Dr. Kehoe said about lead pollution. Therefore, the most innocent-looking and effective way of promoting one's interests is to raise doubt.[5] As made famous by former Secretary of Defense Donald Rumsfeld, in numerous statements on the evidence (or the lack thereof) of Iraqi weapons of mass destruction, absence of evidence is of course not evidence of absence. In regard to chemical safety, the industry claim is that there is no health risk as long as there is no conclusive research to document otherwise. This notion is both erroneous and irresponsible. Nonetheless, the argument supports the view that, in the absence of documentation of a definite hazard, there is no reason to worry.[6]

Some scientists have built a reputation around stringent and skeptical interpretations of research findings. One such prominent critic was the late Yale professor

Alvin Feinstein, who was highly skeptical of so-called black-box epidemiology.[7] Just because there is an apparent association between A and B does not mean that A necessarily causes B, he pointed out. Fair enough. However, science needs to be interpreted in light of everything we know, not just the individual study that seems to connect A and B. Nonetheless, Feinstein disputed the link between smoking and lung cancer and many other associations, despite support from a wealth of evidence.

Stubborn naysayers often express their views with rhetoric that gives the appearance of legitimate debate, where there is very little or none.[8] Disagreements are exaggerated, perhaps with the help of hand-picked academics who support an alternative interpretation in accordance with industry views, and who are (therefore) referred to as experts. With the laudable but naïve aim of covering "both sides," journalists frequently employ this strategy, thus being of much help to the vested interests that promote the "alternative" hypotheses. The ultimate goal of this distraction tactic is to reject a conclusion—which is considered adverse from some vested interest perspective—upon which a scientific consensus already exists.

Historian Naomi Oreskes has researched the climate change debate and documented how a few scientists with strong ties to particular industries and conservative political connections have played a disproportionate role in public debates on controversial issues. The "scientists in their twilight years who had turned to fields in which they had no training or experience" nonetheless managed to raise doubt and affect public opinion and political decisions.[9] The "doubting Thomases" seem not to be deterred by the extreme isolation of their theories but often interpret it as indication of their courage against the dominant orthodoxy and political correctness.[10]

Another angle is to question the personal motives and integrity of the researchers, like the website that called me an "advocate." To discredit unsavory results, industry representatives may blame scientists for having vested interests themselves. Thus, the tobacco industry has portrayed mainstream researchers (who insist, for example, that smoking is a health hazard) as being extremist, unqualified, or politically motivated.[11] The scientists are ridiculed as having conspired against honest critique, which they suppress through "biased" peer review and similar means. The collaboration among scientists is said to represent a cartel, such as the "anti-smoking industry," that behaves dishonestly in promoting erroneous research results. Clearly the opposite is true. That these claims originate from very clear and adversarial interests is often concealed. Organizations, such as the Center for Science and Public Policy, the Center for Indoor Air Research, or the Citizens for Fire Safety Institute, may sound like neutral and honest establishments, but they turned out to be "front groups" for financial interests. These groups usually purport to represent one agenda while in reality they serve some other party or interest whose sponsorship may be hidden. The three groups just mentioned support views of and receive support from certain food industries, the tobacco industry, and the producers of chemical flame retardants.

That can be hard for the average consumer to figure out. I shall now show how successfully their strategies have worked in regard to chemical brain drain.

Staging Controversy

Reverse causality is one of the favorite arguments used by industry interests to counter inconvenient results. That means that B is really the cause of A, and not A that causes B. For example, the reasoning goes, mentally retarded children somehow get exposed to more pollution than other kids. If that does not work and the association may be real, then the critics will insist that there is an independent underlying cause, such as poverty, maternal drinking or smoking, or nutritional deficiencies. The lead research pioneer, Professor Herbert Needleman, was attacked because he had not adjusted his results for all factors that might possibly affect brain development. Needleman responded, saying: "I pointed out that complete covariate control is impossible to achieve, but that many studies controlling for differing factors found a lead effect. This consistency among the many studies published at that time was strong evidence that the lead effect was real and not produced by confounders, and this was strongly buttressed by animal studies, which showed similar changes and effectively destroyed the reverse causality hypothesis."[12] That response did not satisfy Needleman's opponents, who further decided to accuse him of fraud.

Further, if the other strategies fail, then a critic may acknowledge that an exposure may actually cause the particular effects, but that this happens only under the specific circumstances of the study, and not in general. At a 1990 conference on children's need for special consideration in risk assessment, some speakers emphasized examples of how children may be less vulnerable, due to their immature metabolism (as I already mentioned in chapter 1). So the organizers offered the following conclusion: "Differences in sensitivity between children and adults are chemical specific and must be studied and evaluated on a case-by-case basis."[13] Thus, vulnerability during early development does occur, but it is not a general physiological phenomenon—it needs to be evaluated one substance at a time. This conclusion has been reiterated multiple times since then in order to support the notion that children should not be regarded as more vulnerable, unless we can prove it, again and again. In other words, let us continue exposing the next generation and their developing brains unless definite damage can be demonstrated. I find that despicable and unethical.

In fact, critics sometimes raise doubt in regard to little details that are said to be crucial to the validity of the research. When the Food and Drug Administration (FDA) was considering a dietary advisory in regard to seafood, the tuna canners wrote to the FDA: "There are too many important questions currently being answered by the Seychelles study investigators and too many remaining concerns to be addressed by the Faroes study investigators before the public policy can be effectively settled."[14] Several years ago, a legal consultant to one of the major tuna canners paid me a visit at my department in Denmark. He asked what I would recommend his company to do about mercury exposure. I said that, given the serious consequences for brain development, they should seek out the tuna species that accumulated the least mercury, then harvest it from the least polluted waters, and market it as low-mercury tuna. Of course that would not be all that easy to do, so the company lawyer balked. Many years after that conversation, one tuna canner finally started marketing a low-mercury product. So it appears to be less demanding on industry to raise questions with the FDA.

And the FDA seems happy to comply. "There has never been a documented case of adverse effects (i.e. deficits in health and mental faculties) in an individual in the U.S., resulting from eating commercially bought seafood," an FDA spokesperson stated when high mercury concentrations had been found in fish jerky in 2012.[15] The wording of this statement is surprisingly similar to opinions voiced by the tuna industry and related interests.

The resistance against prevention of neurotoxic pollution was also evident in Anniston, one of the most polluted communities in the United States (see chapter 6): More and more studies have identified health problems associated with PCB exposure. A spokesperson for Solutia, the company now responsible for the pollution, recently countered: "Solutia's role in Anniston is not to focus on studies based on loose science, but rather to lead activities to investigate and/or remediate PCB-containing soils as is defined in Solutia's partial consent decree with the U.S. EPA."[16] So the company is doing what it is legally required to do and nothing more. New evidence that might justify further pollution abatement is dismissed as "loose." It may take another multi-million dollar lawsuit for the research findings to be taken seriously.

The Hired Guns

Doubts about neurotoxicity have been raised at different levels of expertise and have sometimes been pushed forward by front groups of hired experts. Sometimes the doubt is occasioned by very meager evidence, such as a new, small study with limited statistical power to document any effects at all. When commenting on the long-term effects of brain drain in 63 lead-exposed children, one group of authors concluded: "The few statistically significant findings of this study are due to methodological difficulties inherent in this area of research.... If there are in fact behavioral and intellectual sequelae of low levels of lead burden ... these effects of lead are minimal."[17] The first author later appeared as a paid consultant on behalf of the lead industry in regulatory and legal settings.

I remember the very obvious industry presence at scientific conferences on lead pollution around 1980, when the use of lead additives in gasoline was hotly debated. Among the frequent participants was Patrick Barry, company medical director from

Associated Octel (now called Innospec), the major European producer of lead additives. Barry often asked questions during the formal discussion periods at these meetings. Although his comments did not at all invalidate the research findings, his point was that a causal relation between lead from car exhausts and adverse effects had not yet been proven. I am sure that his interventions were considered well worth the travel expenses by his employers.

A highly respected pioneer in developmental psychology at Yale, Alan Kaufman, has likewise denounced the neurotoxic effects of lead exposure in children. Kaufman argued that the association between lead exposure and IQ deficits could be explained by uncontrolled confounding due to other causal factors, like poverty, and that the studies carried out contained a variety of methodological flaws.[18] Kaufman had received support for his work from the lead industry. His subsequent critique of studies on PCB neurotoxicity was likewise supported by General Electric, a company responsible for PCB pollution of the Hudson River. Kaufman's points were readily and convincingly countered by colleagues with expertise in human neurotoxicology, but a critique from such a prominent scientist nonetheless created the impression of uncertainty regarding brain-drain effects of chemical exposures.

The innocently named nonprofit Center for Science and Public Policy—one of the front groups mentioned earlier—fervently criticized the exposure limit for mercury adopted by the US Environmental Protection Agency (EPA). The report hailed a non-informative study carried out in the Seychelles as definitive, while blaming mercury-associated neurotoxicity in the Faroes population on other purported exposures:

> It must be recognized that the EPA's safe mercury dose is based on inappropriate studies of people who consume whale meat and blubber (a unique diet very different from typical U.S. consumption) containing multiple chemicals—PCBs, cadmium, pesticides, persistent organic pollutants, DDT, etc.—of which mercury is only one…. Basing enormously consequential energy and health policies—both nationally and internationally—on myth is both irresponsible and harmful.[19]

One of the report's authors was an apparent heavyweight in science, Professor Willie Soon. An astrophysicist by training, Soon received support from industry sources, such as the American Petroleum Institute, and he has worked as a paid consultant for the George C. Marshall Institute, a conservative think tank. As author of an op-ed in the Wall Street Journal in 2011, Soon was identified as an expert on mercury and public health issues, but I am not aware that Soon has any such credentials. The professor is also known as a climate-change denier. Perhaps because coal-fired power plants are important sources of both carbon dioxide and mercury, the mercury issue was linked to the climate change debate.

The Center for Science and Public Policy continues to maintain websites devoted to debunking environmental concerns, such as those regarding mercury in fish. They criticize unwanted results as junk science and interpret uncertainties in the evidence as indication that chemical exposures are safe. As environmental groups claimed that mercury was a real hazard, the Center responded:

> If these organizations were truly concerned with the health and welfare of women and children, they should apply their precautionary approach about the potential indication of harm, not the actual proof of it, to their own public misstatements and regulatory zeal.... It is the science-challenged alarmists who are endangering the health of America's and the world's children.[20]

Another industry-supported source additionally ranted: "In the United States, even the most rabid environmentalist cannot point to one sickened child or doddering old fool made ill from mercury."[21] The term "junk science" has been used extensively in spin generated by science commentator Steve Milloy, who has often appeared on Fox News. He has worked to discredit bothersome research apparently on behalf of a number of industrial corporations and industry groups, including the so-called Advancement of Sound Science Coalition.

Clandestine links between denialists and vested interests may infect international agencies. Among the most trusted sources of chemical risk evaluations, expert committees evaluate pesticides on behalf of the World Health Organization (WHO) and the Food and Agricultural Organization of the UN. Several years ago, when the interests of the tobacco industry were threatened by possible regulation of a particular pesticide used on tobacco fields, they managed to hire the recently retired scientific secretary of the committee, Gaston Vettorazzi, as a consultant. He knew very well all the administrative procedures and maintained friendly ties with his former colleagues. First he developed some background documents that stressed the safety of the pesticide. His successor at the WHO accepted Vettorazzi's collegial assistance and then allowed him to participate as a volunteer expert in the committee meetings. Nobody was told who Vettorazzi's benefactor was. Documentation later showed that the tobacco industry had provided him with an honorarium of $200,000 dollars in addition to $7,000 per month as per diem plus reimbursement of expenses. Following Vettorazzi's intervention, usage of the pesticide was not restricted.[22]

Upon discovery of the plot, the WHO tightened the rules regarding conflicts of interest. Not all organizations have such strict guidelines, and we are left wondering how often clandestine cases like Vettorazzi's are missed or willfully ignored.

Expert Selection

Conclusions by expert committees of course depend on who sits on the committee. So selection of expert members sometimes considers qualifications other than expertise, even within governmental agencies. The Centers for Disease Control and Prevention (CDC) has long provided highly respected advice on lead exposure. The CDC's Advisory Committee on Childhood Lead Poisoning Prevention lowered in 1991 the action level for lead concentrations in blood (to 100 μg/L).[23] As more recent research made the standard outdated, a more protective recommendation was anticipated. However, in 2002, the Health and Human Services secretary decided that the committee membership needed to reflect the views of the administration, and the panel was therefore reconfigured. Four new members were chosen, all of whom had direct or indirect links to the lead industry.[24] The committee decided against lowering the action limit. After a change of membership under a new administration, a formal recommendation was finally made in 2012 to lower the limit by 50%. Unfortunately, at that point, Congress had all but eliminated CDC's budget for lead poisoning prevention.

I had a parallel experience as the author of a draft criteria document on fluoride generated on behalf of WHO's International Programme of Chemical Safety. Most of the committee members were in one way or another associated with the cause for the beneficial use of fluoride in dentistry, and therefore, curtailed any mention of toxic effects in the draft. As I was considered part of the secretariat, I had no vote, and my views were not allowed in the final document. Realizing that I had been taken hostage, I had to disengage myself from the report.

Selection of experts is also important in regard to congressional hearings. To support weakened regulations of mercury releases from power plants—the major source of mercury pollution in the United States—the Bush government in 2003 relied on testimony before the Senate energy committee chaired by Republican senator James Inhofe. As told by Chris Mooney, an investigative journalist, the first speaker at the hearing represented the industry-supported Electric Power Research Institute (EPRI) and argued that much of the mercury pollution in the United States is of foreign origin. Subsequently, the senators were told by pediatrics professor Gary Myers, a main author of reports from the Seychelles that had so far failed to show any clear mercury toxicity: "We do not believe that there is presently good scientific evidence that moderate fish consumption is harmful to the fetus."

The journalist added that EPRI had contributed $486,000 to a project involving Myers's group.[25] On another occasion, Myers downplayed the toxic effects that had been documented: "Finger-tapping and the other reported findings from epidemiological studies are statistical associations that have no clinical relevance for an individual."[26] He also concluded: "Some people are convinced that mercury causes these effects and others are not so confident."[27] I believe that both Senator Inhofe and EPRI were very pleased with Professor Myers's comments.

Such statements tend to attract more attention than they deserve. A main reason that the doubt-raising strategy works so well is the news media aim of presenting a "balanced coverage" of both sides. Science reporting then gets framed as an interesting competition between opposing camps of scientists. Presented this way, the public would not have any reason to believe the party that happens to represent the vast majority of the expertise. And the controversy may even be entertaining. At first.

Buying Influence

Scientific documentation is of course useful only when the information is shared. Unwanted information may never see the light outside the closed walls of a sponsored laboratory. Results deemed potentially deleterious may be suppressed or withheld, depending on who has the access to and control over the data, through a research contract or otherwise. Some instances that have surfaced illustrate a variety of strategies of suppression, such as withdrawing research support, transferring scientists to other jobs, dismissing, denying promotion, or blocking of publications.[28]

A survey carried out in 1993 among biomedical faculty found that 20% for various reasons had withheld research results for more than six months at least once during the last three years.[29] A more recent survey suggested that the most common form of improper conduct was that the researchers had changed design, choice of method, or results following pressure from a sponsor.[30] Further insight into such cases has been obtained from public records in regard to drugs. Up to one-half of drug trials were never published, while other trials (with beneficial outcomes) might be published repeatedly under different names, sometimes including only selected data, thereby augmenting any outcome favorable to the corporate sponsor of the trial.[31]

Although expensive, a common strategy to control science is to sponsor the project. Thus, by commissioning or supporting collaborative scientists, the aim is to obtain results that are beneficial to the funder. This method is probably most often used by drug companies in regard to testing of new pharmaceuticals. But does the identity of the sponsor affect the research outcome? In a review of 1,140 biomedical articles, industry-sponsored studies were significantly more likely to reach conclusions that were favorable to the sponsor than the non-industry studies.[32] For intervention studies on soft-drink beverages, none of the industry-sponsored reports on nutritional impacts carried a conclusion unfavorable to the sponsor, while such conclusions occurred in over one-third of the studies that declared no industry funding.[33]

Although such problems may be less apparent in regard to environmental chemicals, one survey of 115 studies on bisphenol A (a contaminant released from polycarbonate plastic previously used for manufacturing baby bottles) showed that none of the industry-sponsored studies reported adverse effects at low exposures, while the vast majority of government-funded studies did.[34] An apparent bias has also been reported in regard to study of possible adverse effects of cell phone use.[35] It is unclear how many of these discrepancies may result from researchers withholding unwanted results. Whatever its origin, the bias is reason for serious concern, as we have already seen that research on brain toxicity is highly prone to critique or dismissal. If evidence on chemical brain drain is held back or falsified, the available documentation will result in an even greater underestimation of the risks.

To generate publicity on uncertainties of the evidence, commercial interests may commission "product defense" papers that are then submitted as original research articles or reviews to scientific journals. Typically, these documents are written by consultants or consulting firms (probably for large fees), in the hope that the efforts will help defeat liability claims or new regulations.[36] Alternatively, the authors are "hired guns" from academic institutions who are sympathetic to the funder's interests. These commissioned papers quote the evidence that supports the desired conclusions, perhaps supplemented by an apparent science-based critique of any damaging evidence. The interpretation and spin then dismisses some research as flawed and unconfirmed, while portraying other research as sound because it is in accordance with the conclusions desired. Sometimes, the focus is primarily on labeling damaging research as unsound, as in the case of the results obtained by Professor Per Eriksson from Uppsala University in Sweden. His findings on brain toxicity due to chemical flame retardants were attacked by experts representing a major producer of these substances. Their letters of complaint were published in the same scientific journals that had released Eriksson's reports.[37]

Industries that fear tighter regulations may choose to organize or sponsor symposia and similar events to promote their views or generate consensus statements and press releases supporting their preferred opinions. Financial support for scientific conferences may be exchanged for favors of various kinds—for example, but not limited to, exhibition space and brochures. No one knows the total amount of financial support that physicians receive from drug companies, but Marcia Angell, former editor-in-chief of the *New England Journal of Medicine*, suspects that it comes to tens of billions of dollars in America every year.[38] Through this support, the pharmaceutical industry has gained access to physicians, highly respected experts, and senior faculty at prestigious medical schools, with opportunities for influencing research designs, results, and interpretation. It is not known to what extent the chemical industry and other interests may use similar strategies, and only anecdotal evidence suggests that efforts are made to buy influence in regard to chemical brain drainers.

EPRI was a main financial sponsor of an international conference on mercury in 2004. At an official pre-conference event, EPRI staff taught a course on risk assessment. Worse, the two sessions on human health effects of mercury exposures were both chaired by EPRI officials. This is an important function as the chair of conference sessions decides who gets to ask questions and when to cut off the discussion. As EPRI was also represented in the planning committee, perhaps they were involved in the decision allowing me to deliver only one short presentation on the most recent Faroes findings, while the program included three presentations on the Seychelles studies which assured attendees that there were no adverse effects of methylmercury exposure. I have been unable to find out how much EPRI invested in the conference to gain these extraordinary favors from the organizers.

Conference organizers must of course worry about the budget as they aim at providing hearty hospitality to colleagues from out of town. Predictably, a psychiatrist explained to a *Washington Post* writer that without support from industry, the psychiatrists would have to hold their annual meeting at the YMCA basement, to which the journalist asked what exactly was wrong with that.[39] Good point. When entities like the WHO sponsor a scientific conference, no involvement of commercial interests is permitted. Perhaps this is why so few meetings request WHO approval.

Perhaps the most stunning illustration of the purchasing power of vested interests was the promotion of a deadly brain drainer that came to light in 2010. Lead additives to gasoline were still in use in several countries, mainly in Asia. The world's only remaining producer of lead additives is the UK company Innospec (formerly Associated Octel). In connection with the United Nations investigations of fraud within the Oil for Food Program in Iraq, evidence surfaced that Innospec had violated the UN sanctions against Iraq and committed corruption offenses. The company admitted to having bribed officials in both Iraq and Indonesia to delay for several years a planned ban of leaded gasoline.[40] The revenues from exporting lead additives to these developing countries were about $1.8 billion, with profits totaling more than one-third of that. In comparison to the profits, the $9 million used for bribes seems petty, but so does the fine of $40 million imposed by the courts. As phrased by the UK newspaper *The Guardian*, "the only individuals to have suffered penalties have been the nameless children who ... may have inhaled lead dust. But effects on them are bound to prove more difficult to document."[41] As of early 2013, the additives were still exported to Iraq, Afghanistan, North Korea, and Yemen.

One might have expected that Innospec would show some remorse. But the company continues to market lead additives as a product named Tetraboost for certain airplanes and veteran automobiles. Under FAQs at its website, the company offers the following answer to the question: "Am I polluting the environment? Tetraethyl lead waste leaves the exhaust system as tetraethyl lead salts which dissolve harmlessly in the rain." Harmlessly, indeed.

Although the individual victims may remain unknown, science *has* documented the adverse effects from lead pollution. If science seems powerful and if it threatens vested interests, it may stimulate efforts to control it for the simple reason that you are better able to control the decisions if you can control the documentation that regulatory decisions must be based upon. No wonder industry interests aim at suborning the apparatus and authority of science to become their own instrument of profit. It is the potential power of science to lend credibility to environmental positions that makes ownership of scientific knowledge so intensely contested. While the quality of science remains crucial, the possible direct or indirect impact of powerful interests on science means that we must consider what the purpose of the science is and whom it benefits.[42]

Attacking Scientists

A more direct means of discrediting an inconvenient truth is to harass the scientists themselves, just as the tuna industry attacked me and my work. Condemning scientists and questioning their moral character can escalate to an assault on the integrity of a researcher, especially if he has authored several bothersome publications. Allegations of scientific misconduct and unethical behavior can be used to prevent the scientists from conducting any further damaging research or perhaps to intimidate them enough that they will leave the field and escape into early retirement.[43] As early as 1914, when Edward Park had diagnosed a series of lead poisoning cases in Baltimore, his findings were challenged by an industry representative, who visited Park's clinic and insisted that his diagnoses of lead poisoning were all wrong.[44] Although it did not work in Park's case, this strategy has been frequently used ever since.

When Clair Patterson from the California Institute of Technology reported that "natural" exposures to lead were only about 1% of the current levels of intake (see chapter 3),[45] a group from Ethyl Corporation—the major producer of lead additives to gasoline—visited him and offered support for research "that would yield results favorable to their cause" (as expressed in a letter to Herb Needleman). Pat refused the unethical offer, but then his substantial support from the American Petroleum Institute was terminated. Members of the Board of Trustees at CalTech even paid a visit to the chairman of his department asking that Pat be fired.[46]

Having authored pioneering papers on the neurotoxicity of lead from gasoline, Herb was himself accused of fraud. Two scientists took it upon themselves to scrutinize his work for possible flaws. They reported the alleged flaws to the governmental Office of Scientific Integrity, which then requested Herb's university to conduct a special inquiry.[47] Because universities rely on government support, they have good reason to appear receptive to allegations of fraud and other irregularities in research. On the other hand, being forthcoming to critique opens the possibility of abusing the procedures that were originally intended to protect the public against fraud. The unreasonably protracted investigation eventually exonerated Herb Needleman but cost him more than 10 years of frustration and an enormous waste of his time.

Patterson and Needleman were not the only targets. Toxicologist Phyllis Mullenix had developed a promising method for computerized surveillance of rat behavior. Her research colleagues suggested using fluoride as a test of the new methodology. The results were surprising and showed clear neurotoxicity. When Mullenix in 1992 presented her results to dental research colleagues at Forsyth Research Institute in Boston, she was met with disbelief. Fluoride was a widely known anti-cavity agent and therefore sacred. Her supervisor advised her, on the next day, that she "was going against what dentists and everybody have been publishing for fifty years, that this is safe and effective." He also said that she "was jeopardizing the financial support of [the] entire institution."[48] Her results were eventually published in a highly respected scientific journal.[49] Soon thereafter, she was fired. In a letter to the journal, her results were criticized by researchers from Procter & Gamble, maker of fluoride toothpaste (Mullenix and her coauthors countered the critique).[50]

In this case, the researcher inadvertently challenged the promoters of drinking water fluoridation, not a chemical producer. Addition of fluoride to drinking water has been hailed by CDC as one of the 10 greatest health achievements of the 20th century, alongside vaccines and family planning.[51] When first proposed during the cold war, water fluoridation faced fierce objections. Opponents called it "the work of Communists who want to soften the brain of American people and make them pushovers for communism," although neurotoxicity as such was not seriously suspected back then.[52] As fluoride was produced in large amounts as waste in the metals industry, a trusted expert was recruited to defend the sponsors' interest. They chose none other than Robert A. Kehoe, well known for his stand on lead poisoning, or absence thereof (see chapter 3).

Even today, available evidence on any potential long-term harms of fluoride exposure is of rather poor quality and insufficient to rule out all but the most obvious effects.[53] This is unfortunate, as fluoride—like arsenic (chapter 4)—is part of many minerals and can contaminate the groundwater. A large percentage of wells in the United States (and worldwide) contain substantially elevated fluoride concentrations.[54]

Knowing that research on fluoride neurotoxicity in children had been done in China, I asked my Harvard colleague, Anna Choi, who speaks Chinese, if she could help evaluating the studies published in Chinese journals. She managed to locate the reports on fluoride in drinking water and its association with cognitive deficits in children—a total of 27 studies.[55] Only a couple of these studies had been considered in previous reviews. All but one suggested that a higher fluoride content in drinking water was associated with poorer performance on IQ tests at school age. Although this evidence may only reflect brain drain at high intake levels, Mullenix was probably right that fluoride can under certain conditions be toxic to the brain. She should have been praised rather than fired.

I already mentioned Per Eriksson, a Swedish toxicologist, who had developed a screening model in rodents to detect developmental neurotoxicity. When this approach was applied to industrial chemicals of commercial importance, his studies were criticized by researchers employed by a major producer of the compounds. Not only was their critique submitted to scientific journals, but a letter of complaint was also sent to the vice-chancellor at the author's university.[56]

Attacks may even be directed toward government employees. In one case, a state epidemiologist authored a report that recommended discontinuation of aerial spraying with malathion, a neurotoxic pesticide. When he refused to change the conclusion to agree with the official policy, the agency undertook a review of his travel records and, upon finding a possible $12.50 overcharge, fired him.[57]

In that comparison, we have been lucky. As our mercury research at the Faroe Islands was developing, EPRI commissioned a report from a consultant to evaluate our work. The sponsor was kind enough to send me a copy. Not surprisingly, the report concluded that I lacked qualifications, that the design of the Faroes study was inappropriate, and that there was no reason to trust anything that might emanate from this project.[58] Although the report was rather superficial, I am sure that EPRI was eager to identify reasons to distrust our findings. On the other hand, the sponsor perhaps might have been much more supportive had I been unable to find any evidence of brain drain from mercury.

When scientific evidence on brain drain must be considered in connection with legal proceedings, researchers often serve as expert witnesses who can be of critical importance in the decision of the case. Perhaps not surprisingly, industry lawyers have been known to harass the experts with subpoenas. Data-sharing requests may include research materials, including subject results and statistical analyses. This strategy was used in a lawsuit that the state of Rhode Island brought against lead-based paint manufacturers for damages due to lead poisoning in the state's children. The defendants subpoenaed 25 years' worth of raw data and unpublished documents from three scientists, who had agreed to serve as experts for the state.[59]

History professor Gerald Markowitz appeared as an expert on several such cases and had compiled the damaging evidence in a book, *Deceit and Denial, the Deadly Politics of Industrial Pollution*, which the defendants wanted to discredit. In a joint action, several industrial corporations subpoenaed and deposed the book's peer reviewers to provide evidence in court, although this was clearly an intrusion on confidential advice offered by these colleagues to the publisher.[60]

As cases of harassment do not necessarily come to the attention of the experts' colleagues in the field, a group of researchers affiliated with the International Society of Environmental Epidemiology conducted a survey and documented numerous cases where a whistleblower had been fired or otherwise lambasted after releasing information on an environmental hazard.[61] The Society now honors whistleblowers with an award, as does the German Society for Social Responsibility.

Exploiting Scientific Uncertainties

Compared to blitz campaigns in the media and critiques submitted to scientific journals, new research to address any concerns will take a dreadfully long time. This is particularly true in brain-drain science. Moreover, the results will usually not generate the definitive answers that may be desired. For better or for worse, scientists primarily care about the novelty and the methodological qualities of their work rather than the social implications. As part of their academic responsibility, scientists aim at being impartial and objective, thereby also avoiding any suspicion that their conclusions were somehow tainted or even fixed. When dealing with chemical brain drain and similar topics of social interest, scientists must strive to achieve a challenging balance between advocating particular recommendations and maintaining strict ivory-tower neutrality. This becomes particularly difficult when stakes are high, uncertainties are great, and the research becomes a target for narrow-minded criticism. For these reasons, science is easily criticized and appears as vulnerable as a sitting duck targeted by the sharp-shooting vested interests.

Like other branches of science, research on brain-draining chemicals is susceptible to criticism, even when the concerns are unfounded. Some uncertainties will always remain (as I shall discuss further in chapter 10). Thus, if we measure the exposure by analyzing the lead, mercury, or other pollutant concentrations in a blood sample, the result may or may not reflect the total amount of the chemical that has entered the body and reached the brain. The concentrations can vary within the body, and our exposure estimate is no better than an imprecise indicator of the cumulated amount in the brain. In addition, as brain development is rapid during childhood, we need to apply tests appropriate for the developmental stage of the child being examined and take the child's age into consideration in the data analysis. But many factors may influence the child's performance, and all children do not necessarily follow the same developmental trajectory. Many studies have applied intelligence quotient (IQ) tests because they are standardized and easily available. As IQ tests were not developed for the purpose of neurotoxicity assessment, they may be less sensitive to particular types of neurotoxicity than more specific domain-related tests. Subtle or more focal deficits may be missed.

To be informative, a research study must be of a reasonable size and use sensitive methods. In this regard, we refer to statistical power as the likelihood that the study will be able to detect whether the chemical exposure is linked to any effects at all with sufficient confidence. For this purpose, we calculate the likelihood of the results if we were to assume that no effect existed. However, in many cases, we already know that a substance—lead, mercury, or some other brain drainer—is toxic. But the standard procedure is not to consider how serious the effect might be, given the data (the upper confidence limit, as statisticians would say). When our results (or some more extreme) could occur randomly in at least 1 case out of 20 (i.e., with a probability of 5% or more), then we just conclude that the findings are "not significant."

Not significant just means that the study did not have enough power to document whether the effect was beyond doubt. However, such findings are often interpreted as an indication that there is no effect at all. This is a serious error. We would then be acting as if chemicals have the right to be considered innocent, unless we can *prove* otherwise.

I realize that this is perhaps a very technical issue, but it is of profound importance for the use of scientific documentation in policy decisions. But we must also consider the opposite possibility. In principle, a significant association between a brain drain effect and exposure to a chemical could still be incorrect. Let us assume

that 20 studies were carried out, and 1 accidentally showed an apparent and significant association at the 5% significance level. If we only published or considered this
single study, we would mislead our readers and the public because we would not be
revealing all the other results. We could therefore argue that a single report on brain
drain is not necessarily representative. However, that would mean that the single
study with allegedly spurious findings on average is taken out of a total of 20 studies, where the other 19 have been forgotten and left in the drawer. While we should
not be fooled into thinking that this sole study proves the case, we would have to
imagine an enormous number of forgotten studies hidden in very large drawers to
make up for the numerous published reports on brain-draining chemicals. Because
neurotoxicity studies are generally quite expensive, there would be a pressure, at
least within academic institutions, to generate some form of publication from these
substantial efforts.

An additional problem is biological variability and various types of uncertainty
can generate statistical noise that blurs the results and makes it more difficult to document adverse effects. A key issue is that our standard statistical methods assume that
the exposure is known for sure, without any imprecision, which is usually not true.[62]
The greater the imprecision is, the more the study will tend to underestimate the
effect. Ironically, studies on brain drainers are often criticized for imprecision of one
kind or another, as if that could cause an exaggeration of the toxicity risk. On the
contrary, the conclusions are most likely weaker than they would have been had we
had access to more valid measurement or been able to control for the imprecision.

Although the research can be strengthened through better designs and more
sensitive methods,[63] the uncertainties are real. But they generally tend to hide or
underestimate the possible effects of brain drainers and other toxic chemicals—not
the other way around. So we are in a double-whammy situation. Not only is there
insufficient evidence, so that we are only looking at a tiny tip of an iceberg, but at
the same time, our glasses are fogged up. Unfortunately, this situation provides an
almost ideal opportunity for brain-drain deniers to criticize and raise doubt about
the documentation.

Soft-Spoken Scientists

There is one more issue that further worsens the situation—so we are now looking
at a triple whammy. In order to protect themselves against harsh critique, scientists
have become particularly careful about mentioning relevant caveats and downplaying the significance of their findings. Linguists call this type of language "hedging."[64]
The lay reader, who is not familiar with this custom, may erroneously believe that
the results are more uncertain that they really are. When rereading our own 1980s
publications on lead neurotoxicity in children, and the later ones on mercury, I discover with dismay that we way too frequently have used double negations and words

like may, maybe, and perhaps. With the sharp debate and ongoing controversies, our reports were unnecessarily hedged and understated the impact of environmental chemical exposure on brain development.[65] This book also contains a lot of maybes, too, for similar reasons (please feel free to skip those that are clearly superfluous). So although the tuna industry has referred to me as an "advocate," in reality, the vast majority of scientific publications—including mine—are so soft-spoken that it is hard to see how they can represent any danger to corporate interests.

Still, the greatest wish of a scientist is, of course, to discover something new. An ambitious researcher may therefore misinterpret an accidental observation as a breakthrough. Thus, when original articles on medical discoveries in major health science journals were scrutinized several years later, a large proportion of the "new" observations were found to be wrong or inflated.[66] But it is exactly because the findings were novel and surprising that they attracted the interest of the editors of the prestigious journals. Often, the new findings relate to drug therapy of crucial relevance to the pharmaceutical industry. It is very different in regard to environmental chemicals.

Only a minute proportion of industrial pollutants ever gets featured in a major scientific journal, and most potential brain drainers are not even studied. At the same time, researchers in environmental toxicology cannot expect praise from industry for documenting adverse effects of chemical pollutants. As a result, very little research on brain toxicity reaches the most prestigious journals, and brain drain has even been downplayed in articles published in *The Lancet*, the *New England Journal of Medicine*, and *Science*.

Exceptions can occur, such as the rare occasions where fraud is involved. In one very sad case, British physician Andrew Wakefield linked measles vaccination to the development of autism. The vaccine contained a mercury compound that was thought to cause toxic effects. It was later discovered that the study description was erroneous and misleading, and the author failed to disclose funding from a lawyer who hoped to mount a legal action against the vaccine manufacturer. *The Lancet* retracted the publication[67] and Wakefield lost his medical license.

Still, even if a few false alarms may occur, for whatever reason, they will be rare events on an enormous background of absent information. More seriously, when the absence of evidence is interpreted as lack of toxicity, the misinterpretation generates a huge underestimation. So our main concern is not a few exaggerations of possible risks but the lacking or insufficient evidence that results in brain drain being greatly underestimated. We are in acute need of large-scale and long-term studies with detailed assessments of exposure and brain functions. But reality is that most studies are far less comprehensive and less informative, so that they are prone to miss the effects on brain development unless the damage is severe. Such studies often conclude that an effect was not identified for sure. As the effect could easily have been missed, the conclusion may be a false negative finding. But the error is only realized when larger and more decisive studies have been completed. So in technical terms, the most common and serious problems are the insufficient statistical power, overemphasis on a 5% probability level for statistical significance, reliance on exposure data as if no imprecision is present, insensitive effect measures, and short-term and incomplete follow-up. This inherent bias toward the null hypothesis of no effect is not easily overcome.[68]

Given that we are likely underestimating the magnitude of chemical brain drain, should we then believe any research report that suggests neurotoxic effects? Skepticism has a crucial role in science but should not be exaggerated to the extent that no new ideas will be generated. Likewise, gullibility should not be so generous that it prevents the distinction between useful and worthless ideas. However, in regard to brain drainers, scientific skepticism has generally taken precedence, sometimes to the extreme, especially when absence of evidence was erroneously thought to speak against there being any risk at all. So, even if ice is spotted, it is explained away as specks on the glasses, or just a stray ice floe, certainly not an iceberg. It is safe for the *Titanic* to move on, the conclusion goes.

We cannot easily solve the problem of vastly incomplete documentation and our scientific tradition of skepticism. As human experimentation is ruled out, we are left to observe the effects of exposures that actually happen. To get more reliable information, we might want to start tracking the exposure of the mother during the pregnancy and then ascertain the effects on the child's brain functions by examinations through to school age. That means that the research must cover an interval of 7–8 years or more from the time of exposure to the time of clinical testing. The temporal dissociation of exposure from effect has serious implications for the feasibility of the research and its costs. Also, this time frame does not fit into thesis schedules, grant durations, and merit reviews at learned institutions. And it may take even longer before the results are published.

My Faroese colleague Pál Weihe and I started our collaboration on mercury in 1985 and began recruiting pregnant women for the study the following year. But it was not until 1997 that we published our first article on brain drain caused by mercury. Twelve years later! Some of the delay happened in the final stages of communicating the results. The first three scientific journals rejected our manuscript based on concerns raised by one or more anonymous colleagues. Before our findings were tentatively approved for publication in the fourth journal, the text had to go through five rounds of comments, responses, and revisions, with additional caveats, to satisfy the editor and the reviewers.

Our experience illustrates well the triple whammy. There is insufficient evidence on mercury and other brain-draining chemicals. Even the most intensive research involves uncertainties. And the conclusions, when finally published, are expressed in the midst of scientific caveats and disclaimers. All told, such research is an easy target for overzealous critique and undue skepticism. Among questions that can be raised, why blame a single chemical exposure when so many factors could have influenced brain development during childhood? Unfortunately, all of these problems also help scare young researchers away from the field.

Dealing with Conflicts and Inertia

Federal agencies and biomedical journals require that researchers and authors disclose possible conflicts of interest. But at least in the past, this duty has been disregarded more often than can be attributed to tight work schedules or faulty memory. Iowa senator Charles Grassley in 2008 investigated whether scientists were fully and accurately reporting their external incomes to their academic institutions. Among egregious cases, a child psychiatrist, who promoted the use of antipsychotic medicines in children, had earned at least $1.6 million over a period of seven years consulting for drug makers. As part of the health care reform bill enacted in 2010, drug manufacturers now have to report payments to physicians annually. Again, the most dramatic examples come from the pharmaceutical industry, but similar problems have occurred in other fields of research.

Conflicts of interest can also affect government institutions. As epidemiological studies began to suggest that Parkinson's disease was associated with a history of pesticide exposure,[69] a company that conducts research for the pesticide industry came on the scene. The consulting company, Exponent, Inc., donated $60,000 to the CDC for the purpose of carrying out studies that might put the apparent association in doubt. Thus, the company used a loophole in the regulations to recruit government resources for its own purpose.[70]

In a forceful book, *Bending Science; How Special Interests Corrupt Public Health Research*, two legal scholars from the University of Texas argue that scientists are themselves partially responsible for the collision with what has become known as science-based advocacy funded by vested interests.[71] Professors Thomas McGarity and Wendy Wagner blame the independent scientists for not involving themselves in the policy debates on environmental health issues. We already know that advocates representing special interests hail the right to pick the "sound science" that they want policy decisions to be based on. These maneuvers are not being appropriately challenged, unless academic researchers take part in the discussions. So academic researchers must shed some of the hedging and join the world outside the ivory tower.

Conflicts of interest will always occur, no matter the guidelines from WHO and science journals, and financial power will benefit particular interests. Billion-dollar industries with stakes in the brain-drain concerns are as diverse as tuna canners, coal-based power producers, chemical commodities firms, and drug producers. An editor of a major medical journal once said: "Dependence on company money corrupts and cows university researchers" and, to thwart publication of unfavorable research reports, "pharmaceutical firms have threatened researchers, interrupted trials, and blocked publications." Also, to create an impression of a robust body of research, "firms have promoted multiple publication of slender research results, sometimes shuffling the sequence of the researchers' names to disguise the repetition."[72] Academics have a choice either to develop their energies in trade and industry or to stand by their obligation to science. "We do not accept that the two possibilities can be combined," *The Lancet's* editors concluded.[73] While I would agree, an additional problem is that it is often unclear (or secret) who made which choice.

We should not ignore the indirect effects of vested interests. For example, we pay much less attention to the adverse effects of new technology than to its advantages (and then again, the conclusions may be tainted). For example, huge amounts are invested in microelectronics, nanotechnology, communication by electromagnetic fields, genetically modified organisms, and many other promising technologies. However, I very rarely see any reports on possible risks to human health and almost never any on risks to brain development. I would love to believe that there are no risks, but have we looked?

The focus of research at academic institutions can be influenced by possibilities for obtaining external funding. Thus, comparatively little research is devoted to the risks associated with pesticide exposures and likewise the advantages of alternative crop protection methods.[74] Ideally, science should not be defined by what is convenient and advantageous in the short term. However, studies on human brain toxicity take way too long for academic achievement purposes, not to mention time-limited grant support. It is understandable that researchers look for more rewarding research topics that will result in a steady stream of publications likely to be admired, rather than criticized, especially when the ire of powerful interests can be provoked.

As a consequence, academics are tempted to focus on narrowly defined issues for the sake of efficiency. However, this preference can lead to reductionism and to lack of novelty. The safe approach of replication and verification may conveniently result in scientific publications but could lead to inertia. So the same stone is polished more and more. Unfortunately, it takes vision and courage to choose untried research topics and research methods, and there may not be funding available for such risky projects. But how bad is this situation? Are we only studying the same old problems?

I decided to check the databases that list publications in scientific journals. The sad result is that the majority of papers in environmental health journals deal with a limited, rather stable list of pollutants out of the thousands of potential chemical hazards. For example, the National Library of Medicine lists over 3,500 publications in scientific journals on the epidemiology of lead exposure and lead poisoning. To some extent, lead has served as a paradigm in research, but would science and society not have been better served if some of the resources had been used on other topics?

I therefore checked the articles published in the 78 major toxicology and environmental health journals between 2000 and 2009. Unfortunately, lead, mercury, arsenic, and PCBs were among the most popular substances, with thousands of articles.[75] On lead alone, four articles were published each working day (not allowing for vacations). Other pollutants, such as many commonly used pesticides, perfluorooctane sulfonate (a.k.a. C8), flame retardants, and similar substances are barely studied at all, at least according to the published articles. The extent of replication—and the associated conflict avoidance—has clearly gone astray. This is not the sole fault of the academic community, but part of the reason for the continued focus on well-known toxicants is that we are still arguing the risks to public health from these problem chemicals. Although some extent of replication can perhaps be justified, it should not come at the expense of attention to the scores of other potentially serious health hazards that are in critical need of scrutiny.

Adding to this problem, research results can be difficult to access. A bibliometric analysis of European environmental health research during 1995–2005 counted a total of 6,329 articles. But these articles had been published in an amazing total of 711 different scientific journals.[76] Thus, to follow all the research in the field, we would need access to a very large number of scientific sources, not to mention information published as institutional reports, proceedings, and the like. Although digital technology has immensely facilitated literature reviews, only about 10% to 15% of scientific journals are freely accessible on the Internet worldwide. In this regard, much of the published research does not serve the need of the public to have the results available.

Uncertainties will necessarily spur discussions, and controversies may ensue. When scientists disagree for one reason or another, the disagreements may be fortified by interference from vested interests. Weaknesses of the evidence may then be unfairly highlighted as described by prominent biostatistician Irwin Bross: "In recent years research on major public health problems has tended to run into storms of controversy that have delayed or prevented effective action on the health hazard." Although it would apply to brain-drain discussions today, Bross offered these views in regard to thalidomide in an article published almost 50 years ago.[77]

We need to heed the advice, published around the same time by British statistician, Sir Austin Bradford Hill: "All scientific work is incomplete.... All scientific work is liable to be upset or modified by advancing knowledge. That does not confer upon us the freedom to ignore the knowledge we already have, or to postpone the action that it appears to demand at the given time."[78] Given the risks that we have now realized in regard to the next generation's brains, the triple-whammy of uncertainties, underestimations, and soft science language, combined with the uneven battle with vested interests, the time has come to consider some prudent and responsible actions.

CHAPTER 10

Brainy Choices

HOW TO SECURE OPTIMAL BRAIN DEVELOPMENT
FOR THE NEXT GENERATION

The previous nine chapters can be summarized as follows: "We are conducting a massive clinical toxicological trial, and our children and our children's children are the experimental subjects." This wording was used almost 20 years ago by medical professors Herb Needleman and Phil Landrigan, both known for their pioneering research on lead toxicity.[1] I think their conclusion is quite fitting, and it is even more appropriate today, as we are discovering more and more testimonies of this mega-experiment with human brains. We are playing games with the brain power of the next generation, and we do not really know what we are doing.

Our exposure to environmental chemicals amounts to what philosophy professor Carl Cranor refers to as a "chemical invasion."[2] Similar wording was chosen by French journalist Stéphane Horel, who called her book on environmental toxicants *La grande invasion*.[3] The trouble is that we do not know for sure to what extent this invasion is a health hazard. In regard to pharmaceuticals, Cranor notes that we have the right to information on their approved and safe uses, as well as the risk of side effects and their characteristics. When new drugs are being tested, the doctors must ask each patient for a written, informed consent. Treatment can be initiated only when the patient has given his or her approval. Even if your internist prescribes a drug, you still have the choice not to fill the prescription or not to take the tablets. Although we should probably follow the doctor's advice, we still have much autonomy. Not so, in regard to environmental chemicals.

Numerous industrial chemicals enter our bodies because we happen to inhale, eat, drink, or touch these compounds. We are usually unaware of it—the chemicals do not taste or smell or itch in the concentrations that we usually encounter. Exposures to some environmental chemicals have decreased, thanks to national and international regulations and increased vigilance. However, children and pregnant women today are continually in contact with a myriad of new synthetic chemicals,

140

few of which are regulated in any way. Since World War II, at least 70,000 chemical compounds have entered into mass production and been dispersed into consumer products and the environment.

The right to choose is implicit in our moral and legal culture, and this choice should be made based on access to proper information. Cranor refers to the philosopher John Stuart Mill and his book *On Liberty*, published 150 years ago. According to Mill, we should have the freedom to act according to our own wishes, as long as we do not inflict harm on anybody else. The chemical invasion conflicts with this principle. Our body—including the brain—constitutes a possession that we (and our children) share with nobody else. But its integrity is violated by chemical invasion without any informed consent.

Unfortunately, freedom is sometimes interpreted in terms of individualism and libertarianism (in the conservative American meaning of the word) to argue against big government and advocate for as little regulation as possible, while leaving any appropriate control to the market forces. Mill would counter that we should not risk inflicting harm on others. Professor Gerald Markowitz from the City University of New York recently expressed this more bluntly: "It's not in anybody's self-interest to be poisoned by the air we breathe. That's not freedom. That's insanity."[4]

In regard to this pollution, the brain is at particular risk (although chemical brain drain may be hard to detect in the presence of insanity). In contrast to other vital organs, a healthy brain is not just a matter of absence of a neurological diagnosis. Optimal brain function depends on the integrity of the complete organ. Thus, every brain cell needs the best possible conditions for fulfilling its functions. However, brain development involves multiple complex stages that must be completed sequentially, and these processes are uniquely vulnerable to adverse chemical interference (see chapter 1). Any damage is likely to lead to permanent change, even if some compensation occurs. As I stress in this book, you only get one chance to develop a brain. The developing brain therefore needs more protection than any other organ or function. Thus, chemical brain drainers are putting modern society to a serious test, which we are failing. The stakes are exceedingly high, most likely much higher than documented by science so far.

Protecting brains has ethical implications. This dimension first attracted attention in the early 1970s when pediatricians raised the question of whether to withhold treatment of seriously brain-damaged newborns.[5] Although these infants might not survive for very long, a key concern was that the prognosis of a meaningful life was virtually hopeless. So brain function was tied to quality of life. At a time when the anti-abortion movement was just gaining speed, the sanctity of life—and brain function—became hotly debated. Unfortunately, the debate soon came to focus narrowly on the US Supreme Court decision on the legality of abortion, and the obligation to preserve brain function was left out. But would it not be reasonable to couple the right to life with a right to optimal brain development? Whether or not agreeing with the *Roe v. Wade* decision, a woman who chooses to complete her pregnancy should be entitled to having a child whose brain functions are not damaged by environmental chemicals.

Perhaps the time has come for us to revive the discussion addressing the ethical imperative of preserving brain functions in the next generation. We want our children and grandchildren to develop optimally functioning brains and to protect them against any brain drain. To achieve this, we will need information on exposure levels and toxicity, and transparent and fair procedures to ensure that the risks are minimized. So our strategy against brain drain will need to include several elements.

Access to Information

When we conduct studies of children exposed to environmental chemicals, we share our research findings with the families. So the Faroese know very well that they are exposed to mercury and other chemicals from ocean pollution and the Ecuadoreans know about the pesticides from the flower production. But people in general do not have a clue if they—or their children—are exposed to toxic chemicals in their neighborhood, in food, in drinking water.

The availability of information on chemical pollution is required by an international agreement called the Aarhus convention. The formal name is impressive: The UNECE Convention on Access to Information, Public Participation in Decision-making and Access to Justice in Environmental Matters. It grants the public rights to information on environmental pollution and imposes obligations on public authorities regarding access to information and public participation, and access to justice, at least in Europe where the convention was developed.

In the United States, the Environmental Protection Agency (EPA) maintains the Toxics Release Inventory (TRI), a publicly available database on important environmental pollutants. The US government proposed in 2005 to reduce the required reporting frequency from every year to every other year, but this change was withdrawn due to intense criticism. Likewise, an attempt was made in 2008 by the Department of Agriculture to eliminate its recording of pesticide use as part of the Agricultural Chemical Use Reports. Although sometimes inaccurate and incomplete, release data for chemicals constitute an important source of information.

Still, the main problem is that we have no information as to how much pollution has entered our bodies. John Stuart Mill would probably agree that we should have access to such data, but presently no government or convention formally provides us with that right. I only know of one example of access to analyses of one's own pollutant exposure. Since 1985, breast-feeding mothers in the German state Schleswig-Holstein have had the right to get their milk analyzed for persistent contaminants, and thousands of women have taken advantage of this possibility.[6] Based on the pollutant levels in the milk, the mothers could then obtain specific advice concerning breast-feeding. The analysis is still much in demand although concentrations have declined and German doctors recommend no limitation of breast-feeding. However, the results provide useful information on the exposures of a vulnerable population.

Thus, in general, what we know about global chemical burdens comes from scattered individual reports and from population-based studies, such as the National Health and Nutrition Examination Survey (NHANES) in the United States. Blood and urine samples collected from a cross-section of the population have been analyzed for over 200 chemical pollutants at the Centers for Disease Control in Atlanta. The results reflect the extent of exposures in the country as a whole and how they relate to age, sex, residence, and other factors. Cord blood is not included, but most of these substances are capable of passing from the mother to her child (see chapter 2). So analyses of the mother's blood also reflect exposures of the next generation. When compared with the substances known to be neurotoxic to humans (see Appendix), about half of the chemicals currently monitored in NHANES constitutes a neurotoxic risk. On the other hand, a substantial number of the highly likely brain drainers listed in the Appendix are not monitored at all in America, nor are they monitored elsewhere.

Outside the United States, much less information is available on the degree of exposure to possible brain drainers. The European Union decided in 2003 to include biomonitoring in its strategy for health and environment, but progress has been slow, as the European Commission counted on member states to finance this effort while they in turn were waiting for the Commission to act. A pilot study, jointly financed by both parties, finally got started in 2011 to collect information on a handful of substances only. I find that a disgrace.

Changing Toxicity Paradigm

Even if we can assemble better exposure information, that is not enough to establish priorities for action. We need to know the possible consequences of different levels of chemical invasion. The evidence on lead, mercury, and other well-established brain drainers provides plenty of justification that we must protect the next generation's brains against these individual substances. But the perspective goes far beyond a piecemeal focus on single chemicals. We therefore need to resolve the triple whammy of incomplete scientific documentation, the traditional tendency toward false negatives in research, and the softly worded conclusions that researchers favor. Science provides at least two general insights that should inspire a comprehensive strategy to prevent chemical brain drain.

One new discovery is that many diseases and functional deficits seem to have a developmental origin. We now understand that our bodies, organs, and cells are programmed during early development to establish organ functions, but also in regard to disease risks. This new insight has emerged as a true paradigm shift in toxicology, nutrition science, and public health.[7] It supersedes the past belief that development was generally a homogeneous and invariant sequence of genetically coded developmental stages, or in other words, a foregone conclusion. In regard to brain development, we realize now that negative effects on developmental processes can have impacts on an individual's entire life span. Toxicity caused by lead, mercury, and other substances during early life stages is therefore not a unique consequence of these toxicants, but rather a characteristic of a general vulnerability associated with early development (see chapter 1). This knowledge ought to have tremendous impact in general on prevention and pollution abatement.

A second and related component of the paradigm change is that even slight changes in programming can cause important functional deficits, especially in the brain. We can easily survive without the full metabolizing capacity of the liver, and we can safely donate one of our two kidneys for transplantation. But optimal development and complete integrity of the brain are necessary for us to enjoy our brain functions to the full extent. And because brain development is such a complex process, it is also highly vulnerable to adverse influences.

These two insights are only slowly being applied, even within the scientific community. When the European Brain Council in 2006 proposed a new neurology research focus, it highlighted brain functions, disease pathogenesis, and treatment.[8] The Council recognized the importance of normal brain function but decided that better understanding and treatment of brain disease was the priority. While diagnoses, such as Parkinson's disease, are extremely costly to society, we now believe that brain toxicity during early life may be part of the causation.[9] We therefore need to go beyond the mere prevention of individual diseases and aim at securing healthy and optimal brain function. This will require new approaches to address risks to human brains and new research strategies to identify the culprits through systematic testing.

Addressing Brain Drain

Despite our current arsenal of prenatal testing techniques, pregnancy and early human development remain complex processes with uncertain outcomes. When these end in disappointment for the parents and their physicians, they invariably ask what went wrong and what should they have done or not done. These questions may be conducive to further research and may lead to important discoveries (although they are unlikely to console the parents). This is what Australian surgeon Gregg did when he asked questions about the unexplained cataracts in infants, and French pediatrician Lemoine, who saw the disrupted lives of similar-looking children in Brittany. However, physicians today are trained to diagnose and treat individual patients and therefore rarely even think of prevention.

Gregg's discovery eventually bore fruit and spurred action within the public health agencies. In 1969 the first official recommendation was published on the use of German measles (rubella) vaccine. After that, the incidence of reported rubella cases declined dramatically. The licensure and widespread distribution of the attenuated rubella virus vaccines effectively prevented future epidemics of the disease. Since the late 1980s, children in most Western countries have received rubella vaccine during infancy to stop its transmission. In 2004, the CDC declared the disease eliminated in America.

Likewise, following the general acceptance that alcohol can harm not only one's own health but also the next generation's, many countries have chosen to run public education campaigns and to require warning messages on alcoholic beverages. Medical historian Janet Golden has studied the framing of the fetal alcohol syndrome over time. After the initial sympathy with women struggling with substance and alcohol abuse, attention shifted to the unethical behavior of mothers who drink during pregnancy thereby putting their babies at risk. As a consequence, a movement surfaced to punish drinking mothers in order to protect potential future citizens. Despite having a legal right to drink as an adult, in the United States, women can be arrested and charged with child endangerment for drinking while pregnant.[10]

So, to date, we have been able to launch prevention campaigns to protect against agents such as German measles and alcohol that may harm the developing brain. In contrast, the experience with well-documented industrial brain drainers has been much less laudable. Leaded gasoline for automobiles was finally banned in the United States in 1995, a total of 23 years after the phase-out began, and 70 years after lead additives were first introduced. In regard to house paints, the League of Nations already in 1922 had agreed that the use of lead white for interior paint should be banned. A complete ban on lead-containing paints was not enacted in the United States until 1977. Both lead paints and long-banned water pipes made of lead remain in millions of American households and also in many other countries.

Says public health professor Bruce Lanphear, "Lead's impact on public health and social functioning is such that I think in a hundred years we will look back at the 20th century and recognize that lead, tobacco, and air pollution were the choleras and typhoids of this century."[11] I agree, although I would add other brain drainers in addition to lead. In considering how the mistakes were made, Lanphear also noted that "the reasons for the delays in regulation are more complex than the nefarious actions of a few profiteers.... In our quest for scientific certainty, we inadvertently delayed the promulgation of regulations at the expense of public health."[12]

Alas, a key problem is that we know too little about the toxicity risks to the brain—the triple whammy of obstacles that I discussed in chapter 9. The history of the known neurotoxicants indicates that the very first discoveries of clinical toxicity often occurred under occupational exposure circumstances, and that they were later followed by case reports that involved children or pregnant women. As better and larger studies were carried out, pollutant-associated brain toxicity was documented in children exposed to a variety of substances during early development. Subsequently, more subtle deficits were discovered at lower and more widespread exposure levels, thereby suggesting the existence of a silent epidemic of developmental neurotoxicity or, rather, a global brain drain.[13] My own 25-year effort to understand brain drains due to mercury is a potent illustration of the slow pace of scientific insight in this field.

Because the research needed can take decades to accomplish, in the meantime, literally millions of children may harmed by continued exposure to brain drainers. So there is a serious cost of waiting for enough scientific evidence to convince skeptical colleagues, regulators, and industry representatives that prevention is needed. This is exactly the difficult conundrum that we want to solve—that the prevention of brain drain needs to begin with demonstrating the existence of the very brain drain we wanted to prevent.

Regulatory agencies and industry often claim that no convincing evidence of chemical brain drain is available. I have already given several examples of this skepticism, but here is a more recent one. When our review on fluoride neurotoxicity was published in 2012, worried fluoridation proponents and regulators rapidly responded that the toxic effects occurred only at excessive exposures, that the average effect was too small to be of any health significance, that any such effect, if real, would have been discovered in the United States or the European Union long ago (although nobody has looked), that animal studies show no effects even at huge doses, and that any effect in the studies reviewed was likely due to lead and arsenic, not fluoride. When such a misleading fusillade is aimed at the authors of a careful meta-analysis of 27 different studies, what would it take to convince critics like that?

The most reliable documentation required in regard to drugs includes testing in volunteers according to strict guidelines for clinical trials. In theory, I could design a similar study, where healthy experimental subjects would receive a small capsule every day. Half of them would get capsules with corn oil, the other half would get an environmental chemical dissolved in the corn oil. This imaginary experiment would test a substance suspected of causing toxicity to the brain. Even though the doses to be used would be the same as those we may already be exposed to every day, this human subjects study would still need the ethical approval of my university's institutional review board (IRB). These committees operate under national legislation, international conventions, and basic principles of human rights. I am convinced that I would never get their approval for this experiment, should I ever try to obtain it. Had I proposed to carry out the study using pregnant women and infants, I think the IRB would call my dean and tell him that this insane faculty member needs psychiatric supervision (or perhaps a straitjacket). Nobody in his right mind would even think of carrying out an experiment like that.

But as Needleman and Landrigan noted, instead we are conducting an "experiment" with the next generation's brains, although without any research design, certainly without IRB approval, and without proper documentation. As another paradox, citizens are not offered the option of approval or disapproval when exposed to environmental toxicants as part of their daily lives. So the consequences of the chemical invasion cannot be studied by our best research designs, while, nonetheless, the exposures continue without being monitored. We must face this embarrassing conundrum.

Neurotoxicity Testing

We need to generate reliable test data on neurotoxicity using laboratory models that are efficient and reliable. Such methods are indeed available. However, despite the urge to protect brain development and our growing understanding of toxic risks to the brain, only a fraction of the chemicals present in the environment have ever been properly tested. In the early 1980s, the US National Research Council completed a study on toxicity testing and found that 78% of the industrial chemicals most commonly produced had not even been minimally tested for toxicity. The majority had been in use for a long time and had therefore been allowed to escape modern requirements for safety testing (they were "grandfathered" in, as I shall discuss shortly). While some information on neurotoxicity was available for one in three chemicals, very few had been studied in regard to their effects on the developing brain.

These findings were later confirmed by a more detailed study by the US Environmental Protection Agency. As a result, a voluntary testing program was initiated in collaboration with the chemical industry to develop minimum toxicity data for the 3,000 high-production volume chemicals. Even so, this effort has been derailed due to delayed, incomplete, and poor-quality data submissions by the chemical producers.[14] And it involves virtually no testing for developmental neurotoxicity.

In contrast to the United States, the REACH legislation in the European Union requires extensive testing of existing chemicals. Still, this effort is only slowly materializing, and the European Chemicals Agency reports that gaps in safety data remain, mostly because industry has been slow to provide the necessary information, and little has been done to mend the problem.[15] Further, the agency has little capacity to evaluate the quality of the data submitted. Thus, even though the EU legislation is considered the most stringent, only high production volume chemicals have to be tested in some toxicological detail, which, unfortunately, does not include testing for developmental neurotoxicity.

Given the need to protect the development of optimal brain function, we clearly are far from doing enough. Most of the tests conducted to provide the required safety data assess only acute effects, and there is no general obligation to conduct any testing for effects on brain development.[16] Such tests are only triggered by specific criteria that must be met in other tests, such as a decrease in brain weight in newborn pups. Although some toxicologists and industry representatives will insist that brain drainers will be detected by these simple procedures, the validity of these triggers has not been documented.

A related problem is the actual criterion that will trigger action against toxic hazards. Much discussion has focused on how to differentiate between beneficial or "adaptive" responses and true adverse effects. When an industrial chemical perturbs a biochemical pathway, cellular compensation or adaptation is likely to occur, and the change may be balanced out without any adverse effect on overall health. However, this separation can become difficult or inappropriate in regard to brain toxicity, as our aim should be to maintain optimal function. In the past, regulators have accepted a loss of brain weight below 5% as not being a definite adverse effect. Yes, losing 5% of the brain weight! However, as microcephaly—decreased brain size—is one of the most extreme outcomes of brain toxicity in humans, a 5% limit seems unreasonably high. We should worry about much less serious types of brain drain. Thus, the definition of "normal" brain function must agree with the deepening of our understanding of the brain, and we must adjust the triggers used to indicate toxicity in experimental tests. Rather than avoiding abnormal function and deranged morphology, we should emphasize the need to preserve a fully functioning brain and avoid deficits, even if they seem subtle.

An OECD-approved method for developmental neurotoxicity testing in rodents was adopted in 2007, but the expense involved and the large number of animals required means that funding for such studies will be volunteered only rarely. All told, only a couple of hundred chemicals have been tested this way.[17] Hence, the vast majority of environmental chemicals have not been examined for their possible adverse effects on brain development. Much toxicity information is available on several pesticides, and data on developmental neurotoxicity in several cases resulted in a lower exposure limit than routine data would have indicated.[18]

When the Toxic Substances Control Act (TSCA) was passed by the US Congress in 1976, it exempted from regulation about 62,000 chemicals that were in commercial use at the time—they were "grandfathered" in. Thus, about 92% of the most commonly produced chemicals today are allowed for continued use without further review or testing. New chemicals developed since the law's passage can still escape from being tested for safety. Companies are just asked to volunteer information on the health effects of their compounds, and the government can decide whether additional tests are necessary. If a manufacturer possesses data showing that a chemical harms health or the environment, it is required to turn over the findings to the EPA. However, this provision can create a disincentive for manufacturers to test their chemicals, which would seem to be contrary to the very purpose of the TSCA legislation.

These legal requirements are weak, and we have no way of knowing whether the reporting by industry to the EPA is complete. A major chemical company that was using a perfluorinated compound called C8 did not disclose for decades that releases and wastes from the production facilities were contaminating waterways and the environment. The polluter—the world's third largest chemical company—eventually reached a settlement with the EPA in the largest civil administrative penalty in history for withholding information from the agency ($16.5 million). Still, the company admitted no liability for its conduct.[19]

In total, the various environmental statutes in the United States regulate just over 1,000 of the chemicals currently produced. TSCA would allow EPA to tighten the regulations, but the legal standards for demonstrating unreasonable risk are very high. Thus, since 1976, the EPA has issued rules banning or limiting the production of only five existing chemicals or groups of chemicals.[20]

Since TSCA places the burden of collecting safety data on the EPA rather than on manufacturers, the law is clearly insufficient, especially when compared to the stricter chemical legislation in the European Union. For cosmetics, the situation is not much better, as proprietary secrets abound. Among more than 10,000 ingredients in these products, the US Food and Drug Administration (FDA) has banned or restricted only nine during the seven decades that the agency has been responsible for cosmetics safety. The FDA is also responsible for regulation of food containers and packaging materials, which may release chemicals into the food, but again, in this regard, the FDA has hesitated to regulate substances that are suspected of being toxic.

EU chemical producers are allowed to provide the required safety data from sources of their own choosing. Even so, the information is not provided as stipulated. One option would be to take the discretionary testing out of the hands of private companies and place it in governmental agencies or nonprofit, nongovernmental agencies that do not have vested interests in the research outcomes. This model would require the agencies to collect fees from the chemical producers.[21] In regard to drugs, the United States has recently taken the important step of creating the National Center for Advancing Translational Sciences, with the aim of speeding up development of new medicines. Why not establish a central laboratory to examine the risk of adverse effects of chemicals?

From Test to Decision

Even if scientific documentation from laboratory research is available, the results are not always taken seriously. The first confirmation in a rat model that methylmercury was particularly toxic to the developing brain was published in *Science* in 1972. Joan Spyker Cranmer and her colleagues showed that exposure of rats to methylmercury during development—and not in rats exposed only as adults—resulted in brain damage that emerged as the animal matured.[22] At a court hearing that investigated whether the EPA should regulate methylmercury, the researchers described their results and showed pictures of abnormalities in the various behaviors affected, including urination and defecation. This prompted the judge, who had listened to Dr. Cranmer's testimony, to ask: "Do you mean to say that we must regulate mercury because of pee-pee and poo-poo?"[23] Indeed.

However, in-depth experimental testing for brain drain in laboratory animals would require millions of rats and mice. Due to the sheer cost and time requirement, it would be an impractical way to evaluate the safety of thousands of chemicals. Other approaches must be considered. At the EPA, Johns Hopkins University, the EU Joint Research Centre in Ispra, Italy, and elsewhere, cell-based in vitro testing methods are being developed and validated to avoid using live animals. Primary cell cultures based on neuronal stem cells or progenitor cells can be used to assess changes in sensitive parameters, such as cell proliferation, migration, and differentiation, which may be affected by suspected brain toxicants. A main problem is that the cell lines and cultures cannot fully replicate the metabolism that occurs in intact animal (or human being), and that there is no blood-brain barrier. Nonetheless, a promising series of tests is currently being developed as a screening battery.[24] If we were to adopt this screening approach, we could avoid using live animals, and the expenses would be dramatically reduced.

In its report on *Toxicity Testing in the 21st Century*, the US National Research Council called for the development of new approaches to human health-risk assessment that would rely, in part, on computer-based models rather than animal testing and epidemiology.[25] Although these conclusions are both timely and visionary, progress has been slow, as elaborate validation of the models may be necessary before new approaches to predictive toxicology can be adopted. Computational methods have developed further, and chemical data bases have expanded. An advanced computational systems biology approach now seems to be realistic in assessing the potential hazards associated with environmental chemicals. The EPA recently created a National Center for Computational Toxicology to deal with high-throughput screening data, whether *in silico* (computer models) or in vitro (cell cultures). So there are promises for even more expedient testing. These developments can pave the way for decision making on tests that can realistically be extended to the thousands of unstudied potential brain drainers that we are currently assuming to be entirely safe.

Can we learn from the experience obtained from other prevention campaigns, such as cancer? The "war on cancer" was introduced by President Richard Nixon in his State of the Union address in 1971. By that time, geographic studies on cancer incidences had convincingly shown that cancer is not an inherited disease but is primarily due to external or environmental factors. An international effort had therefore been initiated and in 1965 resulted in the formation of the International Agency for Research on Cancer (IARC), under the auspices of the World Health Organization.[26] The IARC conducts and coordinates important cancer research (much of it in collaboration with the National Cancer Institute in the United States), and it evaluates the possible cancer risks associated with chemicals and other environmental exposures. These evaluations are used internationally in decisions on regulating hazardous substances.

We need a similar initiative in regard to brain drainers. It would be much easier to establish than the IARC, which had to rely on an influential Frenchman, who knew then-President Charles de Gaulle and suggested to him that a new cancer research organization should be funded, and that only half a percent of the military budget would be needed. Today, most of the necessary facilities and capabilities already exist to expand and carry out much-needed research on brain toxicity, but the efforts are scattered and only to a limited extent address the most critical concerns. International funding, inspiration, and coordination could accomplish much more and in a shorter time than has been needed for cancer research. This initiative should also include a clearinghouse for collection of neurotoxicity documentation to be applied for evaluation of risks to brain development. It would hardly need to cost as much as half a percent of today's military budget.

Interpreting Uncertainty

Even if we can collate better test data, we must get accustomed to uncertainty as the normal condition. We will not fight chemical brain drain if we keep on asking for a time-out (for example, by appointing an expert committee or funding a project) to await better information. If anything, a delay will just result in greater brain drain. We have to explore the extent to which the existing documentation supports a purported safety, not just the mere presence of a risk. In other words, we need to ask what could possibly be known, given the evidence available. We already know that small and noisy studies with imprecise exposure estimates and insensitive and nonspecific outcome measures are unlikely to detect any but the most serious risks. So the triple whammy should no longer lure us into waiting for final "proof." Thus, the fact that a null hypothesis of no effect could not be rejected with confidence in a particular study may be completely irrelevant.

As part of this evaluation, worst-case scenarios need to be scrutinized at least as carefully as the hypothesis of no effect that we have traditionally compared our results with. Thus, we should begin to ask: How serious could the effect be, and how large an effect can be reasonably ruled out? This will allow us to make a prudent choice where we take into regard both what is known and what is not known.

Because the evidence on brain drain is not definite, all conclusions must be accepted as provisional and temporary. As we may have to act on incomplete evidence, any actions may need adjustment later on, as more definite documentation emerges. In some cases, it may turn out that we overreacted, and the restrictions can be then relaxed. But is this a large risk?

Probably not. So far, we have almost always underestimated the risks from brain drainers. For example, exposure limits have generally decreased with time. Just think of the acceptable blood-lead concentration in children, which has by now decreased 12-fold (see chapter 4). It is big news when, on very rare occasions, the opposite happens (there are a couple of examples from occupational exposure limits). Although new insight is of course beneficial when translated into more protective regulations, the problem is that the higher exposures that were accepted in the past have caused harm for many years, perhaps affecting large groups of people. They paid a price for our unwillingness to interpret uncertainty in terms of providing safety. Just think of the sad consequences of the optimistic approval of high lead exposures as being safe. We can do better than that.

The precautionary principle emerged in Europe as a procedure in environmental and public health to facilitate decision making in the presence of uncertainty. It allows and encourages important decisions that may prevent serious consequences, even if there is no certainty yet. The precautionary principle was included in the first convention on the protection of the North Sea in 1984, later to be followed by many other international agreements, including the EU treaty. Accordingly, appropriate action must be taken in response to limited but plausible and credible evidence of likely and substantial harm. The principle aims at avoiding possible future harm associated with suspected, though not (yet) conclusive, environmental risks, while at the same time shifting the burden of proof from demonstrating the presence of risk toward demonstrating the absence of risk.[27]

The precautionary principle has been ridiculed by the American Chemistry Council (ACC; formerly known as Chemical Manufacturers' Association) in statements like this: "It's no secret that [ACC doesn't] think the precautionary principle is either precautionary or a principle. It's a blunt instrument being used by a number of organizations to essentially ban chemicals."[28] This critique is unfair, as the idea applies equally to alternative options that must be evaluated to minimize the costs of surprises and maximize the benefits of innovation. We should not institute indiscriminate bans on chemicals; neither should we expose the next generation to brain drainers while we wait for significant damage to be documented.

Uncertainty is by no means new to us. We deal with it in our everyday lives and in our functions as physicians and other professionals. We worry about security and the risk of terrorism, and, in turn, use intelligence to obtain better information, and next consider preemptive strikes and other interventions. But we do not sit back and wait for fate or WikiLeaks to spontaneously produce the insight that resolves all the uncertainty. In contrast, insurance agencies calculate the risks, however uncertain, and then diversify and adjust accordingly the premiums that customers must pay. Businessmen or investment bankers optimize gains considering the risks and limit the exposures and cut losses in case a risk turns out to be greater than anticipated.

Even in medicine, in heeding the Hippocratic oath, we operate on children with pain in the lower right side of the belly, even if we are not certain that the appendix is really infected. It is just too risky to ignore the subtle signs that a pathological process may be developing. If there is a risk of a large-scale influenza epidemic, we try to isolate the contagious patients and carriers, and we plan for mass vaccinations. Such large-scale efforts can be extremely expensive and may well be in vain, as they clearly were with the swine flu outbreak in 1976. Nobody could have predicted that, however, and it seemed better to be safe than sorry, especially with a bug that could potentially kill large numbers of people and cause enormous losses to society. That is also the way that we eventually dealt with German measles (see chapter 2).

The concept of precaution is certainly not new. At a conference held as early as 1925 about the possible risks of adding lead compounds to gasoline, Yale professor Yandell Henderson warned that "conditions will grow worse so gradually, and the development of lead poisoning will come on so insidiously ... that leaded petrol will be in nearly universal use before the public and the government awakens to the situation." Henderson therefore recommended: "this substance, this new industrial hazard, should not be put into general use, or its use should not be extended until we have adequate and full information assuring us that we are not introducing another health hazard into our daily lives." So, because of the insidious, though uncertain, risk to public health, Henderson suggested a reversed burden of proof.[29] That was 60 years before the precautionary principle was first enacted in the European Union. However, as recently as 2012, when Senator James Inhofe, ranking member of the Senate Appropriations Committee, was asked about the need to reduce lead exposures, he stated that efforts "must be based on a scientific approach and not on precautionary paranoia."[30] It seems that it is the word "precaution" that somehow triggers paranoia, but I am puzzled why that is. We use precaution when dealing with threats of terrorism and making business decisions—why not use the same strategy when it comes to chemicals that endanger the brains of our children and grandchildren?

In connection with the unsuccessful Copenhagen climate conference in 2009, *New York Times* columnist Thomas Friedman referred to "the one percent doctrine" recommended by then-Vice President Dick Cheney in regard to a Pakistani scientist potentially offering nuclear weapons expertise to Al Qaeda terrorists.[31] "If there's a 1% chance that Pakistani scientists are helping Al Qaeda build or develop a nuclear weapon, we have to treat it as a certainty in terms of our response," Cheney said. Noting that this stance is in accordance with the precautionary principle, Friedman recommended taking climate change seriously: Going Cheney on climate.[32] I would recommend going Cheney on chemical brain drainers.

The Immediate Agenda

Even in regard to the poisons that we already know well, there is a lot to be done to stop the brain drain. The greatest risk of lead exposure in the United States today comes from housing built before 1978, the year the federal government banned leaded paint entirely. Up until 1950, paint used in houses contained as much as 50% lead by weight. Even though it may have been put on 60 or more years ago and painted over many times since, old paint remains a hazard: If the newer paint chips off, the old paint can, too. Lead-paint dust and chips appeal to children because they taste sweet, and even a dime-size chip of pre-1950 lead paint contains enough lead to poison a 2-year-old. There are still 25 million American homes that contain lead paint. Further, water pipes made of lead present in several million American households (and countless others abroad) may release the toxic metal into drinking water. In addition, water contaminated with high arsenic concentration is affecting millions of people. Mercury, PCBs, pesticides, solvents—the problems are obvious, but we have lagged behind in regard to action.

More than 300 pollutants are detectable in community tap water, more than half of which are not subject to US health or safety regulations.[33] These toxicants can therefore legally be present in any amount, and no monitoring is required. The US government has not set a single new drinking water standard since 2001. In contrast, the EU Drinking Water Directive has a general limit value for all pesticides of 0.1 microgram per liter, which at the time of authorization was thought to be the lowest level detectable. Also, the sum of all pesticides must be below 0.5. Although these limits are not based on any specific risk assessment, they help ensure that new substances will not enter the water supplies. On the other hand, this rule is not used very often, as few pesticides are included in the routine monitoring of drinking water. We can do better than that.

After a report from the US National Research Council had highlighted the risks to infants and children from pesticide residues in their diets,[34] Congress approved in 1996 the Food Quality Protection Act requiring consideration of the contaminant risks to infants and children. Accordingly, the special susceptibility of children to pesticides can be taken into account by applying an additional 10-fold safety factor. Unfortunately, this option has rarely been used, allegedly due to lack of evidence—which seems like a paradox. The added protection was intended to be used when there was not enough evidence to identify an exposure level that was known to be safe for children. We should therefore use this already existing option to define lower exposure limits that will protect sensitive developmental processes. Similar approaches should be considered in other connections.

Some progress has already happened. Several countries have now banned the use of bisphenol A in baby bottles, and the European Union has banned phthalates in toys. These decisions reflect a growing attention to the need to protect the youngest members in the population against chemical hazards. They also demonstrate that we already have some of the tools necessary to act.

The very products that cause brain drain, however, are often key parts of industrial activities that are of benefit to society. Each of these activities is carried out by a corporate entity that serves its own interests in profit-making, with little concern about harms and benefits to society.[35] While industrial production as such is not purposely malicious, or innocuous for that matter, the huge externalized costs due to brain toxicity would demand appropriate restrictions for the corporate pursuit of short-term profit. Brain drain has such severe consequences to each victim, and so many people may be affected, that even billion-dollar compensations later awarded to plaintiffs cannot justify reckless behavior when disseminating brain-draining chemicals. The costs to society are simply too enormous to leave decisions solely to corporate bodies or to the courts in regard to compensation awards to victims.

Thus, demands for individual freedom, the need to allow market forces to operate, and the opposition against big government are simply beside the point and certainly counter to John Stuart Mill's teaching. As professor Markowitz has said, it would be insanity to pollute developing brains in the interest of "freedom." Chemical brain drainers must be stopped at every possible level. Useful state-based initiatives include green chemistry in California and New York's list of chemicals to avoid purchasing. They should inspire national and international efforts in a greater scale.

We are in this together. Exposures to neurotoxic chemicals differ across countries and social groups. Some brain drainers are more common in certain populations than in others. But toxicity to brain development is by no means a risk that primarily affects certain subgroups, like the floriculture workers in Ecuador, or the Faroese consumers of pilot whale meat. Some chemicals show higher exposures in the well-to-do, while others show the opposite trend. The children and grandchildren of senators, CEOs, and humble consumers like you and me are all at risk. The key issue is that we, the adult population of today, are responsible for exposures that can negatively impact the brain functions of the next generation.

In addressing chemical brain drain, we must tackle the problems that are common to all decisions on prevention.[36] The benefits lie in the future and may be difficult to quantify. The beneficiaries are generally unknown. Even the benefactors may be unknown. Thus, public health intervention may encounter opposition from various sides. But the business-as-usual or status quo is nonetheless a decision that will allow continued exposure to the potential hazards. I believe that the time has come to push for better protection of developing brains as the precious, yet highly vulnerable targets for toxic chemicals. We generally focus on preventing exposures at home, at work, in the community, and from consumer products, often both through government action and consumer choice. In regard to brain drainers, we have much less information at our disposal than we do concerning carcinogens, for example. So our first goal must be to put the brain on the agenda as a top priority for public health.

Rehabilitation Is Only a Complementary Option

Intelligence is malleable and can be stimulated. Neuroscience documentation supports the impact of education and training on brain development. We know that cortical gray matter expands in people who learn how to juggle (see chapter 1). Learning a second language increases the density of gray matter (left inferior parietal cortex). The degree of structural reorganization in this region depends on the proficiency attained and the age at acquisition.[37] The Head Start program in the United States provides comprehensive education, health, nutrition, and parent involvement services to low-income children and their families. Such programs have shown sub-stantial beneficial effects on children's cognitive development.[38]

So, as toxic chemicals can siphon IQ points out of the brain, the right stimulation and support can add some. But this is not to say that we can forget about chemical brain drain as long as we supply ample support to our schools and special educa-tion. That itself would be an expensive remedy. In addition, brains will benefit more from stimulation if they function optimally to begin with. For children starting at a lower functional level, special education may help them to achieve better skills, but these skills will not compare with those of their unexposed peers. The final outcome hinges on properly functioning brain cells in the right locations and with the right connections. In addition, the stimulation must happen at the right time. Once the brain has matured, rewiring the brain circuitry becomes a lot harder.

Nutrients also play a key role for brain development. The food needed for brain development is rather similar to what we need for our cardiovascular system and for general health. So the dietary advice to pregnant mothers and families with small children is generally a varied and nutritious diet.[39] Children with nutritional deficien-cies of protein, iron, zinc, and other essential nutrients develop cognitive deficits.[40] Pre- and early postnatal supplement of omega-3 fatty acids has been linked to better vision and higher IQs, even among apparently well-fed infants. Seafood is an impor-tant source of the fatty acids, and they are transferred to the infant through human milk. But seafood and breast milk may also be contaminated by brain drainers.[41] Likewise, fruit and vegetables that contain important vitamins and nutrients may also contain pesticide residues.[42] Dietary advice must therefore take into account both the beneficial components and the pollutants as they vary regionally and over time.

Knowing that neurotoxic chemicals can affect behavior, perhaps we need to think of other vulnerable populations. Some success has been achieved with exper-iments to compensate for assumed biochemical imbalances among prison inmates by making dietary treatment part of their rehabilitation.[43] Thus, some criminally violent persons may be seen as victims of neural circuitry gone astray because of genetic predisposition, life experiences, and toxic chemical exposures. The US Supreme Court ruled in 2002 in *Atkins v. Virginia* that executing the mentally retarded violates the Eighth Amendment's ban on cruel and unusual punishments. This decision has inspired the Administrative Office of the United States Courts and its Office of Defender Services to expand its initiatives to help lawyers explore potential mitigating evidence on behalf of clients raised in poverty and exposed to chemicals that are toxic to brain development.[44] As I discussed in chapter 8, delin-quency and crime may in some cases be linked to developmental neurotoxicity, thus again emphasizing the importance of prevention.

Could science develop some kind of antidote to counteract brain drain? That would be hard—there is no quick technofix. We cannot count on pharmaceutical intervention to improve on such complex organs as human brains that have been damaged by toxic chemicals. First, brain damage that has already occurred during development will be very difficult to repair, if it can be done at all. If the cells are not in the right place, in sufficient numbers, with extensions and connections, then the morphological basis is inadequate for drugs to stimulate the brain to function better. Of course, certain drugs currently used for treatment of attention deficit hyperactivity disorder (ADHD) or sleep disturbance, such as Ritalin, Provigil, or Piracetam, may confer some benefits and help the user to concentrate better, but the effects of the so-called neuroenhancers are short term, and they do not seem to change the wiring of the brain. We should also consider the danger of overmedicating those with abnormal behavior. At the risk of sounding overly repetitive, I suggest that prevention would be a better solution.

Inertia in Research

If we decide to apply a precautionary approach to protecting brain development, our research practices and paradigms must also change. We need to address the weaknesses associated with the triple whammy (chapter 9). Part of a revised research agenda will be to explore major uncertainties in our current understanding of chemical brain drain. In contrast to current scientific tradition, extensive replication or repetitive attempts at verification should no longer be essential. As uncertainty must be accepted as an inevitable property of scientific knowledge, the need for further elucidation depends on the potential consequences. Rather than senseless and endless verification, we should use our resources to explore new areas where knowledge is minimal and where the risks to developing brains could be large.

We are not doing very well in generating research information as support for important societal decisions on brain-drain risks. Most published papers in environmental health journals deal with a limited, rather stable list of pollutants out of the thousands of important chemical hazards. The way we are conducting research therefore needs more careful thought, as I argued in chapter 9 and earlier in this chapter. We should no longer conduct statistical tests solely to determine whether a research finding is definitely a deviation from normal background. We also need to explore how bad a worst-case scenario could be, how serious the effect could be, and how large an effect we can reasonably rule out. Instead of concluding that no convincing evidence exists—in accordance with lead industry spokesman Robert Kehoe's fateful dictum (see chapter 3)—we also need to consider what *could* be known, given the research results available.

Thus, lack of evidence should no longer be misinterpreted as evidence that the hazard does not exist. In regard to chemical brain drain, the risks are simply too great to allow ignorance to triumph over prudence. On the contrary, cautious, though sensible, conclusions should build upon the evidence, even though it may be preliminary. The assumptions may later turn out to be false, and earlier actions taken may need to be adjusted, as more definite documentation emerges. But being concerned about over-regulating a few industrial chemicals is no justification for ignoring the possible risks associated with an immense number of industrial chemicals that have been poorly studied so far and which are entering developing brains this very moment.

As socially responsible citizens, scientists must consider the possible implications of their research. Nuclear physicist Alvin Weinberg many years ago emphasized the need to make clear where science ends and "trans-science" begins.[45] Thus, fearing speculation when one transcends the confines of one's research specialty, and in combination with a traditional ideal of a value-free science, researchers have hesitated to comment on trans-scientific implications. If I am perceived as an advocate of a particular solution to a problem in society, how can I remain a neutral scientist? Fortunately, science philosophers have begun to question this ideal, not only because it is unrealistic, but also because it may be irresponsible.[46] It is exactly because of the uncertainties that scientists with their competences and experiences need to weigh in and explain the implications. This can be done without compromising objectivity, transparency, and integrity (as I hope this book illustrates). To the extent that the conclusions rely on values, they have to be declared. Only then can science contribute to an open and fruitful discussion of the possible consequences of brain-toxicant exposures.

Inertia in science is a tremendous obstacle to decision making on brain drainers. Most researchers are guilty to some extent. The inertia is only in part due to our ancient tradition of replication and verification. Judge Richard A. Posner, formerly a leading figure in the conservative Chicago School of economics, expressed it as follows: "Professors have tenure. They have lots of graduate students in the pipeline who need to get their Ph.D.s. They have techniques that they know and are comfortable with. It takes a great deal to drive them out of their accustomed way of doing business."[47] In my field of research, it takes a substantial investment to establish cohorts, chemical analyses, and other methodologies, so investigators will object to changes in research focus. I, myself, have written about 100 scientific articles about mercury. So mea culpa, I know that I am part of the problem. But I need help, as my critics will probably continue to complain that I have not considered this possible source of error and that uncertainty. I need justification to ignore such pledges for more research on the same issue so that we can explore something new, from which we may learn much more.

Learning from the Past

Our current day-to-day chemical exposure profile is very different from that of humans from whom we evolved. Back then, brain development during fetal life was fully safeguarded by the placenta, as there were no chemical perpetrators. According to Native American tradition, we do not inherit the Earth from our ancestors, we borrow it from our children. This saying usually is thought to refer to the environment or the biosphere. So we are violating the moral obligation of leaving the Earth in the same, or better, condition than it was when we entered it.

In addition, our children are inheriting toxic chemicals from us, from the time of their conception—chemicals that negatively affect their chances of good health, optimal functions, and attractive opportunities in life. We have the luxury now of looking back at the narrow-minded (and wrong) decisions that caused disasters like leaded gasoline, Minamata disease, or Morinaga milk poisoning. We can laugh at anecdotes, and we can call the decision makers naïve and Dr. Kehoe a crook, if we want. But, more important, how will people in 20 years, or in 50, think about our lax attitude toward pesticides and other brain drainers and our miserable efforts to protect the brains of the next generation?

There is a lot at stake. Will we make the same mistakes that, some historians say, ancient Romans made? According to some scholars, the Roman Empire collapsed because of lead toxicity, as the Roman rulers were by poisoned by widespread use of metal water cisterns and food containers. If they are right, lead gradually made Patrician families deranged and infertile—leaving no competent leaders to run the Empire.[48] A similar fate seems to have befallen the Samurai regime during the Edo period in Japan. When bones from burials in a castle town were analyzed for lead, high concentrations were found especially in the children, suggesting severe lead poisoning.[49] Given the adverse effects on brain development, the Samurai descendants would likely be incapable of dealing with political crisis, thereby possibly contributing to the downfall of the Shogunate.

In this book, I have collated historical evidence on political follies, irresponsible industrialists, and naïve scientists. The triple whammy of obstacles to brain drain research was expertly exploited by Dr. Kehoe's demands for proof along with reckless claims of real or invented uncertainty. We were lured into thinking that our brains are perfectly safe, as long as the science does not convincingly show otherwise, with persuasive documentation and statistical significance. We need to cut through the paltry arguments about uncertainty and concentrate on the protection that our most valuable organ system deserves.

In the 1700s, the Count of Württemberg decreed capital punishment for causing lead poisoning of the citizens (see chapter 3). While that is unreasonably harsh, we need similar chutzpah to act against chemical brain drain. Why be lenient with modern sources of brain drain? Today, victims are receiving petty compensation for ruined brains, and although the fines imposed upon polluting industries may seem large, they are tiny compared to corporate profits. It would seem to me that the brain power of the future generations is a shared interest that we can all agree on. After all, we care about our children and grandchildren—you and I do, and so should politicians, industrialists, and decision makers, because brain drain also affects the brains of their children and grandchildren.

The Strategy

We need a strategy to counter chemical brain drain. We have underestimated its consequences, and now the time has come to act. Gustave Speth, dean at Yale University, has called for a new consciousness and a transformation in politics.[50] He addressed environmental crisis and climate change, but chemical brain drain is a related challenge of the same magnitude. And it is urgent. One part of our strategy should be to place brains at the top of our promotion of healthy lifestyles, public information, environmental protection, and chemical control agendas:

- *Optimal brain functioning* should be a key focus of health promotion—not just avoidance of neurological disease.
- Because brain development is *extremely vulnerable* to chemical toxicity, children and pregnant women deserve the strongest possible protection.
- The public must have *access to information* on brain toxicity, the sources of exposure, and the actual levels of exposure where they live.
- Many *pesticides, solvents, metals*, and other industrial chemicals are already known to cause brain toxicity; these exposures must be vigorously controlled without further delay.
- Because there is *only one chance to develop a brain*, protection against brain drainers must be promoted as a crucial and joint responsibility in society.

This immediate agenda needs to be supported by investment in new research, new approaches, and new thinking. We must place the protection of brain development as a high priority for research and testing of chemicals, and we need to generate responsible procedures for prudent decision making:

- As most industrial chemicals have not been *tested for toxicity* to brain development, screening should be conducted using existing and improved test methods to identify substances that need tighter control.
- We need new *research to understand* how brain development can be optimized and how best to prevent long-term dysfunctions and deficits linked to brain toxicity.
- As exposures and toxicity do not respect national borders, a *clearinghouse* is needed to collect and evaluate documentation on brain drain and to stimulate international collaboration to prevent their adverse effects.
- *Scientific proof should no longer be demanded* as a prerequisite to act responsibly and ethically in protecting vulnerable populations against brain-draining chemicals.
- On this basis, transparent *procedures and decision rules* need to be devised for acquisition of safety information, public information, improved control of chemicals, and monitoring while innovation in safer technology is stimulated.

These 10 elements involve both a new consciousness regarding the importance of optimal brain function and the need to protect its development. They also involve a transformation in politics and the way we evaluate and manage risks. They require more appropriate safety testing and new research to gain new insight into chemical brain drain. It may seem like an impossibly ambitious agenda.

Is this overambitious? Hopefully not. If anything, we have been far too careless in safeguarding the brains of the next generation against chemical brain drain. We have, for too long, ignored worldwide brain toxicity, as it seems to be "silent," mostly without medical diagnoses. But there is so much at stake that a major and serious effort must be undertaken on a global scale. The silent pandemic demands a loud response. I believe that we can do it, but we need to get this started without further delay.

Before closing, I should admit to having a nightmare. Writing this book is in fact my own remedy to fight this nightmare. In my half-conscious sleep, I watch as we keep releasing toxic chemicals, each of which carves away a tiny part of our brain power. While the total brain drain is increasing, the contribution of each chemical is barely detectable, if at all. In the end, our brains are reduced until nothing is left.

A continuation of this nightmare includes the "historical amnesia," our common inability (or unwillingness) to learn from past experience—in this case, regarding environmental toxicants.[51] We use a particular part of the brain—one that apparently is not present or not functioning the same way in any other species—to plan for the future.[52] As some chemicals, often at a narrow time window during development, affect very specific brain functions, my nightmare is that we are completely losing the capability to plan for the future and thus to prevent the chemical brain drain that is causing the damage.

Anyway, these are just nightmares. At least, I hope so.

APPENDIX

CHEMICALS KNOWN TO BE BRAIN DRAINERS

The following list of chemical brain drainers is an updated version of the list first developed in collaboration with Professor Philip Landrigan and published in *The Lancet* in 2006. Each of the 213 industrial chemicals listed is known to cause brain toxicity and neurological symptoms in humans (generally in adults), thus proving that the substance can reach the brain and exert toxicity to brain cells. Substances that are considered high-production volume (US, EU, or OECD) are labeled with an asterisk (*). In general, the common chemical names are indicated, but when appropriate some common synonyms are also listed. This list is not meant to be exhaustive but includes substances that were known by 2012 to cause adverse effects on the human nervous system.

Metals and Inorganic Compounds

Aluminum compounds*
Arsenic and arsenic compounds
Azides
Barium compounds
Bismuth compounds
Carbon monoxide*
Cyanides
Decaborane
Diborane
Ethylmercury
Fluorides
Hydrazine*
Hydrogen phosphide
Hydrogen sulfide*

Lead and lead compounds*
Lithium compounds
Manganese and manganese
   compounds*
Mercury and mercuric compounds
Methylmercury
Nickel carbonyl
Pentaborane
Phosphine
Phosphorus*
Selenium compounds
Tellurium compounds
Thallium compounds
Tin compounds*

Organic Solvents

Acetone*

Benzene*

Benzyl alcohol*

1-Bromopropane*

Carbon disulfide*

Chloroform*

Cyclohexane*

Cyclohexanol*

Cyclohexanone*

1,2-Dibromo-3-chloropropane (DBCP)

1,2-Dibromoethane*

Dichloroacetic acid

Dichloromethane*

Diethylene glycol*

N,N-Dimethylformamide*

Ethanol (Alcohol)*

Ethyl acetate*

Ethyl chloride

Ethylene glycol*

Ethylene glycol ethyl ether
    (Ethoxyethanol)*

Ethylene glycol methyl ether
    (Methoxyethanol, Methyl cellosolve)*

n-Hexane*

Isophorone*

Isopropyl alcohol*

Methanol (Methyl alcohol)*

Methyl-n-butyl ketone (2-Hexanone)

Methylcyclopentane

Methyl ethyl ketone*

Methyl isobutyl ketone*

2-Methylpropanenitrile*

Nitrobenzene*

2-Nitropropane*

1-Pentanol*

Pyridine*

Styrene*

1,1,2,2-Tetrachloroethane*

Tetrachloroethylene
    (Perchloroethylene)*

Toluene*

1,1,1-Trichloroethane
    (Methylchloroform)*

Trichloroethylene*

Xylene*

Other Organic Substances

Acetone cyanohydrin
    (2-Hydroxy-2-methylpropanenitrile)*

Acrylamide
    (2-Propenamide) *

Acrylonitrile*

Allyl chloride
    (1-Chloro-2-propene)*

Aniline*

1,4-Benzenediamine
    (4-Aminoaniline)*

1,2-Benzenedicarbonitrile (1,2-
    Dicyanobenzene)*

Benzonitrile*

1,3-Butadiene*

Butylated triphenyl phosphate*

Caprolactam
    (Azepan-2-one)*

Chloroprene*

Cumene*

Cyclonite (RDX)*

Diethylene glycol diacrylate*

Di-N-butyl phthalate*

Dimethyl sulfate*

Dimethylhydrazine

3-(Dimethylamino)-propanenitrile*

Dinitrobenzene*

Dinitrotoluene*

Ethylbis(2-chloroethyl)amine
    (HN1)

Ethylene

Ethylene oxide*
Fluoroacetamide
Fluoroacetate*
Hexachlorophene
Hydroquinone*
Methyl chloride (Chloromethane)*
Methyl formate*
Methyl iodide
Methyl methacrylate*
4-Nitroaniline*
Phenol*
Phenylhydrazine*
Polybrominated biphenyls (PBBs)

Polybrominated diphenyl ethers
 (PBDEs)
Polychlorinated biphenyls (PCBs)
1,2-Propylene oxide*
2,3,7,8-Tetrachlorodibenzo-*p*-dioxin
 (TCDD)
Tributyl phosphate*
Tri-*o*-cresylphosphate
Trimethyl phosphate
Triphenyl phosphate*
Tris(2-chloroethyl)amine
 (Trichlormethine)
Vinyl chloride (Chloroethene)*

Pesticides

Acetamiprid
Aldicarb (Temik)
Aldrin
Amitraz
Avermectin
Bensulide
Bromophos (Brofene)
Carbaryl (Sevin)*
Carbofuran (Furadan)*
Carbophenothion (Trithion)
α-Chloralose
Chlordane
Chlorfenvinphos
Chlormephos
Chlorothion
Chlorpyrifos
 (Dursban, Lorsban)*
Coumaphos
Cyhalothrin (Karate)
Cyolane (Phospholan)
Cypermethrin
Deltamethrin
 (Decamethrin)
Demeton-S-methyl
Dialifor
Diazinon*

Dichlofenthion
Dichlorodiphenyltrichloroethane
 (DDT)*
2,4-Dichlorophenoxyacetic acid
 (2,4-D)*
1,3-Dichloropropene*
Dichlorvos (DDVP, Vapona)
Dieldrin
Dimefox
Dimethoate*
4,6-Dinitro-*o*-cresol
Dinoseb*Dioxathion
Disulfoton
Edifenphos
Emamectin
Endosulfan (Thiodan)*
Endothion
Endrin
Ethiofencarb (Croneton)
Ethion
Ethoprop
O-Ethyl O-(4-nitrophenyl)
 phenylphosphonothioate (EPN)
Fenitrothion
Fensulfothion
Fenthion*

Fenvalerate
Fipronil (Termidor)
Fonofos
Formothion
Glyphosate
Heptachlor
Heptenophos
Hexachlorobenzene*
Hexaconazole
Imidacloprid
Isobenzan
Isolan
Isoxathion
Kepone (Chlordecone)
Leptophos
Lindane (γ-Hexachlorocyclohexane)*
Merphos*
Metaldehyde*
Methamidophos*
Methidathion (Suprathion)
Methomyl
Methyl bromide*
Methyl parathion (Parathion-methyl)*
Mevinphos
Mexacarbate (Zectran)
Mipafox

Mirex
Monocrotophos
Naled
Nicotine
Oxydemeton-methyl
Parathion*
Pentachlorophenol
Phorate
Phosphamidon (Dimecron)
Propaphos
Propoxur (Baygon)*
Pyriminil (Pyrinuron, Vacor)
Sarin
Schradan
Soman
Sulprofos
Systox (Demeton)
Tebupirimfos
Tefluthrin
Terbufos
Thiram*
Toxaphene
2,4,5-Trichlorophenoxyacetic acid
    (2,4,5-T)
Trichlorfon
Trichloronate

ACKNOWLEDGMENTS

Brain development is crucially dependent on the early environment, and that these processes are uniquely vulnerable to toxic chemicals during fetal and early postnatal life. Despite these new insights, we often cling to a traditional and catastrophic paradigm that allows chemical pollution to invade our bodies and brains, while any intervention to limit chemical brain drain must be justified by compelling evidence. Our new understanding of the vulnerability and preciousness of brain development must influence the way we shape our environment and how we protect one of the most critical resources of the future: the next generation's brain power.

This book and the achievements that inspired it are due to the committed efforts of many colleagues in environmental medicine, epidemiology, pediatrics, toxicology, and related fields. I have relied on the work of many of these key colleagues in writing this book and have tried to refer to what I consider the most central research publications. I have also asked many of them for advice, and some have read and commented on drafts of full chapters. In particular, I have greatly benefited from the help of Helle Raun Andersen, Anna Bal-Price, Martine Bellanger, David Bellinger, Roberto Bertollini, Esben Budtz-Jørgensen, David Carpenter, Sandra Ceccatelli, Anna Choi, Sylvaine Cordier, Joan Cranmer, Carl Cranor, Frodi Debes, Norvald Fimreite, David Gee, James Hammitt, Raul Harari, Birger Heinzow, Joseph Jacobson, Jordi Julvez, Tord Kjellström, Ora Kofman, Philip Landrigan, Bruce Lanphear, Roberto Lucchini, Troels Lyngbye, Phyllis Mullenix, Katsuyuki Murata, Larry Needham, Herbert Needleman, David Ozonoff, Celine Pichery, Hiroshi Satoh, Joel Schwartz, Ann Streissguth, Pál Weihe, Marc Weisskopf, Roberta White, and Takashi Yorifuji. In addition, David Bellinger, Anna Choi, Birger Heinzow, David Ozonoff, and Marc Weisskopf commented on the full manuscript. I apologize if I have forgotten anyone who provided inspiration, or whose seminal publications I failed to include in the bibliography. Any errors or misunderstandings should be blamed on me only.

I have benefited greatly from dual appointments at universities in the United States and in Denmark. Colleagues at the schools of public health both at Boston University and at Harvard University have contributed superbly inspiring academic environments as a prerequisite for putting this book together. Katie Herz saw the book through multiple stages and helped make it legible, while Sandra Tøttenborg organized the references. My colleagues at the University of Southern Denmark helped me directly and indirectly, especially in regard to the empathy and support that a book author needs, when multiple overlapping commitments seem to prevent any time for writing. My special thanks are due to Helle Raun Andersen, Karin Cederberg, Christine Dalgård, Tina Kold Jensen, and Flemming Nielsen. The final version benefited greatly from the constructive suggestions of series editor Kristin Shrader-Frechette, three anonymous reviewers, and associate editor Lucy Randall at Oxford University Press. Throughout the writing process, Ida Hasselbalch kept our spirits high.

My research into developmental neurotoxicity has been supported since 1992 by the National Institute of Environmental Health Sciences (NIEHS) of the US National Institutes of Health and by several grants from the European Commission and the Danish Research Councils. The only private source of support was the 2010 Research Award from the Order of Odd Fellows. A few years before that, I received a special "Mercury Madness Award" for excellence in science in the public interest, from eight US environmental organizations. It entitled me to a very enjoyable, and free, lunch. I am grateful for the confidence that the funding agencies and my colleagues have had in me.

A final tribute goes to the children and poisoning victims who taught me about the reality of chemical brain drain. One of them, Shinobu Sakamoto, has shared her suffering in public. Others have not, and in respect of their privacy and dignity, I use only first names if at all referring to them by name. More than two thousand children have participated in our clinical studies in the Americas, Asia, and Europe. I am grateful to all of them, and their parents, for their willingness to help and for their trust in our ability to learn and to share our insights. This book would not have been possible without their support and inspiration.

NOTES

Introduction

1. Herculano-Houzel, 2009
2. Herculano-Houzel, 2009
3. Sanes et al., 2006
4. Bloom et al., 2010; Boyle et al., 1994
5. Grandjean and Landrigan, 2006
6. Kovarik, 2005
7. Grandjean and Landrigan, 2006
8. Speth, 2008, 199–200

Chapter 1

1. Sanes et al., 2006
2. Lauder and Schambra, 1999
3. Sur and Rubenstein, 2005
4. Sjostrom et al., 2008
5. Huttenlocher and Dabholkar, 1997
6. Ruediger and Bolz, 2007
7. Gregg et al., 2010
8. Vreugdenhil et al., 2002
9. Johnston et al., 2001
10. Wurtz, 2009
11. Higley and Strittmatter, 2010
12. Martin et al., 2004
13. Martin et al., 2005
14. Blakemore, 2005
15. Nelson, 2004
16. Nelson et al., 2007
17. Mechelli et al., 2004
18. Draganski et al., 2004
19. Fields, 2010
20. Chaddock et al., 2010
21. Langer et al., 2012
22. Marin-Burgin et al., 2012
23. O'Farrell, 2009
24. World Health Organization, 2006

25. Augusti-Tocco et al., 2006
26. Pinker, 2003, p. 47
27. Davies et al., 2011
28. Francis et al., 2003
29. Guzelian et al., 1992, p. 2
30. Sly and Flack, 2008
31. Grandjean, 2008a

Chapter 2

1. Seidman and Warren, 2002
2. Bross, 1964
3. Dally, 1998
4. DeSesso et al., 2012
5. Streissguth, 1997, p. 36
6. Warner and Rosett, 1975
7. Warner and Rosett, 1975
8. Jones and Smith, 1973
9. Gregg, 1941
10. Webster, 1998
11. Gregg, 1941
12. Banatvala, 2001
13. Editorial, 1941
14. Swan et al., 1943
15. Lancaster, 1951
16. Editorial, 1944
17. Editorial, 1945
18. Ulleland, 1972
19. Lemoine et al., 2003
20. Sadoun et al., 1965
21. Lemoine, 1994
22. Koren and Navioz, 2003
23. Ernhart et al., 1985
24. Streissguth and Kanter, 1997, p. 72
25. Cooper et al., 1969
26. Menser et al., 1967
27. Burgess, 1991; Forrest et al., 2002
28. Munroe, 2006
29. O'Donnell, 1991
30. World Health Organization., 2009
31. Lemoine, 1992
32. Streissguth, 1997, pp. 102–103
33. Hill et al., 1989
34. Streissguth and Kanter, 1997, p. 26
35. Lee et al., 2004
36. Carter et al., 2005
37. Streissguth et al., 2004
38. Fryer et al., 2009
39. Wolf et al., 1939
40. Ho-Yen and Joss, 1992
41. Weiss and Dubey, 2009
42. Stern et al., 1969
43. Revello and Gerna, 2002

44. Hornig and Lipkin, 2001
45. Dally, 1998
46. Ito et al., 2010
47. Boseley, 2010
48. Webster, 1998
49. Environmental Working Group, 2005
50. Needham et al., 2011
51. Centers for Disease Control and Prevention, 2009
52. World Wildlife Fund, 2004
53. Barr et al., 2006
54. Grandjean and Jensen, 2004
55. Evenhouse and Reilly, 2005
56. World Health Organization, 2002

Chapter 3

1. U.S. Public Health Service, 1925, p. 70
2. Needleman, 1997
3. McNeill, 2000, p. 111
4. Needleman, 2000
5. Lanphear, 2007
6. Byers and Lord, 1943
7. Hardy, 1966, pp. 73–83
8. Needleman, 1998
9. Kehoe, 1961
10. Barltrop, 1975
11. Marshall, 1984
12. Kehoe et al., 1935
13. Lead Industries Association, 1968
14. Patterson, 1965
15. Grandjean and Holma, 1973
16. US Public Health Service, 1970
17. Facchetti, 1990
18. Annest et al., 1983; Jones et al., 2009
19. Markowitz and Rosner, 2000
20. Fassin and Naude, 2004
21. Hunt et al., 1982
22. Rabin, 1989
23. International Lead Zinc Research Organization, 1979, p. 37
24. International Programme on Chemical Safety, 1977
25. Advisory Group on Lead, 1988
26. Kaufman, 2001
27. Bryce-Smith et al., 1978
28. Murozumi et al., 1969
29. National Research Council, 1980
30. Chisolm, 1984
31. Landrigan et al., 1975
32. Wynn, 1982
33. Joint Expert Committee on Food Additives, 1986
34. World Health Organization, 2002
35. Centers for Disease Control and Prevention, 1991
36. Committee on Toxicity of Chemicals in Food, 2008
37. Agency for Toxic Substances and Disease Registry, 2007

38. EFSA Panel on Contaminants in the Food Chain (CONTAM), 2010
39. Kovarik, 2005; Rabin, 1989
40. Markowitz and Rosner, 2002, p. 59; Rabin, 1989;
41. Kovarik, 2005; Markowitz and Rosner, 2002, p. 63
42. Needleman et al., 1979
43. Marshall, 1983
44. US Environmental Protection Agency, 1986
45. Needleman, 1998
46. Bellinger and Bellinger, 2006
47. Kotok, 1972
48. Needleman et al., 1979
49. Budtz-Jørgensen et al., 2012; Lanphear et al., 2005
50. Hornung et al., 2009
51. Kordas et al., 2006; Min et al., 2009; Pawlas et al., 2012; Tellez-Rojo et al., 2006
52. Mazumdar et al., 2011
53. Nevin, 2009
54. Needleman et al., 1996
55. Fergusson et al., 2008; Wright et al., 2008
56. Cecil et al., 2008
57. Grandjean and Klein, 2005
58. Moore, 1977
59. Troesken, 2006
60. Rabin, 2008
61. Renner, 2009
62. Young, 2012
63. Haefliger et al., 2009
64. Blacksmith Institute, 2012

Chapter 4

1. Harada, 2004
2. Social Scientific Study Group on Minamata Disease, 1999
3. Harada, 1977a
4. United Nations Environment Programme, 2009
5. Takeuchi and Eto, 1999
6. Harada, 1977b
7. Edwards, 1865
8. Hepp, 1887
9. Hunter et al., 1940
10. Hook et al., 1954
11. Herner, 1945
12. Hunter and Russell, 1954
13. Grandjean et al., 2010
14. Hunter and Russell, 1954
15. Eto et al., 2001
16. Spyker et al., 1972
17. Engleson and Herner, 1952
18. Bakir et al., 1973; Jalili and Abbasi, 1961; Ordonez et al., 1966
19. Giles, 2003; Hightower, 2009
20. Amin-Zaki et al., 1978
21. Marsh et al., 1987
22. Jensen and Jernelöv, 1967
23. Wood et al., 1968

24. Shkilnyk AM, 1985, p. 187
25. Fimreite and Reynolds, 1973
26. Erikson, 1994, p. 34
27. Hutchison, 1977, p. 72
28. Wheatley et al., 1997
29. Erikson, 1994, p. 38
30. I have signed a confidentiality agreement and therefore cannot reveal details of the findings.
31. Sellers, 2010
32. McKeown-Eyssen et al., 1983
33. Weihe et al., 2002
34. Dietz et al., 2009
35. Kjellström et al., 1986; Kjellström et al., 1989
36. Crump et al., 1998
37. Grandjean et al., 1997
38. Egeland and Middaugh, 1997
39. Myers and Davidson, 1998
40. Budtz-Jørgensen, 2007
41. Spulber et al., 2010
42. Budtz-Jørgensen et al., 2004; Grandjean and Budtz-Jørgensen, 2010
43. Joint Expert Committee on Food Additives, 1972
44. Joint Expert Committee on Food Additives, 1978
45. Tejning and Vesterberg, 1964
46. http://water.epa.gov/scitech/swguidance/fishshellfish/fishadvisories/technical_factsheet_2010.cfm
47. National Institute of Environmental Health Sciences, 1998
48. National Research Council, 2000a
49. Joint Expert Committee on Food Additives, 2003
50. Biodiversity Research Institute, 2012; Mahaffey et al., 2011
51. Mishima, 1992, pp. 151–152
52. Shkilnyk AM, 1985, p. 190
53. Myers et al., 2003
54. Myers et al., 1995
55. Davidson et al., 1995
56. Gorman, 2003
57. Lyketsos, 2003
58. Tsubaki et al., 1969
59. D'Itri and D'Itri, 1978
60. Grandjean et al., 2010

Chapter 5

1. Mari et al., 2004
2. Dakeishi et al., 2006
3. Frankel et al., 2009
4. Dakeishi et al., 2006; Nakagawa and Libuchi, 1970;
5. Dakeishi et al., 2006; Yamashita et al., 1972
6. Dakeishi et al., 2006; Ohira and Aoyama, 1973
7. Dakeishi et al., 2006; Yamashita et al., 1972
8. National Research Council, 1999
9. International Programme on Chemical Safety, 2001
10. Brown, 1900
11. Whorton, 2010, pp. 307–309

12. Smith et al., 2000
13. Fendorf et al., 2010; United Nations Children's Fund., 2010
14. International Agency for Research on Cancer, 2004; University of Cambridge, 2007
15. Calderon et al., 2001; Tsai et al., 2003; Wasserman et al., 2004; Wasserman et al., 2007; Wright et al., 2006
16. Alan et al., 2000
17. Flanagan et al., 2012
18. Natural Resources Defense Council, 2009

Chapter 6

1. Love, 2006, p. 216
2. Drinker et al., 1937
3. Francis, 1994
4. Jensen, 1972; Jensen is known by few researchers in the field, even though he was also involved in the discovery of the mercury methylation (chapter 4)
5. Jensen, 1972
6. Love, 2006, p. 69
7. Love, 2006, p. 93
8. Grunwald, 2002
9. Francis, 1994
10. Kely, 2000
11. Guo et al., 2004
12. Jacobson et al., 1990; Jacobson and Jacobson, 1996
13. Gladen et al., 1988
14. Patandin et al., 1999; Walkowiak et al., 2001
15. Schantz et al., 2003; Stewart et al., 2012
16. Boix et al., 2010
17. Yang et al., 2009
18. Letter from Elisabeth A. Whelan to Producers of *60 Minutes*, 2002.
19. Love, 2006, p. 288
20. Gentle, 2009
21. www.epa.gov/pcbsincaulk/
22. Liebl et al., 2004
23. MacIntosh et al., 2012; www.pcbinschools.org; www.nycsca.org/Community/Programs/EPA-NYC-PCB/Pages/default.aspx
24. Herrick et al., 2004
25. Dallaire et al., 2009; Lopez-Espinosa et al., 2010; Ribas-Fito et al., 2006
26. Eskenazi et al., 2013; Herbstman et al., 2010; Roze et al., 2009
27. Clapp and Hoppin, 2011
28. Mariussen, 2012
29. Gump et al., 2011; Stein and Savitz, 2011

Chapter 7

1. Grandjean and Landrigan, 2006
2. Grandjean et al., 2006; Harari et al., 2010
3. Angle et al., 1968
4. Dahlgren et al., 2004
5. Kofman et al., 2006
6. Ruckart et al., 2004
7. Eskenazi et al., 2007; Young et al., 2005;
8. Berkowitz et al., 2004; Engel et al., 2007

9. Rauh et al., 2006
10. Bouchard et al., 2011; Engel et al., 2011; Rauh et al., 2011
11. Horton et al., 2011
12. Rauh et al., 2012
13. Barr et al., 2005; Heudorf et al., 2006; Ye et al., 2008
14. www.nass.usda.gov/Surveys/Guide_to_NASS_Surveys/Chemical_Use/
15. U.S. Environmental Protection Agency, 2011
16. European Commission, 2007
17. Bjørling-Poulsen et al., 2008
18. Qiao et al., 2003
19. Vidair, 2004
20. Gollamudi et al., 2012
21. Garry, 2004
22. Colborn, 2004; Cooper and Kavlock, 1997; Zoeller and Crofton, 2000
23. Bjørling-Poulsen et al., 2008
24. Jacobsen et al., 2010
25. Schafer and Marquez, 2012
26. www.ecpa.be/website/page.asp?mi=1&cust=3<=en&news=17994
27. Arnold et al., 1994; Hersh et al., 1985; Julvez and Grandjean, 2009; Pearson et al., 1994; Péle et al., 2013
28. Aschengrau et al., 2012; Janulewicz et al., 2012
29. Erikson, 1994
30. Ericson et al., 2007; Lucchini et al., 2012
31. Patel and Sun, 2009; Rappaport et al., 2011
32. Kurth and Haussmann, 2011
33. Ackerman et al., 2010
34. Clifford et a., 2012; Gatzke-Kopp and Beauchaine, 2007; Swan and Lessov-Schlaggar, 2007
35. Devine et al., 2002; Dix-Cooper et al., 2012
36. Grandjean and Landrigan, 2006
37. Calderon-Garciduenas et al., 2008; Perera et al., 2009
38. Vrijheid et al., 2012
39. Colborn, 2004; Zoeller and Crofton, 2000
40. Cho et al., 2010; Engel et al., 2010
41. Heiervang et al., 2010

Chapter 8

1. Grosse et al., 2002 ; Salkever, 1995
2. Levine, 2010
3. Grandjean and Landrigan, 2006
4. World Health Organization, 2006
5. Institute of Medicine, 1981
6. Smith et al., 1999
7. Prüss-Üstün and Corvalán, 2006
8. Nevin, 2009
9. Trasande et al., 2006
10. National Research Council, 2000b
11. Landrigan et al., 2002
12. Salkever, 1995
13. Murray, 2002
14. Gould, 2009; Pichery et al., 2011
15. Trasande et al., 2005

16. Bellanger et al., 2013; Rice et al., 2010
17. Pichery et al., 2012
18. Bellinger, 2012
19. Jensen, 2000
20. Duckworth and Seligman, 2005
21. Nelson et al., 2007
22. Nisbett, 2009, pp. 121–122, 148
23. Heckman, 2006
24. Lyngbye et al., 1990
25. Schwartz, 1994
26. Chambers et al., 2004
27. Pichery et al., 2011
28. White et al., 2011
29. Carpenter and Nevin, 2010; Drum, 2013
30. Needleman et al., 1996; Nevin, 2009
31. Denno, 1990
32. Fergusson et al., 2008; Wright et al., 2008
33. Pekkanen, 2006
34. Gould, 2009
35. Tsai and Hatfield, 2011
36. Lynn and Vanhanen, 2002
37. Eppig et al., 2010
38. Flynn, 2007
39. Herrnstein and Murray, 1994
40. Eyferth, 1961
41. Nisbett, 2009, pp. 21–38
42. Moore, 1986
43. Turkheimer et al., 2003
44. Miranda et al., 2009
45. Martin, 2002
46. MacIntosh et al., 2012
47. US Environmental Protection Agency, 1985
48. Gould, 2009
49. Rice and Hammitt, 2005
50. Gayer and Hahn, 2005
51. Sundseth et al., 2010
52. Bahr and Janson, 2004
53. www.theolympian.com/2011/11/08/1868238/the-asarco-smelters-toxic-legacy.html#storylink=cpy
54. www.ecpa.be/website/page.asp?mi=1&cust=3<=en&news=17899

Chapter 9

1. McGarity and Wagner, 2008, p. 282
2. Rodgers, 2005
3. Michaels, 2008; Union of Concerned Scientists, 2012
4. Kurland, 2002; Landman and Glantz, 2009
5. Michaels, 2005
6. Grandjean, 2008b
7. Feinstein, 1988
8. Diethelm and McKee, 2009
9. Oreskes and Conway, 2010, p. 36
10. Diethelm and McKee, 2009

11. Landman and Glantz, 2009
12. Needleman, 2000
13. Guzelian et al., 1992, p. 2
14. Letter of 31 October 2000 to the FDA from the United States Tuna Foundation, www.fda.gov/OHRMS/DOCKETS/ac/02/briefing/3872_Stake%2025.pdf
15. Cocke, 2012
16. Israel, 2012
17. Ernhart et al., 1981
18. Kaufman, 2001
19. Soon and Ferguson, 2005
20. Ferguson, 2004
21. Gough, 1999
22. www.who.int/tobacco/en/who_inquiry.pdf
23. Centers for Disease Control and Prevention, 1991
24. McGarity and Wagner, 2008, p. 184
25. Mooney, 2004
26. Myers et al., 2006
27. Pearson, 2004
28. Kuehn, 2004
29. Blumenthal et al., 1997
30. Martinson et al., 2005
31. Schott et al., 2010
32. McGarity and Wagner, 2008, p. 96
33. Lesser et al., 2007
34. vom Saal and Hughes, 2005
35. Huss et al., 2007
36. Michaels, 2005
37. Eriksson, 2008
38. Angell, 2009
39. Brody, 2007, p. 218
40. Serious Fraud Office, 2010
41. Leigh et al., 2010
42. Kuehn, 2004; Jasanoff, 2010
43. McGarity and Wagner, 2008, p. 168
44. Markowitz and Rosner, 2002, p. 57
45. Patterson, 1965
46. Needleman, 1998
47. Silbergeld, 1995
48. Bryson, 2004, p. 22
49. Mullenix et al., 1995
50. Ross and Daston, 1995
51. Centers for Disease Control and Prevention, 1999
52. Illson, 1955
53. Cheng et al., 2007; National Research Council, 2006
54. National Research Council, 2006
55. Choi et al., 2012
56. Eriksson, 2008
57. Kuehn, 2004
58. I understand from EPRI that, at my request, all copies of this report have been destroyed.
59. Kaiser, 2005
60. Rosner and Markowitz, 2009
61. Richter et al., 2001
62. Grandjean and Budtz-Jørgensen, 2010

63. Bellinger, 2009
64. Hyland, 1998
65. Grandjean, 2008a
66. Ioannidis, 2008
67. The editors of *The Lancet*, 2010
68. Grandjean, 2008b
69. Freire and Koifman, 2012
70. Kaplan, 2011
71. McGarity and Wagner, 2008, p. 96
72. Greenberg, 2003
73. James et al., 2004; London et al., 2013
74. Krimsky, 2003, p. 78
75. Grandjean et al., 2011
76. Tarkowski, 2007
77. Bross, 1964
78. Hill, 1965

Chapter 10

1. Needleman and Landrigan, 1994
2. Cranor, 2008
3. Horel, 2008
4. Holtcamp, 2012
5. Duff and Campbell, 1973
6. Schade and Heinzow, 1998
7. Barouki et al., 2012; Grandjean et al., 2008
8. Olesen et al., 2006
9. Freire and Koifman, 2012; Gollamudi et al., 2012
10. Hoffman, 2005
11. Pekkanen, 2006
12. Lanphear, 2007
13. Grandjean and Landrigan, 2006
14. Wilson and Schwarzman, 2009
15. Gilbert, 2011
16. Claudio et al., 2000
17. Makris et al., 2009
18. Raffaele et al., 2010
19. Clapp and Hoppin, 2011
20. Government Accounting Office, 2005; Schwarzman and Wilson, 2009
21. McGarity and Wagner, 2008, p. 297
22. Spyker et al., 1972
23. E-mail from Professor Joan Spyker Cranmer, 12 November 2008.
24. Bal-Price et al., 2010
25. National Research Council, 2007
26. Higginson, 1998
27. European Environment Agency, 2001
28. Anon., 2003
29. US Public Health Service, 1925
30. Young, 2012
31. Suskind, 2006
32. Friedman, 2009
33. Environmental Working Group, 2010a
34. National Research Council, 1993

35. Wiist, 2006
36. Hemenway, 2010
37. Mechelli et al., 2004
38. Heckman, 2006; Nisbett, 2009, pp. 121–122
39. Logan, 2006
40. Walker et al., 2007
41. Grandjean and Jensen, 2004; Mahaffey et al., 2011
42. Environmental Working Group, 2010b
43. Bohannon, 2009
44. Office of Defender Services of the Administrative Office of the U.S. Courts www.fd.org/odstb_supreme.htm
45. Weinberg, 1972
46. Douglas, 2009, pp. 66–86; Shrader-Frechette, 2012
47. Cassidy, 2010
48. Gilfillan, 1965
49. Nakashima et al., 2011
50. Speth, 2008, pp. 199–200
51. Kovarik, 2005
52. McClure et al., 2004

BIBLIOGRAPHY

Ackerman JP, Riggins T, and Black MM. (2010) A review of the effects of prenatal cocaine exposure among school-aged children, *Pediatrics* 125, 554–565.

Advisory Group on Lead. (1988) *The neuropsychological effects of lead in children: A review of the research, 1984–1988*, Medical Research Council, London.

Agency for Toxic Substances and Disease Registry. (2007) *Toxicological profile for lead*. Atlanta, GA, ATSDR. www.atsdr.cdc.gov/toxprofiles/tp13.pdf.

Alan HW, Sharon A, Dennis RH, and Michael JF. (2000) *Arsenic in ground-water resources of the United States: U.S. Geological Survey.* http://pubs.usgs.gov/fs/2000/fs063-00/pdf/fs063-00.pdf.

Amin-Zaki L, Majeed MA, Clarkson TW, and Greenwood MR. (1978) Methylmercury poisoning in Iraqi children: Clinical observations over two years, *Br Med J* 1, 613–616.

Angell M. (2009) Drug companies and doctors: A story of corruption, *New York Review of Books*, 15 January.

Angle CR, McIntire MS, and Meile RL. (1968) Neurologic sequelae of poisoning in children, *J Pediatr* 73, 531–539.

Annest JL, Pirkle JL, Makuc D, Neese JW, Bayse DD, and Kovar MG. (1983) Chronological trend in blood lead levels between 1976 and 1980, *N Engl J Med* 308, 1373–1377.

Anon. (2003) ACC, EWG square off over precautionary principle, *Pesticide & Toxic Chemical News*, 1 December.

Arnold GL, Kirby RS, Langendoerfer S, and Wilkins-Haug L. (1994) Toluene embryopathy: Clinical delineation and developmental follow-up, *Pediatrics* 93, 216–220.

Aschengrau A, Weinberg JM, Janulewicz PA, Romano ME, Gallagher LG, Winter MR, Martin BR, Vieira VM, Webster TF, White RF, and Ozonoff DM. (2012) Occurrence of mental illness following prenatal and early childhood exposure to tetrachloroethylene (PCE)-contaminated drinking water: A retrospective cohort study, *Environ Health* 11, 2.

Augusti-Tocco G, Biagioni S, and Tata AM. (2006) Acetylcholine and regulation of gene expression in developing systems, *J Mol Neurosci* 30, 45–48.

Bahr J, and Janson J. (2004) Cost of late action—the case of PCB, *TemaNord* 556, 43.

Bakir F, Damluji SF, Amin-Zaki L, Murtadha M, Khalidi A, al-Rawi NY, Tikriti S, Dahahir HI, Clarkson TW, Smith JC, and Doherty RA. (1973) Methylmercury poisoning in Iraq, *Science* 181, 230–241.

Bal-Price AK, Hogberg HT, Buzanska L, Lenas P, van Vliet E, and Hartung T. (2010) In vitro developmental neurotoxicity (DNT) testing: Relevant models and endpoints, *Neurotoxicology* 31, 545–554.

Banatvala JE. (2001) Congenital cataract following German measles in the mother, *Rev Med Virol* 11, 277–285.

Barltrop D. (1975) International Symposium on Environmental Lead Research, *Arh Hig Rada Toksikol* 26 (suppl), 248.

Barouki B, Gluckman PD, Grandjean P, Hanson M, and Heindel JJ. (2012) Developmental origins of non-communicable diseases and dysfunctions: Implications for research and public health, *Environ Health* 11, 42.

Barr DB, Allen R, Olsson AO, Bravo R, Caltabiano LM, Montesano A, Nguyen J, Udunka S, Walden D, Walker RD, Weerasekera G, Whitehead RD, Jr., Schober SE, and Needham LL. (2005) Concentrations of selective metabolites of organophosphorus pesticides in the United States population, *Environ Res* 99, 314–326.

Barr DB, Weihe P, Davis MD, Needham LL, and Grandjean P. (2006) Serum polychlorinated biphenyl and organochlorine insecticide concentrations in a Faroese birth cohort, *Chemosphere* 62, 1167–1182.

Bellanger M, Pichery C, Aerts D, Berglund M, Castano A, Cejchanova M, Crettaz P, Davidson F, Esteban M, Fischer ME, Gurzau AE, Halzlova K, Katsonouri A, Knudsen LE, Kolossa-Gehring M, Koppen G, Ligocka D, Miklavcic A, Reis MF, Rudnai P, Tratnik JS, Weihe P, Budtz-Jørgensen E, and Grandjean P. (2013) Economic benefits of methylmercury exposure control in Europe: Monetary value of neurotoxicity prevention, *Environ Health* 12, 3.

Bellinger DC, and Bellinger AM. (2006) Childhood lead poisoning: The torturous path from science to policy, *J Clin Invest* 116, 853–857.

Bellinger DC. (2009) Interpreting epidemiologic studies of developmental neurotoxicity: Conceptual and analytic issues, *Neurotoxicol Teratol* 31, 267–274.

Bellinger DC. (2012) A strategy for comparing the contributions of environmental chemicals and other risk factors to neurodevelopment of children, *Environ Health Perspect* 120, 501–507.

Berkowitz GS, Wetmur JG, Birman-Deych E, Obel J, Lapinski RH, Godbold JH, Holzman IR, and Wolff MS. (2004) In utero pesticide exposure, maternal paraoxonase activity, and head circumference, *Environ Health Perspect* 112, 388–391.

Biodiversity Research Institute. (2012) Mercury in the Global Environment: Patterns of Global Seafood Mercury Concentrations and their Relationship with Human Health. Gorham, ME. http://www.briloon.org/hgcenter.

Bjørling-Poulsen M, Andersen HR, and Grandjean P. (2008) Potential developmental neurotoxicity of pesticides used in Europe, *Environ Health* 7, 50.

Blacksmith Institute. (2012) The world's worst pollution problems: Assessing health risks at hazardous waste sites. New York. www.worstpolluted.org/files/FileUpload/files/WWPP_2012.pdf.

Blakemore C. (2005) In celebration of cerebration, *Lancet* 366, 2035–2057.

Bloom B, Cohen RA, and Freeman G. (2010) Summary health statistics for U.S. children: National Health Interview Survey, 2009, *Vital Health Stat* 10, 1–82.

Blumenthal D, Campbell EG, Anderson MS, Causino N, and Louis KS. (1997) Withholding research results in academic life science. Evidence from a national survey of faculty, *JAMA* 277, 1224–1228.

Bohannon J. (2009) Psychology. The theory? Diet causes violence. The lab? Prison, *Science* 325, 1614–1616.

Boix J, Cauli O, and Felipo V. (2010) Developmental exposure to polychlorinated biphenyls 52, 138 or 180 affects differentially learning or motor coordination in adult rats. Mechanisms involved, *Neuroscience* 167, 994–1003.

Boseley S. (2010) 50 years on, an apology to thalidomide scandal survivors, *The Guardian*, 14 January.

Bouchard MF, Chevrier J, Harley KG, Kogut K, Vedar M, Calderon N, Trujillo C, Johnson C, Bradman A, Barr DB, and Eskenazi B. (2011) Prenatal exposure to organophosphate pesticides and IQ in 7-year old children, *Environ Health Perspect* 119, 1189–1195.

Boyle CA, Decoufle P, and Yeargin-Allsopp M. (1994) Prevalence and health impact of developmental disabilities in US children, *Pediatrics* 93, 399–403.

Brody BA. (2007) *Hooked: How medicine's dependence on the pharmaceutical industry undermines professional ethics*, Rowman & Littlefeld, Lanham, MD.

Bross ID. (1964) Prisoners of jargon, *Am J Public Health Nations Health* 54, 918–927.

Brown J. (1900) Case in a child of two years, *British Medical Journal* ii, 1683.

Bryce-Smith D, Stephens R, and Mathews J. (1978) Mental health effects of lead on children, *Ambio* 7, 192–203.

Bryson C. (2004) *The fluoride deception*, Seven Stories Press, New York.

Budtz-Jørgensen E. (2007) Estimation of the benchmark dose by structural equation models, *Biostatistics* 8, 675–688.

Budtz-Jørgensen E, Grandjean P, Jørgensen PJ, Weihe P, and Keiding N. (2004) Association between mercury concentrations in blood and hair in methylmercury-exposed subjects at different ages, *Environ Res* 95, 385–393.

Budtz-Jørgensen E, Bellinger D, Lanphear B, and Grandjean P, on behalf of the International Pooled Lead Study Investigators. (2012) An international pooled analysis for obtaining a benchmark dose for environmental lead exposure in children, *Risk Anal* (in press).

Burgess MA. (1991) Gregg's rubella legacy 1941–1991, *Med J Aust* 155, 355–357.

Byers R, and Lord E. (1943) Late effects of lead poisoning on mental development, *Am J Dis Child* 66, 471–494.

Calderon J, Navarro ME, Jimenez-Capdeville ME, Santos-Diaz MA, Golden A, Rodriguez-Leyva I, Borja-Aburto V, and Diaz-Barriga F. (2001) Exposure to arsenic and lead and neuropsychological development in Mexican children, *Environ Res* 85, 69–76.

Calderon-Garciduenas L, Mora-Tiscareno A, Ontiveros E, Gomez-Garza G, Barragan-Mejia G, Broadway J, Chapman S, Valencia-Salazar G, Jewells V, Maronpot RR, Henriquez-Roldan C, Perez-Guille B, Torres-Jardon R, Herrit L, Brooks D, Osnaya-Brizuela N, Monroy ME, Gonzalez-Maciel A, Reynoso-Robles R, Villarreal-Calderon R, Solt AC, and Engle RW. (2008) Air pollution, cognitive deficits and brain abnormalities: A pilot study with children and dogs, *Brain Cogn* 68, 117–127.

Carpenter DO, and Nevin R. (2010) Environmental causes of violence, *Physiol Behav* 99, 260–268.

Carter RC, Jacobson SW, Molteno CD, Chiodo LM, Viljoen D, and Jacobson JL. (2005) Effects of prenatal alcohol exposure on infant visual acuity, *J Pediatr* 147, 473–479.

Cassidy J. (2010) After the blowup, *New Yorker*, 11 January, 28–33.

Cecil KM, Brubaker CJ, Adler CM, Dietrich KN, Altaye M, Egelhoff JC, Wessel S, Elangovan I, Hornung R, Jarvis K, and Lanphear BP. (2008) Decreased brain volume in adults with childhood lead exposure, *PLoS Med* 5, e112.

Centers for Disease Control and Prevention. (1991) *Preventing lead poisoning in young children.* Atlanta, GA. www.cdc.gov/nceh/lead/publications/prevleadpoisoning.pdf.

Centers for Disease Control and Prevention. (1999) Ten great public health achievements—United States, 1900–1999, *Morb Mortal Wkly Rep* 48, 241–243.

Centers for Disease Control and Prevention. (2009) *Fourth national report on human exposure to environmental chemicals*, Atlanta, GA.

Chaddock L, Erickson KI, Prakash RS, Kim JS, Voss MW, Vanpatter M, Pontifex MB, Raine LB, Konkel A, Hillman CH, Cohen NJ, and Kramer AF. (2010) A neuroimaging investigation of the association between aerobic fitness, hippocampal volume, and memory performance in preadolescent children, *Brain Res* 1358, 172–183.

Chambers JG, Parrish TB, and Harr JJ. (2004) *What are we spending on special education services in the United States, 1999–2000?* United States Department of Education, Office of Special Education Programs. http://csef.air.org/publications/seep/national/AdvRpt1.pdf.

Cheng KK, Chalmers I, and Sheldon TA. (2007) Adding fluoride to water supplies, *BMJ* 335, 699–702.

Chisolm JJ. (1984) The continuing hazard of lead exposure and its effects in children, *Neurotoxicology* 5, 23–42.

Cho SC, Bhang SY, Hong YC, Shin MS, Kim BN, Kim JW, Yoo HJ, Cho IH, and Kim HW. (2010) Relationship between environmental phthalate exposure and the intelligence of school-age children, *Environ Health Perspect* 118, 1027–1032.

Choi AL, Sun G, Zhang Y, and Grandjean P. (2012) Developmental fluoride neurotoxicity: A systematic review and meta-analysis, *Environ Health Perspect* 120, 1362–1368.

Clapp R, and Hoppin P. (2011) Perfluorooctanoic acid. *Defending Science.* www.defendingscience. org/case-studies/perfluorooctanoic-acid.

Claudio L, Kwa WC, Russell AL, and Wallinga D. (2000) Testing methods for developmental neurotoxicity of environmental chemicals, *Toxicol Appl Pharmacol* 164, 1–14.

Clifford A, Lang L, and Chen R. (2012) Effects of maternal cigarette smoking during pregnancy on cognitive parameters of children and young adults: A literature review, *Neurotoxicol Teratol* 34, 560–570.

Cocke S. (2012) New tests show Hawaii fish jerky is safe but questions remain, *Honolulu Civil Beat,* 6 August.

Colborn T. (2004) Neurodevelopment and endocrine disruption, *Environ Health Perspect* 112, 944–949.

Committee on Toxicity of Chemicals in Food. (2008) *Statement on the 2006 UK total diet study of metals and other elements,* London. http://cot.food.gov.uk/pdfs/cotstatementtds200808.pdf.

Cooper LZ, Ziring PR, Ockerse AB, Fedun BA, Kiely B, and Krugman S. (1969) Rubella, clinical manifestations and management, *Am J Dis Child* 118, 18–29.

Cooper RL, and Kavlock RJ. (1997) Endocrine disruptors and reproductive development: A weight-of-evidence overview, *J Endocrinol* 152, 159–166.

Cranor C. (2008) Do you want to bet your children's health on post-market harm principles? An argument for a trespass or permission model for regulating toxicants, *Villanova Environmental Law Journal* 19, 251–314.

Crump KS, Kjellström T, Shipp AM, Silvers A, and Stewart A. (1998) Influence of prenatal mercury exposure upon scholastic and psychological test performance: Benchmark analysis of a New Zealand cohort, *Risk Anal* 18, 701–713.

D'Itri PA, and D'Itri FM. (1978) Mercury contamination: A human tragedy, *Environmental Management* 2, 3–16.

Dahlgren JG, Takhar HS, Ruffalo CA, and Zwass M. (2004) Health effects of diazinon on a family, *J Toxicol Clin Toxicol* 42, 579–591.

Dakeishi M, Murata K, and Grandjean P. (2006) Lessons from arsenic poisoning of infants due to contaminated dried milk: A review, *Environ Health* 5, 31.

Dallaire R, Muckle G, Dewailly E, Jacobson SW, Jacobson JL, Sandanger TM, Sandau CD, and Ayotte P. (2009) Thyroid hormone levels of pregnant Inuit women and their infants exposed to environmental contaminants, *Environ Health Perspect* 117, 1014–1020.

Dally A. (1998) Thalidomide: Was the tragedy preventable? *Lancet* 351, 1197–1199.

Davidson PW, Myers GJ, Cox C, Shamlaye CF, Marsh DO, Tanner MA, Berlin M, Sloane-Reeves J, Cernichiari E, Choisy O, et al. (1995) Longitudinal neurodevelopmental study of Seychellois children following in utero exposure to methylmercury from maternal fish ingestion: Outcomes at 19 and 29 months, *Neurotoxicology* 16, 677–688.

Davies G, Tenesa A, Payton A, Yang J, Harris SE, Liewald D, Ke X, Le Hellard S, Christoforou A, Luciano M, McGhee K, Lopez L, Gow AJ, Corley J, Redmond P, Fox HC, Haggarty P, Whalley LJ, McNeill G, Goddard ME, Espeseth T, Lundervold AJ, Reinvang I, Pickles A, Steen VM, Ollier W, Porteous DJ, Horan M, Starr JM, Pendleton N, Visscher PM, and Deary IJ. (2011) Genome-wide association studies establish that human intelligence is highly heritable and polygenic, *Mol Psychiatry* 10, 996–1005.

Denno DW. (1990) *Biology and violence: From birth to adulthood,* Cambridge University Press, Cambridge, UK.

DeSesso JM, Williams AL, Ahuja A, Bowman CJ, and Hurtt ME. (2012) The placenta, transfer of immunoglobulins, and safety assessment of biopharmaceuticals in pregnancy, *Crit Rev Toxicol* 42, 185–210.

Devine SA, Kirkley SM, Palumbo CL, and White RF. (2002) MRI and neuropsychological correlates of carbon monoxide exposure: A case report, *Environ Health Perspect* 110, 1051–1055.

Diethelm P, and McKee M. (2009) Denialism: What is it and how should scientists respond? *Eur J Public Health* 19, 2–4.

Dietz R, Outridge PM, and Hobson KA. (2009) Anthropogenic contributions to mercury levels in present-day Arctic animals—a review, *Sci Total Environ* 407, 6120–6131.

Dix-Cooper L, Eskenazi B, Romero C, Balmes J, and Smith KR. (2012) Neurodevelopmental performance among school age children in rural Guatemala is associated with prenatal and postnatal exposure to carbon monoxide, a marker for exposure to woodsmoke, *Neurotoxicology* 33, 246–254.

Douglas H. (2009) *Science, policy, and the value-free ideal*, University of Pittsburgh Press, Pittsburgh, PA.

Draganski B, Gaser C, Busch V, Schuierer G, Bogdahn U, and May A. (2004) Neuroplasticity: Changes in grey matter induced by training, *Nature* 427, 311–312.

Drinker CK, Warren MF, and Bennett GA. (1937) The problem of possible systemic effects from certain chlorinated hydrocarbons, *J Industr Hyg Toxicol* 19, 283–311.

Drum K. (2013) America's Real Criminal Element: Lead. *Mother Jones* January/February issue.

Duckworth AL, and Seligman ME. (2005) Self-discipline outdoes IQ in predicting academic performance of adolescents, *Psychol Sci* 16, 939–944.

Duff RS, and Campbell AG. (1973) Moral and ethical dilemmas in the special-care nursery, *N Engl J Med* 289, 890–894.

Editorial. (1941) Congenital cataract following German measles in the mother, *Med J Aust* 2, 651–652.

Editorial. (1944) Rubella and congenital malformations, *Lancet* 1, 316.

Editorial. (1945) Congenital defects and rubella, *Brit Med J* 1, 635–636.

Edwards GN. (1865) Two cases of poisoning by mercuric methide, *Saint Bartholomew's Hospital Reports* 1, 141–150.

Egeland GM, and Middaugh JP. (1997) Balancing fish consumption benefits with mercury exposure, *Science* 278, 1904–1905.

Engel SM, Berkowitz GS, Barr DB, Teitelbaum SL, Siskind J, Meisel SJ, Wetmur JG, and Wolff MS. (2007) Prenatal organophosphate metabolite and organochlorine levels and performance on the Brazelton Neonatal Behavioral Assessment Scale in a multiethnic pregnancy cohort, *Am J Epidemiol* 165, 1397–1404.

Engel SM, Miodovnik A, Canfield RL, Zhu C, Silva MJ, Calafat AM, and Wolff MS. (2010) Prenatal phthalate exposure is associated with childhood behavior and executive functioning, *Environ Health Perspect* 118, 565–571.

Engel SM, Wetmur J, Chen J, Zhu C, Barr DB, Canfield RL, and Wolff MS. (2011) Prenatal exposure to organophosphates, paraoxonase 1, and cognitive development in childhood, *Environ Health Perspect* 119, 1182–1188.

Engleson G, and Herner T. (1952) Alkyl mercury poisoning, *Acta Paediatr* 41, 289–294.

Environmental Working Group. (2005) *Body burden—the pollution in newborns*. Washington, DC. www.ewg.org/reports/bodyburden2/execsumm.php.

Environmental Working Group. (2010a) *National drinking water database*. Washington, DC. www.ewg.org/tap-water/fullreport.

Environmental Working Group. (2010b) *EWG's 2010 Shopper's guide to pesticides*. Washington, DC. www.ewg.org/agmag/2010/06/shoppers-guide-to-pesticides/.

Eppig C, Fincher CL, and Thornhill R. (2010) Parasite prevalence and the worldwide distribution of cognitive ability, *Proc Biol Sci* 277, 3801–3808.

Ericson JE, Crinella FM, Clarke-Stewart KA, Allhusen VD, Chan T, and Robertson RT. (2007) Prenatal manganese levels linked to childhood behavioral disinhibition, *Neurotoxicol Teratol* 29, 181–187.

Erikson K. (1994) *A new species of trouble*, Norton, New York.

Eriksson P. (2008) Reply to the letter to the editor, *Toxicology* 248, 162–163.

Ernhart CB, Landa B, and Schell NB. (1981) Subclinical levels of lead and developmental deficit—a multivariate follow-up reassessment, *Pediatrics* 67, 911–919.

Ernhart CB, Wolf AW, Sokol RJ, Brittenham GM, and Erhard P. (1985) Fetal lead exposure: Antenatal factors, *Environ Res* 38, 54–66.

Eskenazi B, Chevrier J, Rauch SA, Kogut K, Harley KG, Johnson C, Trujillo C, Sjödin A, and Bradman A. (2013) In utero and childhood polybrominated diphenyl ether (PBDE) exposures and neurodevelopment in the CHAMACOS study, *Environ Health Perspect* (in press).

Eskenazi B, Marks AR, Bradman A, Harley K, Barr DB, Johnson C, Morga N, and Jewell NP. (2007) Organophosphate pesticide exposure and neurodevelopment in young Mexican-American children, *Environ Health Perspect* 115, 792–798.

Eto K, Yasutake A, Nakano A, Akagi H, Tokunaga H, and Kojima T. (2001) Reappraisal of the historic 1959 cat experiment in Minamata by the Chisso Factory, *Tohoku J Exp Med* 194, 197–203.

European Commission. (2007) *The use of plant protection products in the European Union*. Data 1992–2003. http://epp.eurostat.ec.europa.eu/cache/ITY_OFFPUB/KS-76-06-669/EN/KS-76-06-669-EN.PDF.

European Environment Agency. (2001) *Late lessons from early warnings: The precautionary principle 1896–2000*, Copenhagen, Denmark.

European Food Safety Authority. (2010) EFSA Panel on Contaminants in the Food Chain (CONTAM); Scientific opinion on lead in food, *EFSA Journal* 2010 8, 1570.

Evenhouse E, and Reilly S. (2005) Improved estimates of the benefits of breastfeeding using sibling comparisons to reduce selection bias, *Health Serv Res* 40, 1781–1802.

Eyferth K. (1961) Performance of different groups of children of occupation forces on the Hamburg—Wechsler Intelligence test for children (HAWIK) (in German), *Archiv für die gesamte Psychologie* 113, 222–241.

Facchetti S. (1990) Isotopic lead experiment, *Sci Total Environ* 93, 537–538.

Fassin D, and Naude AJ. (2004) Plumbism reinvented: Childhood lead poisoning in France, 1985–1990, *Am J Public Health* 94, 1854–1863.

Feinstein AR. (1988) Scientific standards in epidemiologic studies of the menace of daily life, *Science* 242, 1257–1263.

Fendorf S, Michael HA, and van Geen A. (2010) Spatial and temporal variations of groundwater arsenic in South and Southeast Asia, *Science* 328, 1123–1127.

Ferguson R. (2004) White paper: *Analysis of the Sierra Clubs alarmist claims about the health impacts of mercury*, Frontiers of Freedom, Center for Science and Public Policy, Washington, DC.

Fergusson DM, Boden JM, and Horwood LJ. (2008) Dentine lead levels in childhood and criminal behaviour in late adolescence and early adulthood, *J Epidemiol Community Health* 62, 1045–1050.

Fields RD. (2010) Neuroscience. Change in the brain's white matter, *Science* 330, 768–769.

Fimreite N, and Reynolds L. (1973) Mercury contamination of fish in Northwestern Ontario, *J Wildl Manage* 37, 62–68.

Flanagan SM, Ayotte JD, and Robinson GR Jr. (2012) *Quality of water from crystalline rock aquifers in New England, New Jersey, and New York, 1995–2007*, Scientific Investigations Report 2011–5220, US Geological Survey.

Flynn JR. (2007) *What is intelligence? Beyond the Flynn effect*, Cambridge University Press, Cambridge, UK.

Forrest JM, Turnbull FM, Sholler GF, Hawker RE, Martin FJ, Doran TT, and Burgess MA. (2002) Gregg's congenital rubella patients 60 years later, *Med J Aust* 177, 664–667.

Francis DD, Szegda K, Campbell G, Martin WD, and Insel TR. (2003) Epigenetic sources of behavioral differences in mice, *Nat Neurosci* 6, 445–446.

Francis E. (1994) *Conspiracy of silence: The story of how three corporate giants—Monsanto, GE and Westinghouse—covered their toxic trail*. Sierra Club. www.sierraclub.org/sierra/200103/conspiracy.asp.

Frankel S, Concannon J, Brusky K, Pietrowicz E, Giorgianni S, Thompson WD, and Currie DA. (2009) Arsenic exposure disrupts neurite growth and complexity in vitro, *Neurotoxicology* 30, 529–537.

Freire C, Koifman S. (2012) Pesticide exposure and Parkinson's disease: Epidemiological evidence of association, *Neurotoxicology* 33, 947–971.

Friedman TL. (2009) Going Cheney on climate, *New York Times*, 9 December.

Fryer SL, Schweinsburg BC, Bjorkquist OA, Frank LR, Mattson SN, Spadoni AD, and Riley EP. (2009) Characterization of white matter microstructure in fetal alcohol spectrum disorders, *Alcohol Clin Exp Res* 33, 514–521.

Garry VF. (2004) Pesticides and children, *Toxicol Appl Pharmacol* 198, 152–163.

Gatzke-Kopp LM, and Beauchaine TP. (2007) Direct and passive prenatal nicotine exposure and the development of externalizing psychopathology, *Child Psychiatry Hum Dev* 38, 255–269.

Gayer T, and Hahn RW. (2005) Regulating mercury: What's at stake? *Science* 309, 244–245.

Gentle ECI. (2009) Administration of the 2003 Tolbert PCB settlement in Anniston, Alabama: An attempted collaborative and holistic remedy, *Alabama Law Review* 60, 1249–1264.

Gilbert N. (2011) Data gaps threaten chemical safety law, *Nature* 475, 150–151.

Giles J. (2003) Iraqis draw up blueprint for revitalized science academy, *Nature* 426, 484.

Gilfillan SC. (1965) Lead poisoning and the fall of Rome, *J Occup Med* 7, 53–60.

Gladen BC, Rogan WJ, Hardy P, Thullen J, Tingelstad J, and Tully M. (1988) Development after exposure to polychlorinated biphenyls and dichlorodiphenyl dichloroethene transplacentally and through human milk, *J Pediatr* 113, 991–995.

Gollamudi S, Johri A, Calingasan NY, Yang L, Elemento O, and Beal MF. (2012) Concordant signaling pathways produced by pesticide exposure in mice correspond to pathways identified in human Parkinson's disease, *PLoS One* 7, e36191.

Gorman J. (2003) Does mercury matter? Experts debate the big fish question, *New York Times*, 29 July.

Gough M. (1999) Competitive Enterprise Institute, in *Los Angeles Times*, 31 October.

Gould E. (2009) Childhood lead poisoning: Conservative estimates of the social and economic benefits of lead hazard control, *Environ Health Perspect* 117, 1162–1167.

Government Accounting Office. (2005) *Options exist to improve EPA's ability to assess health risks and manage its chemical review program*, Washington, DC. www.gao.gov/new.items/d05458.pdf.

Grandjean P. (2008a) Late insights into early origins of disease, *Basic Clin Pharmacol Toxicol* 102, 94–99.

Grandjean P. (2008b) Seven deadly sins of environmental epidemiology and the virtues of precaution, *Epidemiology* 19, 158–162.

Grandjean P, and Budtz-Jørgensen E. (2010) An ignored risk factor in toxicology: The total imprecision of exposure assessment, *Pure Appl Chem* 82, 383–391.

Grandjean P, and Holma B. (1973) A history of lead retention in the Danish population, *Environ Biochem Physiol* 3, 268–273.

Grandjean P, and Jensen AA. (2004) Breastfeeding and the weanling's dilemma, *Am J Public Health* 94, 1075; author reply 1075–1076.

Grandjean P, and Klein G. (2005) Epidemiology and precaution 150 years before Snow, *Epidemiology* 16, 271–272.

Grandjean P, and Landrigan PJ. (2006) Developmental neurotoxicity of industrial chemicals, *Lancet* 368, 2167–2178.

Grandjean P, Bellinger D, Bergman A, Cordier S, Davey-Smith G, Eskenazi B, Gee D, Gray K, Hanson M, van den Hazel P, Heindel JJ, Heinzow B, Hertz-Picciotto I, Hu H, Huang TT, Jensen TK, Landrigan PJ, McMillen IC, Murata K, Ritz B, Schoeters G, Skakkebaek NE, Skerfving S, and Weihe P. (2008) The Faroes statement: Human health effects of developmental exposure to chemicals in our environment, *Basic Clin Pharmacol Toxicol* 102, 73–75.

Grandjean P, Eriksen ML, Ellegaard O, and Wallin JA. (2011) The Matthew effect in environmental science publication: A bibliometric analysis of chemical substances in journal articles, *Environ Health* 10, 96.

Grandjean P, Harari R, Barr DB, and Debes F. (2006) Pesticide exposure and stunting as independent predictors of neurobehavioral deficits in Ecuadorian school children, *Pediatrics* 117, e546–556.

Grandjean P, Satoh H, Murata K, and Eto K. (2010) Adverse effects of methylmercury: Environmental health research implications, *Environ Health Perspect* 118, 1137–1145.

Grandjean P, Weihe P, White RF, Debes F, Araki S, Yokoyama K, Murata K, Sørensen N, Dahl R, and Jørgensen PJ. (1997) Cognitive deficit in 7-year-old children with prenatal exposure to methylmercury, *Neurotoxicol Teratol* 19, 417–428.

Greenberg DS. (2003) Conference deplores corporate influence on academic science. Speakers argue that corporate funds should be separated from science to prevent undue influence, *Lancet* 362, 302–303.

Gregg C, Zhang J, Butler JE, Haig D, and Dulac C. (2010) Sex-specific parent-of-origin allelic expression in the mouse brain, *Science* 329, 682–685.

Gregg NM. (1941) Congenital cataract following German measles in the mother, *Trans Opthalmol Soc Aust* 3, 35–46.

Grosse SD, Matte TD, Schwartz J, and Jackson RJ. (2002) Economic gains resulting from the reduction in children's exposure to lead in the United States, *Environ Health Perspect* 110, 563–569.

Grunwald M. (2002) Monsanto hid decades of pollution, *Washington Post*, 1 January.

Gump BB, Wu Q, Dumas AK, and Kannan K. (2011) Perfluorochemical (PFC) exposure in children: Associations with impaired response inhibition, *Environ Sci Technol* 45, 8151–8159.

Guo YL, Lambert GH, Hsu CC, and Hsu MM. (2004) Yucheng: Health effects of prenatal exposure to polychlorinated biphenyls and dibenzofurans, *Int Arch Occup Environ Health* 77, 153–158.

Guzelian PS, Henry CJ, and Olin SS. (1992) *Similarities and differences between children and adults: Implication for risk assessment*, ILSI Press, Washington, DC.

Haefliger P, Mathieu-Nolf M, Lociciro S, Ndiaye C, Coly M, Diouf A, Faye AL, Sow A, Tempowski J, Pronczuk J, Filipe Junior AP, Bertollini R, and Neira M. (2009) Mass lead intoxication from informal used lead-acid battery recycling in Dakar, Senegal, *Environ Health Perspect* 117, 1535–1540.

Harada M. (2004) *Minimata disease* (translated by Sachie Y, George TS), Vol. first published in Japanese 1972, Iwanami Shoten, Tokyo.

Harada M. (1977a) A study on methylmercury concentration in the umbilical cords of the inhabitants born in the Minamata area [in Japanese], *Nhoto Hattatsu* 9, 79–84.

Harada Y. (1977b) Congenital alkyl mercury-poisoning (congenital Minimata Disease), *Paediatrician* 6, 58–68.

Harari R, Julvez J, Murata K, Barr D, Bellinger DC, Debes F, and Grandjean P. (2010) Neurobehavioral deficits and increased blood pressure in school-age children prenatally exposed to pesticides, *Environ Health Perspect* 118, 890–896.

Hardy HL. (1966) Lead, in *symposium on environmental lead contamination*, pp. 73–83, US Dept. of Health, Education, and Welfare, Public Health Service, Washington, DC.

Heckman JJ. (2006) Skill formation and the economics of investing in disadvantaged children, *Science* 312, 1900–1902.

Heiervang KS, Mednick S, Sundet K, and Rund BR. (2010) Effect of low dose ionizing radiation exposure in utero on cognitive function in adolescence, *Scand J Psychol* 51, 210–215.

Hemenway D. (2010) Why we don't spend enough on public health, *N Engl J Med* 362, 1657–1658.

Hepp P. (1887) Über quecksilberäthylverbindungen und über das verhältniss der quecksilberäthyl-zur quecksilbervergiftung, *Naunyn Schmiedebergs Archives of Experimental Pathology and Pharmacology* 23, 91–128.

Herbstman JB, Sjödin A, Kurzon M, Lederman SA, Jones RS, Rauh V, Needham LL, Tang D, Niedzwiecki M, Wang RY, and Perera F. (2010) Prenatal exposure to PBDEs and neurodevelopment, *Environ Health Perspect* 118, 712–719.

Herculano-Houzel S. (2009) The human brain in numbers: A linearly scaled-up primate brain, *Front Hum Neurosci* 3, 31.

Herner T. (1945) Poisoning from organic compounds of mercury [in Swedish], *Nordisk Medicin* 26, 833–836.

Herrick RF, McClean MD, Meeker JD, Baxter LK, and Weymouth GA. (2004) An unrecognized source of PCB contamination in schools and other buildings, *Environ Health Perspect* 112, 1051–1053.

Herrnstein RJ, and Murray C. (1994) *The bell curve*, Free Press, New York.

Hersh JH, Podruch PE, Rogers G, and Weisskopf B. (1985) Toluene embryopathy, *J Pediatr* 106, 922–927.

Heudorf U, Butte W, Schulz C, and Angerer J. (2006) Reference values for metabolites of pyrethroid and organophosphorous insecticides in urine for human biomonitoring in environmental medicine, *Int J Hyg Environ Health* 209, 293–299.

Higginson J. (1998) The International Agency for Research on Cancer. A brief review of its history, mission, and program, *Toxicol Sci* 43, 79–85.

Hightower JM. (2009) *Diagnosis mercury: Money, politics, and poison*, Island Press/Shearwater Books, Washington, DC.

Higley MJ, and Strittmatter SM. (2010) Neuroscience. Lynx for braking plasticity, *Science* 330, 1189–1190.

Hill AB. (1965) The environment and disease: Association or causation? *Proc R Soc Med* 58, 295–300.

Hill RM, Hegemier S, and Tennyson LM. (1989) The fetal alcohol syndrome: A multihandicapped child, *Neurotoxicology* 10, 585–595.

Ho-Yen DO, and Joss AWL. (1992) *Human toxoplasmosis*, Oxford University Press, Oxford, UK.

Hoffman J. (2005) A conversation with Janet Golden, Sorting out ambivalence over alcohol and pregnancy, *New York Times*, 25 January.

Holtcamp W. (2012) Flavors of uncertainty: The difference between denial and debate, *Environ Health Perspect* 120, a314–319.

Hook O, Lundgren KD, and Swensson A. (1954) On alkyl mercury poisoning; with a description of two cases, *Acta Med Scand* 150, 131–137.

Horel S. (2008) *La grande invasion*, Edition du moment, Paris.

Hornig M, and Lipkin WI. (2001) Infectious and immune factors in the pathogenesis of neurodevelopmental disorders: Epidemiology, hypotheses, and animal models, *Ment Retard Dev Disabil Res Rev* 7, 200–210.

Hornung RW, Lanphear BP, and Dietrich KN. (2009) Age of greatest susceptibility to childhood lead exposure: A new statistical approach, *Environ Health Perspect* 117, 1309–1312.

Horton MK, Rundle A, Camann DE, Boyd Barr D, Rauh VA, and Whyatt RM. (2011) Impact of prenatal exposure to piperonyl butoxide and permethrin on 36-month neurodevelopment, *Pediatrics* 127, e699–706.

Hunt TJ, Hepner R, and Seaton KW. (1982) Childhood lead poisoning and inadequate child care, *Am J Dis Child* 136, 538–542.

Hunter D, and Russell DS. (1954) Focal cerebellar and cerebellar atrophy in a human subject due to organic mercury compounds, *J Neurol Neurosurg Psychiatry* 17, 235–241.

Hunter D, Bomford RR, and Russell DS. (1940) Poisoning by methyl mercury compounds, *Quarterly Journal of Medicine* 9, 193–U111.

Huss A, Egger M, Hug K, Huwiler-Müntener K, and Röösli M. (2007) Source of funding and results of studies of health effects of mobile phone use: Systematic review of experimental studies, *Environ Health Perspect* 115, 1–4.

Hutchison G. (1977) *Grassy Narrows*, Van Nostrand Reinhold, Toronto.

Huttenlocher PR, and Dabholkar AS. (1997) Regional differences in synaptogenesis in human cerebral cortex, *J Comp Neurol* 387, 167–178.

Hyland K. (1998) *Hedging in scientific research articles*, John Benjamins, Amsterdam, The Netherlands.

Illson M. (1955) Fluoride's value in water argued, *New York Times*, 11 April.

Institute of Medicine. (1981) *Cost of environment-related health effects: A plan for continuing study*, National Academy Press, Washington, DC.

International Agency for Research on Cancer. (2004) *Some drinking-water disinfectants and contaminants, including arsenic,* Working Group on the Evaluation of Carcinogenic Risks to Humans, Lyon, France. http://monographs.iarc.fr/ENG/Monographs/vol84/volume84.pdf.

International Lead Zinc Research Organization. (1979) *Lead Research Digest,* 37.

International Programme on Chemical Safety. (1977) *Lead.* World Health Organization, Geneva. www.inchem.org/documents/ehc/ehc/ehc003.htm.

International Programme on Chemical Safety. (2001) *Arsenic and arsenic compounds.* WHO, Geneva. www.who.int/ipcs/publications/ehc/ehc_224/en/.

Ioannidis JP. (2008) Why most discovered true associations are inflated, *Epidemiology* 19, 640–648.

Israel B. (2012) Dirty soil and diabetes: Anniston's toxic legacy, *Environmental Health News,* 13 June. www.environmentalhealthnews.org/ehs/news/2012/pollution-poverty-people-of-color-day-6-diabetes/.

Ito T, Ando H, Suzuki T, Ogura T, Hotta K, Imamura Y, Yamaguchi Y, and Handa H. (2010) Identification of a primary target of thalidomide teratogenicity, *Science* 327, 1345–1350.

Jacobsen PR, Christiansen S, Boberg J, Nellemann C, and Hass U. (2010) Combined exposure to endocrine disrupting pesticides impairs parturition, causes pup mortality and affects sexual differentiation in rats, *Int J Androl* 33, 434–442.

Jacobson JL, and Jacobson SW. (1996) Intellectual impairment in children exposed to polychlorinated biphenyls in utero, *N Engl J Med* 335, 783–789.

Jacobson JL, Jacobson SW, and Humphrey HE. (1990) Effects of in utero exposure to polychlorinated biphenyls and related contaminants on cognitive functioning in young children, *J Pediatr* 116, 38–45.

Jalili MA, and Abbasi AH. (1961) Poisoning by ethyl mercury toluene sulphonanilide, *Br J Ind Med* 18, 303–308.

James A, Horton R, Collingridge D, McConnell J, and Butcher J. (2004) The Lancet's policy on conflicts of interest—2004, *Lancet* 363, 2–3.

Janulewicz PA, White RF, Martin BM, Winter MR, Weinberg JM, Vieira V, and Aschengrau A. (2012) Adult neuropsychological performance following prenatal and early postnatal exposure to tetrachloroethylene (PCE)-contaminated drinking water, *Neurotoxicol Teratol* 34, 350–359.

Jasanoff S. (2010) Science and society. Testing time for climate science, *Science* 328, 695–696.

Jensen AR. (2000) The g factor: Psychometrics and biology, *Novartis Found Symp* 233, 37–47; discussion 47–57, 116–121.

Jensen S, and Jernelöv A. (1967) Biosynthesis of methylmercury [in Swedish], *Nordforsk Biocidinformation* 10, 4–5.

Jensen S. (1972) The PCB story, *Ambio* 1, 123–131.

Johnston MV, Nishimura A, Harum K, Pekar J, and Blue ME. (2001) Sculpting the developing brain, *Adv Pediatr* 48, 1–38.

Joint Expert Committee on Food Additives. (1972) *Evaluation of mercury, lead, cadmium and the food additives amaranth, diethylpyrocarbonate, and octyl gallate.* Geneva. http://whqlibdoc.who.int/trs/WHO_TRS_505.pdf.

Joint Expert Committee on Food Additives. (1978) *Evaluation of certain food additives and contaminants* (Twenty-second report of the Joint FAO/WHO Expert Committee on Food Additives). Geneva. http://whqlibdoc.who.int/trs/WHO_TRS_631.pdf.

Joint Expert Committee on Food Additives. (1986) *Evaluation of certain food additives and contaminants* (Twenty-ninth report). www.who.int/ipcs/publications/jecfa/reports/trs940.pdf.

Joint Expert Committee on Food Additives. (2003) Summary and conclusions. Sixty-first meeting of the Joint FAO/WHO Expert Committee on Food Additives held in Rome, 10–19 June 2003. www.who.int/pcs/jecfa/Summary61.pdf.

Jones KL, and Smith DW. (1973) Recognition of the fetal alcohol syndrome in early infancy, *Lancet* 302, 999–1001.

Jones RL, Homa DM, Meyer PA, Brody DJ, Caldwell KL, Pirkle JL, and Brown MJ. (2009) Trends in blood lead levels and blood lead testing among US children aged 1 to 5 years, 1988–2004, *Pediatrics* 123, e376–385.

Julvez J, and Grandjean P. (2009) Neurodevelopmental toxicity risks due to occupational exposure to industrial chemicals during pregnancy, *Ind Health* 47, 459–468.

Kaiser J. (2005) Lead paint experts face a barrage of subpoenas, *Science* 309, 362–363.

Kaplan S. (2011) Company pays government to challenge pesticide research showing link to Parkinson's, In *Investigative Reporting Workshop*, American University School of Communication, 11 February.

Kaufman AS. (2001) Do low levels of lead produce IQ loss in children? A careful examination of the literature, *Arch Clin Neuropsychol* 16, 303–341.

Kehoe RA, Thamann F, and Cholak J. (1935) Normal absorption and excretion of lead, *JAMA* 104, 90–92.

Kehoe RA. (1961) The Harben Lectures, 1960: The metabolism of lead in man in health and disease. 3. Present hygienic problems relating to the absorption of lead, *J R Inst Public Health* 24, 177–203.

Kely RGI. (2000) PCBs fell on Alabama (letter), *The Nation*, 15 June.

Kjellström T, Kennedy P, Wallis S, and Mantell C. (1986) *Physical and mental development of children with prenatal exposure to mercury from fish. State 1: Preliminary tests at age 4*, National Swedish Environmental Protection Board, Solna. Report 3080.

Kjellström T, Kennedy P, Wallis S, Stewart A, Friberg L, and Lind B. (1989) *Physical and mental development of children with prenatal exposure to mercury from fish. Stage II: Interviews and psychological tests at age 6*, National Swedish Environmental Protection Board, Solna. Report 3642.

Kofman O, Berger A, Massarwa A, Friedman A, and Jaffar AA. (2006) Motor inhibition and learning impairments in school-aged children following exposure to organophosphate pesticides in infancy, *Pediatr Res* 60, 88–92.

Kordas K, Canfield RL, Lopez P, Rosado JL, Vargas GG, Cebrian ME, Rico JA, Ronquillo D, and Stoltzfus RJ. (2006) Deficits in cognitive function and achievement in Mexican first-graders with low blood lead concentrations, *Environ Res* 100, 371–386.

Koren G, and Navioz Y. (2003) Historical perspective: The original description of fetal alcohol spectrum disorder in France, 1967, *Ther Drug Monit* 25, 131.

Kotok D. (1972) Development of children with elevated blood lead levels: A controlled study, *J Pediatr* 80, 57–61.

Kovarik W. (2005) Ethyl-leaded gasoline: How a classic occupational disease became an international public health disaster, *Int J Occup Environ Health* 11, 384–397.

Krimsky S. (2003) *Science in the private interest*, Rowman & Littlefield, Lanham, MD.

Kuehn RR. (2004) Suppression of environmental science, *Am J Law Med* 30, 333–369.

Kurland J. (2002) The heart of the precautionary principle in democracy, *Public Health Rep* 117, 498–500.

Kurth L, and Haussmann R. (2011) Perinatal pitocin as an early ADHD biomarker: Neurodevelopmental risk? *J Atten Disord* 15, 423–431.

Lancaster HO. (1951) Deafness as an epidemic disease in Australia; a note on census and institutional data, *Br Med J* 2, 1429–1432.

Landman A, and Glantz SA. (2009) Tobacco industry efforts to undermine policy-relevant research, *Am J Public Health* 99, 45–58.

Landrigan PJ, Schechter CB, Lipton JM, Fahs MC, and Schwartz J. (2002) Environmental pollutants and disease in American children: Estimates of morbidity, mortality, and costs for lead poisoning, asthma, cancer, and developmental disabilities, *Environ Health Perspect* 110, 721–728.

Landrigan PJ, Whitworth RH, Baloh RW, Staehling NW, Barthel WF, and Rosenblum BF. (1975) Neuropsychological dysfunction in children with chronic low-level lead absorption, *Lancet* 1, 708–712.

Langer N, Hanggi J, Muller NA, Simmen HP, and Jancke L. (2012) Effects of limb immobilization on brain plasticity, *Neurology* 78, 182–188.

Lanphear BP, Hornung R, Khoury J, Yolton K, Baghurst P, Bellinger DC, Canfield RL, Dietrich KN, Bornschein R, Greene T, Rothenberg SJ, Needleman HL, Schnaas L, Wasserman G, Graziano J, and Roberts R. (2005) Low-level environmental lead exposure and children's intellectual function: An international pooled analysis, *Environ Health Perspect* 113, 894–899.

Lanphear BP. (2007) The conquest of lead poisoning: A Pyrrhic victory, *Environ Health Perspect* 115, A484–485.

Lauder JM, and Schambra UB. (1999) Morphogenetic roles of acetylcholine, *Environ Health Perspect* 107 Suppl 1, 65–69.

Lead Industries Association. (1968) *Facts about lead and the atmosphere*, Milwaukee, WI.

Lee KT, Mattson SN, and Riley EP. (2004) Classifying children with heavy prenatal alcohol exposure using measures of attention, *J Int Neuropsychol Soc* 10, 271–277.

Leigh D, Evans R, and Mahmood M. (2010) Killer chemicals and greased palms—the deadly 'end game' for leaded petrol, *The Guardian*, 30 June.

Lemoine P, Harousseau H, Borteyru JP, and Menuet JC. (2003) Children of alcoholic parents—observed anomalies: Discussion of 127 cases, *Ther Drug Monit* 25, 132–136.

Lemoine P. (1992) Outcome of children of alcoholic mothers (study of 105 cases followed to adult age) and various prophylactic findings [in French], *Ann Pediatr* (Paris) 39, 226–235.

Lemoine P. (1994) The letter from Professor Lemoine, *Addiction* 89, 1021–1023.

Lesser LI, Ebbeling CB, Goozner M, Wypij D, and Ludwig DS. (2007) Relationship between funding source and conclusion among nutrition-related scientific articles, *PLoS Med* 4, e5.

Levine AD. (2010) Self-regulation, compensation, and the ethical recruitment of oocyte donors, *Hastings Cent Rep* 40, 25–36.

Liebl B, Schettgen T, Kerscher G, Broding HC, Otto A, Angerer J, and Drexler H. (2004) Evidence for increased internal exposure to lower chlorinated polychlorinated biphenyls (PCB) in pupils attending a contaminated school. *Int J Hyg Environ Health* 207, 315–324.

Logan A. (2006) *The brain diet*, Cumberland, Nashville, TN.

London L, Matzopoulos R, Corrigall J, Myers JE, Maker A, and Parry CDH. (2012) Conflict of interest: A tenacious ethical dilemma in public health policy, not only in clinical practice/research. *South African Journal of Bioethics and Law* 5, 102–108.

Lopez-Espinosa MJ, Vizcaino E, Murcia M, Fuentes V, Garcia AM, Rebagliato M, Grimalt JO, and Ballester F. (2010) Prenatal exposure to organochlorine compounds and neonatal thyroid stimulating hormone levels, *J Expo Sci Environ Epidemiol* 20, 579–588.

Love D. (2006) *My city was gone*, HarperCollins, New York.

Lucchini RG, Guazzetti S, Zoni S, Donna F, Peter S, Zacco A, Salmistraro M, Bontempi E, Zimmerman NJ, and Smith DR. (2012) Tremor, olfactory and motor changes in Italian adolescents exposed to historical ferro-manganese emission, *Neurotoxicology* 33, 687–696.

Lyketsos CG. (2003) Should pregnant women avoid eating fish? Lessons from the Seychelles, *Lancet* 361, 1667–1668.

Lyngbye T, Hansen ON, Trillingsgaard A, Beese I, and Grandjean P. (1990) Learning disabilities in children: Significance of low-level lead-exposure and confounding factors, *Acta Paediatr Scand* 79, 352–360.

Lynn R, and Vanhanen T. (2002) *IQ and the wealth of nations*, Praeger, Westport, CT.

Mahaffey KR, Sunderland EM, Chan HM, Choi AL, Grandjean P, Mariën K, Oken E, Sakamoto M, Schoeny R, Weihe P, Yan CH, Yasutake A. (2011) Balancing the benefits of n-3 polyunsaturated fatty acids and the risks of methylmercury exposure from fish consumption, *Nutr Rev* 69, 493–508.

MacIntosh DL, Minegishi T, Fragala MA, Allen JG, Coghlan KM, Stewart JH, and McCarthy JF. (2012) Mitigation of building-related polychlorinated biphenyls in indoor air of a school, *Environ Health* 11, 24.

Makris SL, Raffaele K, Allen S, Bowers WJ, Hass U, Alleva E, Calamandrei G, Sheets L, Amcoff P, Delrue N, and Crofton KM. (2009) A retrospective performance assessment of the developmental neurotoxicity study in support of OECD test guideline 426, *Environ Health Perspect* 117, 17–25.

Mari F, Bertol E, Fineschi V, and Karch SB. (2004) Channelling the emperor: What really killed Napoleon? *J R Soc Med* 97, 397–399.

Marin-Burgin A, Mongiat LA, Pardi MB, and Schinder AF. (2012) Unique processing during a period of high excitation/inhibition balance in adult-born neurons, *Science* 335, 1238–1242.

Mariussen E. (2012) Neurotoxic effects of perfluoroalkylated compounds: Mechanisms of action and environmental relevance, *Arch Toxicol* 86, 1349–1367.

Markowitz G, and Rosner D. (2000) "Cater to the children": The role of the lead industry in a public health tragedy, 1900–1955, *Am J Public Health* 90, 36–46.

Markowitz G, and Rosner D. (2002) Deceit and denial: The deadly politics of industrial pollution, University of California Press, Berkeley.

Marsh DO, Clarkson TW, Cox C, Myers GJ, Amin-Zaki L, and Al-Tikriti S. (1987) Fetal methylmercury poisoning. Relationship between concentration in single strands of maternal hair and child effects, *Arch Neurol* 44, 1017–1022.

Marshall E. (1983) EPA faults classic lead poisoning study. A review questions a study linking lead in teeth with low IQ scores; EPA finds other grounds for regulation, *Science* 222, 906–907.

Marshall E. (1984) Senate considers lead gasoline ban, *Science* 225, 34–35.

Martin JH, Choy M, Pullman S, and Meng Z. (2004) Corticospinal system development depends on motor experience, *J Neurosci* 24, 2122–2132.

Martin JH, Engber D, and Meng Z. (2005) Effect of forelimb use on postnatal development of the forelimb motor representation in primary motor cortex of the cat, *J Neurophysiol* 93, 2822–2831.

Martin MT. (2002) A strange ignorance: The role of lead poisoning in failing schools. Arizona School Boards Association. www.azsba.org/static/index.cfm?action=group&contentID=148.

Martinson BC, Anderson MS, and de Vries R. (2005) Scientists behaving badly, *Nature* 435, 737–738.

Mazumdar M, Bellinger DC, Gregas M, Abanilla K, Bacic J, and Needleman HL. (2011) Low-level environmental lead exposure in childhood and adult intellectual function: A follow-up study, *Environ Health* 10, 24.

McClure SM, Laibson DI, Loewenstein G, and Cohen JD. (2004) Separate neural systems value immediate and delayed monetary rewards, *Science* 306, 503–507.

McGarity TO, and Wagner WE. (2008) *Bending science: How special interests corrupt public health research*, Harvard University Press, Boston, MA.

McKeown-Eyssen GE, Ruedy J, and Neims A. (1983) Methyl mercury exposure in northern Quebec. II. Neurologic findings in children, *Am J Epidemiol* 118, 470–479.

McNeill J. (2000) *Something new under the sun. An environmental history of the twentieth-century world*, Norton, New York.

Mechelli A, Crinion JT, Noppeney U, O'Doherty J, Ashburner J, Frackowiak RS, and Price CJ. (2004) Neurolinguistics: Structural plasticity in the bilingual brain, *Nature* 431, 757.

Menser MA, Dods L, and Harley JD. (1967) A twenty-five-year follow-up of congenital rubella, *Lancet* 2, 1347–1350.

Michaels D. (2008) *Doubt is their product: How industry's assault on science threatens your health*, Oxford University Press, Oxford, UK.

Michaels D. (2005) Doubt is their product, *Sci Am* 292, 96–101.

Min MO, Singer LT, Kirchner HL, Minnes S, Short E, Hussain Z, and Nelson S. (2009) Cognitive development and low-level lead exposure in poly-drug exposed children, *Neurotoxicol Teratol* 31, 225–231.

Miranda ML, Kim D, Reiter J, Overstreet Galeano MA, and Maxson P. (2009) Environmental contributors to the achievement gap, *Neurotoxicology* 30, 1019–1024.

Mishima A. (1992) *Bitter sea, the human cost of Minamata disease* (translated by Gage RL and Murata SB), Kosei, Tokyo.

Mooney C. (2004) Earth last: James Inhofe proves "flat Earth" doesn't refer to Oklahoma, *American Prospect*, 7 May.

Moore EGJ. (1986) Family socialization and the IQ test performance of traditionally and transracially adopted black children, *Developm Psychol* 22, 317–326.

Moore MR. (1977) Lead in drinking water in soft water areas—health hazards, *Sci Total Environ* 7, 109–115.

Mullenix PJ, Denbesten PK, Schunior A, and Kernan WJ. (1995) Neurotoxicity of sodium fluoride in rats, *Neurotoxicol Teratol* 17, 169–177.

Munroe S. (2006) *Congenital rubella syndrome in Canada—report on current status and late manifestations.* Presented at a meeting of the Immunization Unit of the Pan American Health Organization (PAHO). Washington, DC, 10–11 July. www.cdbanational.com/PDFs/Congenital%20Rubella%20Study%20(English).pdf.

Murozumi M, Chow TJ, and Patterson C. (1969) Chemical concentrations of pollutant lead aerosols, terrestrial dusts and sea salts in Greenland and Antarctic snow, *Geochim Cosmochim Acta* 33, 1247–1294.

Murray C. (2002) IQ and income inequality in a sample of sibling pairs from advantaged backgrounds, *Am Econ Rev* 92, 339–343.

Myers GJ, and Davidson PW. (1998) Prenatal methylmercury exposure and children: neurologic, developmental, and behavioral research, *Environ Health Perspect* 106 Suppl 3, 841–847.

Myers GJ, Davidson PW, and Shamlaye CF. (2006) Developmental disabilities following prenatal exposure to methyl mercury from maternal fish consumption: A review of the evidence, *Int Rev Res Ment Retard* 30, 141–169.

Myers GJ, Davidson PW, Cox C, Shamlaye CF, Palumbo D, Cernichiari E, Sloane-Reeves J, Wilding GE, Kost J, Huang LS, and Clarkson TW. (2003) Prenatal methylmercury exposure from ocean fish consumption in the Seychelles child development study, *Lancet* 361, 1686–1692.

Myers GJ, Marsh DO, Davidson PW, Cox C, Shamlaye CF, Tanner M, Choi A, Cernichiari E, Choisy O, and Clarkson TW. (1995) Main neurodevelopmental study of Seychellois children following in utero exposure to methylmercury from a maternal fish diet: Outcome at six months, *Neurotoxicology* 16, 653–664.

Nakagawa R, and Libuchi Y. (1970) Follow-up survey of Morinaga poisoning [in Japanese], *Igaku No Ayumi* 74, 1–3.

Nakashima T, Matsuno K, Matsushita M, and Matsushita T. (2011) Severe lead contamination among children of samurai families in Edo period Japan, *J Archaeol Sci* 38, 23–28

National Institute of Environmental Health Sciences. (1998) *Scientific issues relevant to assessment of health effects from exposure to methylmercury.* Workshop organized by Committee on Environmental and Natural Resources (CENR), Office of Science and Technology Policy (OSTP), White House, 18–20 November, 1998. http://ntp.niehs.nih.gov/index.cfm?objectid=03614B65-BC68-D231-4E915F93AF9A6872.

National Research Council. (1980) *Lead in the human environment*, National Academy Press, Washington, DC.

National Research Council. (1993) *Pesticides in the diet of infants and children*, National Academy Press, Washington, DC.

National Research Council. (1999) *Arsenic in drinking water*, National Academy Press, Washington, DC.

National Research Council. (2000a) *Toxicological effects of methylmercury*, National Academy Press, Washington, DC.

National Research Council. (2000b) *Scientific frontiers in developmental toxicology and risk assessment*, National Academy Press, Washington, DC.

National Research Council. (2006) *Fluoride in drinking water: A scientific review of EPA's standards*, National Academy Press, Washington, DC.

National Research Council. (2007) *Toxicity testing in the 21st century: A vision and a strategy*, National Academy Press, Washington, DC.

Natural Resources Defense Council. (2009) *Arsenic in drinking water.* www.nrdc.org/water/drinking/qarsenic.asp.

Needham LL, Grandjean P, Heinzow B, Jørgensen PJ, Nielsen F, Patterson DG, Jr., Sjödin A, Turner WE, and Weihe P. (2011) Partition of environmental chemicals between maternal and fetal blood and tissues, *Environ Sci Technol* 45, 1121–1126.

Needleman HL. (1997) Clamped in a straitjacket: The insertion of lead into gasoline, *Environ Res* 74, 95–103.

Needleman HL. (1998) Clair Patterson and Robert Kehoe: Two views of lead toxicity, *Environ Res* 78, 79–85.

Needleman HL. (2000) The removal of lead from gasoline: Historical and personal reflections, *Environ Res* 84, 20–35.

Needleman HL, Gunnoe C, Leviton A, Reed R, Peresie H, Maher C, and Barrett P. (1979) Deficits in psychologic and classroom performance of children with elevated dentine lead levels, *N Engl J Med* 300, 689–695.

Needleman HL, and Landrigan PJ. (1994) *Raising children toxic free*, Farrar, Straus and Giroux, New York.

Needleman HL, Riess JA, Tobin MJ, Biesecker GE, and Greenhouse JB. (1996) Bone lead levels and delinquent behavior, *JAMA* 275, 363–369.

Nelson CA, 3rd, Zeanah CH, Fox NA, Marshall PJ, Smyke AT, and Guthrie D. (2007) Cognitive recovery in socially deprived young children: The Bucharest Early Intervention Project, *Science* 318, 1937–1940.

Nelson CA. (2004) Brain development during puberty and adolescence: Comments on part II, *Ann N Y Acad Sci* 1021, 105–109.

Nevin R. (2009) Trends in preschool lead exposure, mental retardation, and scholastic achievement: Association or causation? *Environ Res* 109, 301–310.

Nisbett R. (2009) *Intelligence and how to get it*, Norton, New York.

O'Donnell N. (1991) *Report on a survey on late emerging manifestations of congenital rubella syndrome.* New York, Helen Keller National Center

O'Farrell P. (2009) Lead exposure, brain damage linked, *Cincinnati Enquirer*, 1 December.

Ohira M, and Aoyama H. (1973) Epidemiological studies on the Morinaga powdered milk poisoning [in Japanese with English abstract], *Jpn. J. Hyg.* 27, 500–531.

Olesen J, Baker MG, Freund T, di Luca M, Mendlewicz J, Ragan I, and Westphal M. (2006) Consensus document on European brain research, *J Neurol Neurosurg Psychiatry* 77 Suppl 1, i1–49.

Ordonez JV, Carrillo JA, Miranda M, and Gale JL. (1966) Epidemiologic study of a disease believed to be encephalitis in the region of the highlands of Guatemala [in Spanish] *Bol Oficina Sanit Panam* 60, 510–519.

Oreskes N, and Conway EM. (2010) *Merchants of doubt*, Bloomsbury, New York.

Patandin S, Lanting CI, Mulder PG, Boersma ER, Sauer PJ, and Weisglas-Kuperus N. (1999) Effects of environmental exposure to polychlorinated biphenyls and dioxins on cognitive abilities in Dutch children at 42 months of age, *J Pediatr* 134, 33–41.

Patel P, and Sun L. (2009) Update on neonatal anesthetic neurotoxicity: Insight into molecular mechanisms and relevance to humans, *Anesthesiology* 110, 703–708.

Patterson CC. (1965) Contaminated and natural lead environments of man, *Arch Environ Health* 11, 344–360.

Pawlas N, Broberg K, Olewinska E, Prokopowicz A, Skerfving S, and Pawlas K. (2012) Modification by the genes ALAD and VDR of lead-induced cognitive effects in children, *Neurotoxicology* 33, 37–43.

Pearson H. (2004) Mercury affects brains of adolescents, *Nature*, 6 February.

Pearson MA, Hoyme HE, Seaver LH, and Rimsza ME. (1994) Toluene embryopathy: Delineation of the phenotype and comparison with fetal alcohol syndrome, *Pediatrics* 93, 211–215.

Pekkanen J. (2006) Why is lead still poisoning our children? *Washingtonian*, 1 August.

Pelé F, Muckle G, Costet N, Garlantézec R, Monfort C, Multigner L, Rouget F, and Cordier S. (2013) Occupational solvent exposure during pregnancy and child behaviour at age 2. *Occup Environ Med* 70, 114–119.

Perera FP, Li Z, Whyatt R, Hoepner L, Wang S, Camann D, and Rauh V. (2009) Prenatal airborne polycyclic aromatic hydrocarbon exposure and child IQ at age 5 years, *Pediatrics* 124, e195–202.

Pichery C, Bellanger M, Zmirou-Navier D, Fréry N, Cordier S, Roue-LeGall A, Hartemann P, and Grandjean P. (2012) Economic evaluation of health consequences of prenatal methylmercury exposure in France, *Environ Health* 11, 53.

Pichery C, Bellanger M, Zmirou-Navier D, Glorennec P, Hartemann P, and Grandjean P. (2011) Childhood lead exposure in France: Benefit estimation and partial cost-benefit analysis of lead hazard control, *Environ Health* 10, 44.

Pinker S. (2003). *The blank slate: The modern denial of human nature*, Penguin, New York.

Prüss-Üstün A, and Corvalán C. (2006) Preventing disease through healthy environments— Towards an estimate of the environmental burden of disease. World Health Organization, Geneva. www.who.int/quantifying_ehimpacts/publications/preventingdisease.pdf.

Qiao D, Seidler FJ, Tate CA, Cousins MM, and Slotkin TA. (2003) Fetal chlorpyrifos exposure: Adverse effects on brain cell development and cholinergic biomarkers emerge postnatally and continue into adolescence and adulthood, *Environ Health Perspect* 111, 536–544.

Rabin R. (1989) Warnings unheeded: A history of child lead poisoning, *Am J Public Health* 79, 1668–1674.

Rabin R. (2008) The lead industry and lead water pipes "A Modest Campaign," *Am J Public Health* 98, 1584–1592.

Raffaele KC, Rowland J, May B, Makris SL, Schumacher K, and Scarano LJ. (2010) The use of developmental neurotoxicity data in pesticide risk assessments, *Neurotoxicol Teratol* 32, 563–572.

Rappaport B, Mellon RD, Simone A, and Woodcock J. (2011) Defining safe use of anesthesia in children, *N Engl J Med* 364, 1387–1390.

Rauh V, Arunajadai S, Horton M, Perera F, Hoepner L, Barr DB, and Whyatt R. (2011) 7-year neurodevelopmental scores and prenatal exposure to chlorpyrifos, a common agricultural pesticide, *Environ Health Perspect* 119, 1196–1201.

Rauh VA, Garfinkel R, Perera FP, Andrews HF, Hoepner L, Barr DB, Whitehead R, Tang D, and Whyatt RW. (2006) Impact of prenatal chlorpyrifos exposure on neurodevelopment in the first 3 years of life among inner-city children, *Pediatrics* 118, e1845–1859.

Rauh VA, Perera FP, Horton MK, Whyatt RM, Bansal R, Hao X, Liu J, Barr DB, Slotkin TA, and Peterson BS. (2012) Brain anomalies in children exposed prenatally to a common organophosphate pesticide, *Proc Natl Acad Sci USA* 109, 7871–7876.

Renner R. (2009) Out of plumb: When water treatment causes lead contamination, *Environ Health Perspect* 117, A542–547.

Revello MG, and Gerna G. (2002) Diagnosis and management of human cytomegalovirus infection in the mother, fetus, and newborn infant, *Clin Microbiol Rev* 15, 680–715.

Ribas-Fito N, Torrent M, Carrizo D, Munoz-Ortiz L, Julvez J, Grimalt JO, and Sunyer J. (2006) In utero exposure to background concentrations of DDT and cognitive functioning among preschoolers, *Am J Epidemiol* 164, 955–962.

Rice G, and Hammitt JK. (2005) *Economic valuation of human health benefits of controlling mercury emissions from US coal-fired power plants*. Northeast States for Coordinated Air Use Management. www.nescaum.org.

Rice GE, Hammitt JK, and Evans JS. (2010) A probabilistic characterization of the health benefits of reducing methyl mercury intake in the United States, *Environ Sci Technol* 44, 5216–5224.

Richter E, Soskolne CL, and LaDou J. (2001) Efforts to stop repression bias by protecting whistleblowers, *Int J Occup Environ Health* 7, 68–71.

Rodgers T. (2005) As canned tuna sales dive, companies plan ad blitz to reel buyers back in, *San Diego Union-Tribune*, 27 July.

Rosner D, and Markowitz G. (2009) The trials and tribulations of two historians: Adjudicating responsibility for pollution and personal harm, *Med Hist* 53, 271–292.

Ross JF, and Daston GP. (1995) To the editor, *Neurotox Teratol* 17, 685–686.

Roze E, Meijer L, Bakker A, Van Braeckel KN, Sauer PJ, and Bos AF. (2009) Prenatal exposure to organohalogens, including brominated flame retardants, influences motor, cognitive, and behavioral performance at school age, *Environ Health Perspect* 117, 1953–1958.

Ruckart PZ, Kakolewski K, Bove FJ, and Kaye WE. (2004) Long-term neurobehavioral health effects of methyl parathion exposure in children in Mississippi and Ohio, *Environ Health Perspect* 112, 46–51.

Ruediger T, and Bolz J. (2007) Neurotransmitters and the development of neuronal circuits, *Adv Exp Med Biol* 621, 104–115.

Sadoun R, Lolli G, and Silverman M. (1965) *Drinking in the French culture,* Monographs of the Rutgers Center of Alcohol Studies (No. 5), College and University Press, New Haven, CT.

Salkever DS. (1995) Updated estimates of earnings benefits from reduced exposure of children to environmental lead, *Environ Res* 70, 1–6.

Sanes DH, Reh TA, and Harris WA. (2006) *Development of the nervous system,* 2nd ed., Elsevier, Amsterdam, The Netherlands.

Schade G, Heinzow B. (1998) Organochlorine pesticides and polychlorinated biphenyls in human milk of mothers living in northern Germany: Current extent of contamination, time trend from 1986 to 1997 and factors that influence the levels of contamination, *Sci Total Environ* 215 (1–2), 31–39.

Schafer KS, and Marquez EC. (2012) *A generation in jeopardy.* Pesticide Action Network North America. www.panna.org/sites/default/files/KidsHealthReportOct2012.pdf .

Schantz SL, Widholm JJ, and Rice DC. (2003) Effects of PCB exposure on neuropsychological function in children, *Environ Health Perspect* 111, 357–576.

Schott G, Pachl H, Limbach U, Gundert-Remy U, Lieb K, and Ludwig WD. (2010) The financing of drug trials by pharmaceutical companies and its consequences: Part 2: A qualitative, systematic review of the literature on possible influences on authorship, access to trial data, and trial registration and publication, *Dtsch Arztebl Int* 107, 295–301.

Schwartz J. (1994) Societal benefits of reducing lead exposure, *Environ Res* 66, 105–124.

Schwarzman MR, and Wilson MP. (2009) Science and regulation. New science for chemicals policy, *Science* 326, 1065–1066.

Seidman L, and Warren N. (2002) Frances Kelsey & thalidomide in the US: A case study relating to pharmaceutical regulations, *Am Biol Teach* 64, 495–500.

Sellers P. (2010) *A survey of chemical contaminants in wild meat harvested from the traditional territories of Wabauskang First Nation (Wabauskang), Asubpeechoseewagong Netum Anishinabek (Grassy Narrows), and Wabaseemong Independent Nation (Whitedog).* Grassy Narrows First Nation: First Nations Environmental Contaminants Program (National). http://freegrassy.org/wp-content/uploads/2012/03/Final-Report-2010-Wild-Meat-HQ0900055-REVISED-1-1.pdf.

Serious Fraud Office. (2010) Innospec Limited prosecuted for corruption by the SFO. Press release, 18 March. www.sfo.gov.uk/press-room/latest-press-releases/press-releases-2010/innospec-limited-prosecuted-for-corruption-by-the-sfo.aspx

Shkilnyk AM. (1985) *A poison stronger than love. The destruction of an Ojibwa community,* Yale University Press, New Haven, CT.

Shrader-Frechette KS. (2012) Taking action on developmental toxicity: Scientists' duties to protect children, *Environ Health* 11, 61.

Silbergeld EK. (1995) Annotation: Protection of the public interest, allegations of scientific misconduct, and the Needleman case, *Am J Public Health* 85, 165–166.

Sjostrom PJ, Rancz EA, Roth A, and Hausser M. (2008) Dendritic excitability and synaptic plasticity, *Physiol Rev* 88, 769–840.

Sly PD, and Flack F. (2008) Susceptibility of children to environmental pollutants, *Ann NY Acad Sci* 1140, 163–183.

Smith AH, Lingas EO, and Rahman M. (2000) Contamination of drinking-water by arsenic in Bangladesh: A public health emergency, *Bull World Health Organ* 78, 1093–1103.

Smith KR, Corvalan CF, and Kjellström T. (1999) How much global ill health is attributable to environmental factors? *Epidemiology* 10, 573–584.

Social Scientific Study Group on Minamata Disease. (1999) *In the hope of avoiding repetition of tragedy of Minamata Disease.* Minamata: National Institute for Minamata Disease. www.nimd. go.jp/syakai/webversion/SSSGMDreport.html.

Soon W, and Ferguson R. (2005) Eat more fish! *Wall Street Journal,* 15 August.

Speth JG. (2008) *The bridge at the edge of the world: Capitalism, the environment, and crossing from crisis to sustainability,* Yale University Press, New Haven, CT.

Spulber S, Rantamäki T, Nikkila O, Castrén E, Weihe P, Grandjean P, and Ceccatelli S. (2010) Effects of maternal smoking and exposure to methylmercury on brain-derived neurotrophic factor concentrations in umbilical cord serum, *Toxicol Sci* 117, 263–269.

Spyker JM, Sparber SB, and Goldberg AM. (1972) Subtle consequences of methylmercury exposure: Behavioral deviations in offspring of treated mothers, *Science* 177, 621–623.

Stein CR and Savitz DA. (2011) Serum perfluorinated compound concentration and attention deficit/hyperactivity disorder in children 5–18 years of age, *Environ Health Perspect* 119, 1466–1471.

Stern H, Booth JC, Elek SD, and Fleck DG. (1969) Microbial causes of mental retardation. The role of prenatal infections with cytomegalovirus, rubella virus, and toxoplasma, *Lancet* 2, 443–448.

Stewart PW, Reihman J, Lonky E, and Pagano J. (2012) Issues in the interpretation of associations of PCBs and IQ, *Neurotoxicol Teratol* 34, 96–107.

Streissguth AP. (1997) *Fetal alcohol syndrome. A guide for families and communities,* Paul H. Brookes, Baltimore.

Streissguth AP, and Kanter J. (1997) *The challenge of fetal alcohol syndrome: Overcoming secondary disabilities,* University of Washington Press, Seattle.

Streissguth AP, Bookstein FL, Barr HM, Sampson PD, O'Malley K, and Young JK. (2004) Risk factors for adverse life outcomes in fetal alcohol syndrome and fetal alcohol effects, *J Dev Behav Pediatr* 25, 228–238.

Sundseth K, Pacyna JM, Pacyna EG, Munthe J, Belhaj M, and Astrom S. (2010) Economic benefits from decreased mercury emissions: Projections for 2020, *Journal of Cleaner Production* 18, 386–394.

Sur M, and Rubenstein JL. (2005) Patterning and plasticity of the cerebral cortex, *Science* 310, 805–810.

Suskind R. (2006) *The one percent doctrine,* Simon & Schuster, New York.

Swan C, Tostevin AL, Moore B, Mayo H, and Black GHB. (1943) Congenital defects in infants following infectious disease during pregnancy, *Med J Aust* 2, 201–210.

Swan GE, and Lessov-Schlaggar CN. (2007) The effects of tobacco smoke and nicotine on cognition and the brain, *Neuropsychol Rev* 17, 259–273.

Takeuchi T, and Eto K. (1999) *The pathology of Minamata Disease. A tragic story of water pollution,* Kyushu University Press, Fukuoka, Japan.

Tarkowski SM. (2007) Environmental health research in Europe: Bibliometric analysis, *Eur J Public Health* 17 Suppl 1, 14–18.

Tejning S, and Vesterberg R. (1964) Alkyl mercury-treated seed in food grain, *Poultry Science* 43, 6–11.

Tellez-Rojo MM, Bellinger DC, Arroyo-Quiroz C, Lamadrid-Figueroa H, Mercado-Garcia A, Schnaas-Arrieta L, Wright RO, Hernandez-Avila M, and Hu H. (2006) Longitudinal associations between blood lead concentrations lower than 10 microg/dL and neurobehavioral development in environmentally exposed children in Mexico City, *Pediatrics* 118, e323–330.

The Editors of the *Lancet.* (2010) Retraction—Ileal-lymphoid-nodular hyperplasia, non-specific colitis, and pervasive developmental disorder in children, *Lancet* 375, 445.

Trasande L, Landrigan PJ, and Schechter C. (2005) Public health and economic consequences of methyl mercury toxicity to the developing brain, *Environ Health Perspect* 113, 590–596.

Trasande L, Schechter C, Haynes KA, and Landrigan PJ. (2006) Applying cost analyses to drive policy that protects children: Mercury as a case study, *Ann NY Acad Sci* 1076, 911–923.

Troesken W. (2006) *The great lead water pipe disaster*, MIT Press, Cambridge.

Tsai P, and Hatfield TH. (2011) Global benefits from phaseout of leaded fuel, *Journal of Environmental Health* 74, 8–14.

Tsai SY, Chou HY, The HW, Chen CM, and Chen CJ. (2003) The effects of chronic arsenic exposure from drinking water on the neurobehavioral development in adolescence, *Neurotoxicology* 24, 747–753.

Tsubaki T, Shirakawa K, Kambayashi K, and Hirota K. (1969) Clinical features of organic mercury poisoning in the Agano River area [in Japanese], *Shinkei Kenkyu No Shimpo* 13, 85–88.

Turkheimer E, Haley A, Waldron M, D'Onofrio B, and Gottesman, II. (2003) Socioeconomic status modifies heritability of IQ in young children, *Psychol Sci* 14, 623–628.

U.S. Environmental Protection Agency. (1986) *Air quality criteria for lead.* Washington, DC. http://cfpub.epa.gov/ncea/cfm/recordisplay.cfm?deid=32647.

U.S. Environmental Protection Agency. (1985) *Costs and benefits of reducing lead in gasoline: Final regulatory impact analysis.* Washington, DC. http://yosemite.epa.gov/ee/epa/eerm.nsf/vwAN/EE-0034-1.pdf/$file/EE-0034-1.pdf.

U.S. Environmental Protection Agency. (2011) *Pesticide News Story: EPA Releases Report Containing Latest Estimates of Pesticide Use in the United States.* Washington, DC. www.epa.gov/oppfead1/cb/csb_page/updates/2011/sales-usage06–07.html.

U.S. Public Health Service. (1925) *Proceedings of a conference to determine whether or not there is a public health question in the manufacture, distribution or use of tetraethyl lead gasoline,* Vol. 158, Washington, DC.

U.S. Public Health Service. (1970) *Survey of lead in the atmosphere of three urban communities,* Vol. No. 999-AP-12, Raleigh, NC.

Ulleland CN. (1972) The offspring of alcoholic mothers, *Ann NY Acad Sci* 197, 167–169.

Union of Concerned Scientists. (2012) *Heads they win, tails we lose. How corporations corrupt science at the public's expense,* Union of Concerned Scientists, Cambridge, MA.

United Nations Children's Fund. (2010) *Towards an arsenic safe environment in Bangladesh.* New York. www.unicef.org/media/files/Towards_an_arsenic_safe_environ_summary%28english%29_22Mar2010.pdf.

United Nations Environment Programme. (2009) *Legally binding instrument on mercury.* Geneva. www.chem.unep.ch/mercury/OEWG/Meeting.htm.

University of Cambridge. (2007) *Arsenic in drinking water a global threat to health.* http://news.admin.cam.ac.uk/news/2007/08/29/arsenicindrinkingwateraglobalthreattohealth/.

Vidair CA. (2004) Age dependence of organophosphate and carbamate neurotoxicity in the postnatal rat: Extrapolation to the human, *Toxicol Appl Pharmacol* 196, 287–302.

vom Saal FS, and Hughes C. (2005) An extensive new literature concerning low-dose effects of bisphenol A shows the need for a new risk assessment, *Environ Health Perspect* 113, 926–933.

Vreugdenhil HJ, Slijper FM, Mulder PG, and Weisglas-Kuperus N. (2002) Effects of perinatal exposure to PCBs and dioxins on play behavior in Dutch children at school age, *Environ Health Perspect* 110, A593–8.

Vrijheid M, Martinez D, Aguilera I, Bustamante M, Ballester F, Estarlich M, Fernandez-Somoano A, Guxens M, Lertxundi N, Martinez MD, Tardon A, and Sunyer J. (2012) Indoor air pollution from gas cooking and infant neurodevelopment, *Epidemiology* 23, 23–32.

Walker SP, Wachs TD, Gardner JM, Lozoff B, Wasserman GA, Pollitt E, and Carter JA. (2007) Child development: Risk factors for adverse outcomes in developing countries, *Lancet* 369, 145–157.

Walkowiak J, Wiener JA, Fastabend A, Heinzow B, Kramer U, Schmidt E, Steingruber HJ, Wundram S, and Winneke G. (2001) Environmental exposure to polychlorinated biphenyls and quality of the home environment: Effects on psychodevelopment in early childhood, *Lancet* 358, 1602–1607.

Warner RH, and Rosett HL. (1975) The effects of drinking on offspring: An historical survey of the American and British literature, *J Stud Alcohol* 36, 1395–1420.

Wasserman GA, Liu X, Parvez F, Ahsan H, Factor-Litvak P, Kline J, van Geen A, Slavkovich V, Loiacono NJ, Levy D, Cheng Z, and Graziano JH. (2007) Water arsenic exposure and intellectual function in 6-year-old children in Araihazar, Bangladesh, *Environ Health Perspect* 115, 285–289.

Wasserman GA, Liu X, Parvez F, Ahsan H, Factor-Litvak P, van Geen A, Slavkovich V, LoIacono NJ, Cheng Z, Hussain I, Momotaj H, and Graziano JH. (2004) Water arsenic exposure and children's intellectual function in Araihazar, Bangladesh, *Environ Health Perspect* 112, 1329–1333.

Webster WS. (1998) Teratogen update: Congenital rubella, *Teratology* 58, 13–23.

Weihe P, Hansen JC, Murata K, Debes F, Jørgensen P, Steuerwald U, White RF, and Grandjean P. (2002) Neurobehavioral performance of Inuit children with increased prenatal exposure to methylmercury, *Int J Circumpolar Health* 61, 41–49.

Weinberg AM. (1972) Science and trans-science, *Science* 177, 211.

Weiss LM, and Dubey JP. (2009) Toxoplasmosis: A history of clinical observations, *Int J Parasitol* 39, 895–901.

Wheatley B, Paradis S, Lassonde M, Giguere M, and Tanguay S. (1997) Exposure patterns and long term sequelae on adults and children in two Canadian indigenous communities exposed to methylmercury, *Water Air Soil Pollut* 97, 63–73.

White RF, Palumbo CL, Yurgelun-Todd DA, Heaton KJ, Weihe P, Debes F, and Grandjean P. (2011) Functional MRI approach to developmental methylmercury and polychlorinated biphenyl neurotoxicity, *Neurotoxicology* 32, 975–980.

Whorton JC. (2010) *The arsenic century*, Oxford University Press, Oxford, UK.

Wiist WH. (2006) Public health and the anticorporate movement: Rationale and recommendations, *Am J Public Health* 96, 1370–1375.

Wilson MP, and Schwarzman MR. (2009) Toward a new U.S. chemicals policy: Rebuilding the foundation to advance new science, green chemistry, and environmental health, *Environ Health Perspect* 117, 1202–1209.

Wolf A, Cowen D, and Paige B. (1939) Human toxoplasmosis: Occurrence in infants as an encephalomyelitis verification by transmission to animals, *Science* 89, 226–227.

Wood JM, Kennedy FS, and Rosen CG. (1968) Synthesis of methyl-mercury compounds by extracts of a methanogenic bacterium, *Nature* 220, 173–174.

World Health Organization. (2002) World Health Assembly Resolution 25. *Infant and young children nutrition.* Geneva. www.who.int/nutrition/topics/WHA55.25_iycn_en.pdf.

World Health Organization. (2006) *Neurological disorders, public health challenges.* Geneva. www.who.int/mental_health/neurology/chapter1_neuro_disorders_public_h_challenges.pdf.

World Health Organization. (2009) *WHO vaccine-preventable diseases: Monitoring system—2009 global summary.* Geneva. www.who.int/immunization/documents/WHO_IVB_2009/en/index.html.

World Wildlife Fund. (2004) *Bad blood? A survey of chemicals in the blood of European ministers.* Gland. www.wwf.fi/wwf/www/uploads/pdf/baqdblood.pdf.

Wright JP, Dietrich KN, Ris MD, Hornung RW, Wessel SD, Lanphear BP, Ho M, and Rae MN. (2008) Association of prenatal and childhood blood lead concentrations with criminal arrests in early adulthood, *PLoS Med* 5, e101.

Wright RO, Amarasiriwardena C, Woolf AD, Jim R, and Bellinger DC. (2006) Neuropsychological correlates of hair arsenic, manganese, and cadmium levels in school-age children residing near a hazardous waste site, *Neurotoxicology* 27, 210–216.

Wurtz RH. (2009) Recounting the impact of Hubel and Wiesel, *J Physiol* 587, 2817–2823.

Wynn J. (1982) Lead in petrol, clear risks, *Nature* 297, 175.

Yamashita N, Doi M, Nishio M, Hojo H, and Tanaka M. (1972) Recent observations of Kyoto children poisoned by arsenic tainted "Morinaga Dry Milk" [in Japanese with English abstract], *Nippon Eiseigaku Zasshi* 27, 364–399.

Yang D, Kim KH, Phimister A, Bachstetter AD, Ward TR, Stackman RW, Mervis RF, Wisniewski AB, Klein SL, Kodavanti PR, Anderson KA, Wayman G, Pessah IN, and Lein PJ. (2009) Developmental exposure to polychlorinated biphenyls interferes with experience-dependent dendritic plasticity and ryanodine receptor expression in weanling rats, *Environ Health Perspect* 117, 426–435.

Ye X, Pierik FH, Hauser R, Duty S, Angerer J, Park MM, Burdorf A, Hofman A, Jaddoe VW, Mackenbach JP, Steegers EA, Tiemeier H, and Longnecker MP. (2008) Urinary metabolite concentrations of organophosphorous pesticides, bisphenol A, and phthalates among pregnant women in Rotterdam, the Netherlands: The Generation R study, *Environ Res* 108, 260–267.

Young A. (2012) EPA, CDC officials testify to Senate on child lead poisoning, *USA Today*, 12 July.

Young JG, Eskenazi B, Gladstone EA, Bradman A, Pedersen L, Johnson C, Barr DB, Furlong CE, and Holland NT. (2005) Association between in utero organophosphate pesticide exposure and abnormal reflexes in neonates, *Neurotoxicology* 26, 199–209.

Zoeller RT, and Crofton KM. (2000) Thyroid hormone action in fetal brain development and potential for disruption by environmental chemicals, *Neurotoxicology* 21, 935–945.

INDEX